Political Systems of East Asia

Political Systems of East Asia

China, Korea, and Japan

Louis D. Hayes

An East Gate Book

Routledge
Taylor & Francis Group

LONDON AND NEW YORK

東
An East Gate Book
Consulting Editor: Doug Merwin

First published 2012 by M.E. Sharpe

Published 2015 by Routledge
2 Park Square, Milton Park, Abingdon, Oxon OX14 4RN
711 Third Avenue, New York, NY 10017, USA

Routledge is an imprint of the Taylor & Francis Group, an informa business

Library of Congress Cataloging-in-Publication Data

Hayes, Louis D.
 Political systems of East Asia : China, Korea, and Japan / by Louis D. Hayes.
  p. cm.
 "An East Gate Book."
 Includes bibliographical references and index.
 ISBN 978-0-7656-1785-9 (cloth : alk. paper) — ISBN 978-0-7656-1786-6 (pbk. : alk. paper)
 1. East Asia—Politics and government. 2. Confucianism and state—East Asia.
3. Comparative government. I. Title.

JQ1499.A58H39 2008
320.95—dc22
                                                              2008011299

ISBN 13: 9780765617866 (pbk)
ISBN 13: 9780765617859 (hbk)

Contents

Appendices

Preface

Perhaps more than any other part of the world, East Asia has experienced conflict, turmoil, and transformation over the past century and a half. The dynamism of the area continues today, taking on new and unforeseen patterns. This introduction is intended to acquaint the reader with the basic elements of the East Asian political experience, including not only current developments but also a brief historical review.

China, Korea, and Japan differ in many ways, but the relevance of Confucianism, not only to China but to Korea and Japan as well, is felt even today despite revolution, economic development, and war, both hot and cold. The experience with imperialism is another common theme. Yet another is the impact of World War II, the consequences of which were of enormous significance for all three.

There are two distinctive features of twentieth-century East Asia. One is Japan's rapid ascendancy and pivotal role in the region. Another is the perhaps even more spectacular rise of contemporary China. Japan's preeminence generated considerable interest in its approaches to economic development, education, and law enforcement, among other things. It was also an imperial power, leaving its mark especially on Korea. As for Korea, the North has been mired for decades in an authoritarian system with a dilapidated economy. South Korea has recently entered upon a democratic political path with significant economic growth. And China's revolutionary period, while important, is receding into the past. Neither China nor North Korea has been a major player in international relations until recently. South Korea and Japan were, and still are, important fixtures in the American strategic system and thus played supportive roles in the Cold War.

China, Korea, and Japan differ in many ways, but in discussing them here I have tried to maintain a consistent format and cover similar topics. The section on Japan draws from my *Introduction to Japanese Politics,* 5th ed. (2009), and *Japan and the Security of Asia* (2001).

I wish to acknowledge the help of student assistants Kimberley Hannon, Ryan Swantner, and William Stodden. Also, the advice and guidance provided by Makiko Parsons and Doug Merwin of M.E. Sharpe have been invaluable.

Introduction

China produced the intellectual foundations that shaped not only its own history, but those of its neighbors Korea and Japan. The Confucian legacy defined social, political, and economic institutions. These three countries, while sharing this legacy, followed different historical trajectories. For China, Confucianism defined nearly everything for centuries. Although it had a lesser impact in Korea and Japan, it provided the essence of identity and the moral basis of social interaction.

China's trajectory can be divided into four phases. The first is that of the empire based on the classical Confucian model. The empire lasted for centuries, during which it experienced periods of upheaval and dynastic change while the Confucian core remained intact. By the mid-nineteenth century the empire had became enfeebled with age and corruption and lacked the ability to renew itself yet again in the face of increasing challenges. Unfortunately for China, this enfeeblement came at a time when Western countries were relatively young and energetic. When the old and infirm collided with the young and assertive, it was China that lost.

This encounter with the West is the second phase of China's historical trajectory. Western countries, eventually joined by Japan, systematically exploited China's growing weakness. Defeated in one military confrontation after another and made to pay compensation as a result, imperial China simply collapsed, ushering in the third phase: revolution.

China's imperial system was not overthrown by a revolutionary movement; in fact no such movement even existed at the time. China's post-imperial leaders were hard pressed to come up with a replacement for the old order. But a new model would soon come to hand in the form of Russian Marxism. During the 1920s and 1930s, China developed its own version of Marxist revolution. This third phase bears the distinctive imprint of Mao Zedong and the Chinese Communist Party.

From the mid-1930s, when Mao established his ascendancy, until his death in 1976, China was in a state of almost perpetual turmoil. Ultimately, Mao's severe methods proved ineffective and counterproductive. The passing of Mao marks the fourth period in China's historical trajectory, the emergence of the modern state.

Korea's experience has been much different. In the first place, Korea did not attain the levels of cultural, political, and economic development of its much larger neighbor. For most of its history, Korea was a tributary state of China, although Japan tried on occasion to extend its influence to Korea. That began to change with the advent of Western imperialism. Several countries— Russia, Germany, and Japan in particular—sought to gain control over Korea. Japan succeeded in 1910, making Korea a Japanese colony.

Not only was Japanese rule exploitative, Tokyo also sought to expunge Korean culture. World War II created disastrous conditions for Korea. Japan's defeat led to partition and occupation by the Soviet Union and the United States. The Chinese Communist movement had influenced anti-Japanese activities among Koreans. When the war ended, the Communists were positioned to take over Korea. To block this from happening, the United States promoted political independence in South Korea. The result was the Korean War.

The Korean War solidified the partition of the Korean peninsula. While the possibility of reunification arose from time to time, by the end of the century the situation seemed to have become permanent. The history of Korea is thus marked by two trajectories: that of the North and that of the South.

Communism is now gone from its country of origin, but its legacy remains in North Korea. Unfortunately, adherence to the Stalinist model has not served North Korea well. With the loss of its Soviet patron, North Korea experienced economic deprivation and international isolation. Pyongyang developed increasingly hostile relations with the United States and Japan. While South Korea has developed economically, North Korea has remained mired in poverty.

The South Korean trajectory has been a happier one, although it has not been without difficulty. For years, South Korea was governed by the iron hand of authoritarianism, with heavy military involvement. In many respects it was a puppet of the United States. South Korea has become an "Asian Tiger," experiencing substantial economic growth. In recent years, it has moved in a more open democratic direction.

The story of Japan differs markedly from the other two. Like Korea, Japan has not had the rich history of China. Its tributary status was much less significant than that of Korea. Nonetheless, Japan's culture bears the distinctive stamp of Confucianism.

Japan's historical trajectory departed from those of its neighbors during the period of imperialism. While China was being carved up like a melon and Korea was being annexed, Japan emulated the imperialists and became one of them. Transforming itself from a feudal backwater, Japan became a modern state with all of the attributes of political, economic, and military power. These it used to acquire an empire, at the expense of China, Korea, and other Asian countries. But it was eventually done in by its own imperial overreach, which led to the Pacific theater of World War II and ultimate defeat and occupation.

World War II produced revolution in China, partition in Korea, and crushing defeat in Japan. But unlike the other two, Japan, like a phoenix, quickly rose from the ashes. Within a generation, Japan was back challenging the West on its own terms. By the 1980s, there was talk of Japan as "number one," the world's dominant economy. This, however, faded with the bursting of the "bubble" economy in the 1990s.

While the Communist Party keeps a lock on political control in China and authoritarianism has prevailed to differing extents in both Koreas, Japan established a democracy following the war, although it has generated no small amount of skepticism as to just how democratic it really is. In comparison to its neighbors, civil liberties and democratic privilege exist in large measure in Japan as almost nowhere else in East Asia, although South Korea has in recent years become much more liberal.

Given their widely disparate historical trajectories and differing current circumstances, it is necessary to treat these East Asian countries separately. It is important, however, to stress the commonalities and particularly to note their differing responses to similar circumstances.

An overriding theme for each of these countries is the role of the United States. The legitimacy of the People's Republic of China was denied by Washington until the 1970s. The United States fought a war with North Korea (and China) that ended in an armistice in 1953 but has still not produced a peace settlement. North Korea has developed a nuclear weapon capability along with missile delivery systems, provoking an energetic American response. The United States formed an alliance with Japan in 1951 in order to facilitate the containment of the Soviet Union. The Soviet Union is now gone but the alliance remains and in fact has been invigorated. For its part, Japan is seeking ways to expand its international security involvement and has been seriously considering changing the constitutional prohibition that, in theory at least, limits military activity.

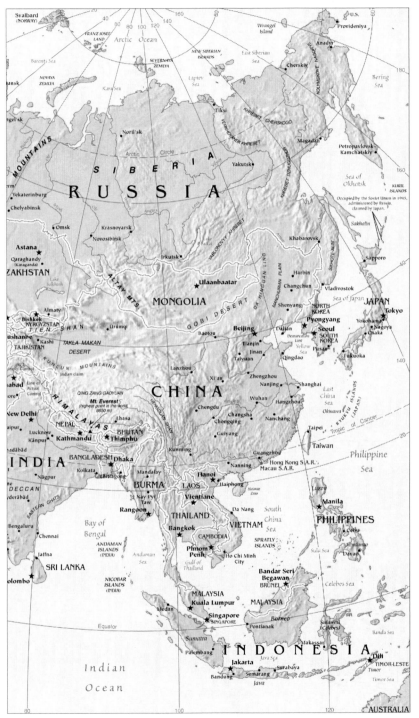

I

China

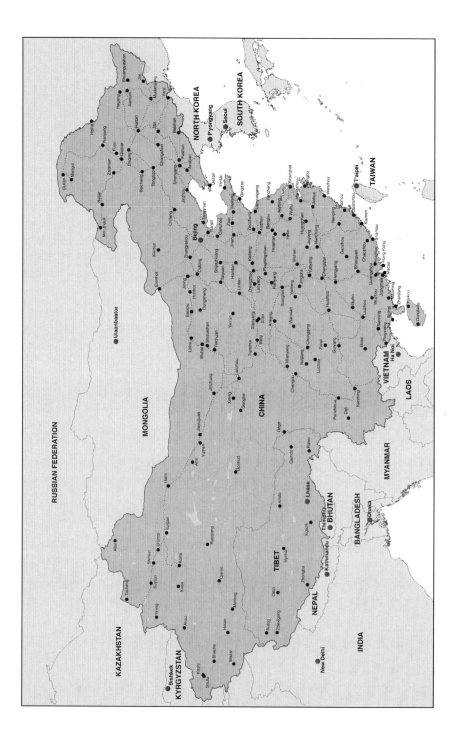

1

The Confucian Tradition

The recorded history of China's civilization is not only one of the most extensive, it is also one of the richest in tradition. That this traditional civilization endured for millennia substantially unchanged is an experience without parallel. The long-term survival of China's institutions is attributable in part to its physical isolation. Other parts of the ancient world that had achieved high levels of sophistication were not in contact with China, thus precluding intellectual cross-pollination. With few exceptions, China was untouched by neighboring cultures. In the sixth century B.C.E. in the Tarai region of Nepal, Prince Gautama contemplated the mysteries of life and in so doing attained enlightenment and established a religion. Buddhism spread throughout South Asia and was known in China by the second century B.C.E. It spread throughout the country by the second century C.E. and from China extended to Korea and Japan.

China was also spared the effects of conquest as it encountered few enemies throughout its long history capable of defeating, subduing, and transforming Chinese institutions and practices. In addition to its endurance, China attained impressive levels of accomplishment in all areas of human endeavor. Given these factors, it is little wonder that China regarded itself as the center of the universe, the "celestial kingdom." Yet while it possessed an amazing capacity for survival, it was also inflexible. Ultimately, traditional China collapsed under its own weight, having in its last century become intellectually and institutionally petrified.

Confucius and the Chinese Way

It is customary to refer to the ideology of traditional China as Confucianism. Confucius supposedly lived from 551 to 479 B.C.E. The Confucian school of philosophy laid the intellectual foundations that would serve China for millennia. It was made the official ideology of the country during the Han dynasty (206 B.C.E.–220 C.E.).

The essentials of Confucius's philosophy were simple. While he saw men struggling with each other everywhere, he refused to believe this situation to be a natural or proper state of society. Normal living is to cooperate, to promote common welfare. Social problems should be dealt with in a reasonable, moral fashion. Agents of the government ought to cooperate on behalf of the general

Confucius

welfare, which he defined as a pattern of harmonious relations. The ruler's success should be measured by his ability to bring welfare and happiness to all people. To achieve these ends, Confucius favored government in the hands of virtuous, trained ministers chosen on the basis of merit. Superior men must rule. "It was a daring step for him to insist that the highest ministers should be appointed for their virtue and ability, regardless of birth."[1]

Confucianism's rationale for organizing society began with the cosmic order and its hierarchy of superior-inferior relationships. Parents were superior to children, men to women, rulers to subjects. Each person therefore had a role to perform collectively as defined by convention, establishing a fixed set of social expectations. These expectations were defined by authority, which guided individual conduct along lines of proper ceremonial behavior. Confucius said, "let the ruler rule as he should and the minister be a minister as he should. Let the father act as a father should and the son act as a son should." If all people conducted themselves according to their proper social role, all would be well. To do otherwise would not only bring on disorder but discredit. "Being thus known to others by their observable conduct, the elite were dependent upon the opinion and moral judgment of the collectivity around them. To be disesteemed by the group meant a disastrous loss of face and self-esteem for which one remedy was suicide."[2]

In contrast to the Western Christian notion of the corruptibility of mankind, evident in the fall from grace idea, Confucius held to the principle that man is perfectible. In the Warring States Period (421–279 B.C.E.), the notion that men are qualitatively different at birth was replaced by the idea that men are by nature good and have an innate moral sense. Men can be led along the right path through education, and especially through their own efforts at self-cultivation. To this end they need to be provided with appropriate models to emulate. "The individual, in his own effort to do the right thing, can be influenced by the example of the sages and superior men who have succeeded in putting right conduct ahead of all other considerations. This ancient Chinese stress on the moral educability of man has persisted down to the present and still inspires the government to do moral educating."[3]

Another important tenet of Confucius's philosophy was a code of behavior that stressed the idea of proper conduct according to social status (*li*). There existed an elite made up of superior, noble men who were guided by *li*. The precepts of *li* were written in ancient records that became the Classics. The code was less relevant to the common people, whose conduct was to be regulated by rewards and punishments, rather than by moral principles. The code was essential for the elite, who were responsible for the management of public affairs. Confucius emphasized right conduct on the part of the ruler and those subordinate to him. The main point of this theory of government by good example was the idea of the virtue that was attached to right conduct. To conduct oneself according to the rules of propriety or *li* in itself gave one a moral status or prestige. This moral prestige in turn gave one influence over the people. "The people are like grass, the ruler like the wind; as the wind blew, so the grass was inclined. Right conduct gave the ruler power. Confucius said: When a prince's personal conduct is correct, his government is effective without the issuing of orders. If his personal conduct is not correct, he may issue orders but they will not be followed."[4]

In the hierarchical arrangement of society, everyone should know his place and the nature of his relationships with others. Everyone should serve the one above him and the one above should protect his inferior. Harmonious linkage of relationships creates obligations to maintain social bonds; these bonds are maintained by convention. There are no preconceived rules, only the ruling elite, the gentry, decide for the moment what is the right thing to do. "From the arbitration of disputes to the sponsorship of public works to the organization of local defenses, the gentry performed an indispensable function in their home areas."[5]

In the West, the tradition was established during the time of the Roman Empire that there are objective rules governing behavior that are codified into law and enforced by the state. Over the past few centuries, the "Roman Law" approach has been augmented by the idea of a contractual relationship among consenting individuals. In the larger political sense, this took the form of the "social contract" that provided the theoretical basis of constitutions. Thus, in the West, rules are formal, legal, and mechanical. In East Asia, under the Confucian philosophy (and in most of the rest of the world in fact), rules are based on moral understanding.

Many in the West who wished to transcend the Old Testament idea of a vengeful God or the Hobbesian idea of the state as a mechanism to keep people in line, have been attracted to Confucius's ideas. "Western observers, looking only at the texts of the Confucian classics, were early impressed with their agnostic this-worldliness," write Fairbank and Goldman in *China: A New History*. "As a philosophy of life, we have generally associated with Confucianism the quiet virtues of patience, pacifism, and compromise; the golden mean; reverence for the ancestors, the aged, and the learned; and above all a mellow humanism—taking man, not God as the center of the universe."[6] This is by no means a radical philosophy although it does remove theology from the equation. "But if we take this Confucian view of life in its social and political context, we will see that its esteem for age over youth, for the past over the present, for established authority over innovation has in fact provided one of the great historic answers to the problem of social stability. It has been the most successful of all systems of conservatism."[7] At the same time, Confucianism did not try to make each individual "a moral being, ready to act on moral grounds, to uphold virtue against human error, even including evil rulers. There were many Confucian scholars of moral grandeur, uncompromising foes of tyranny. But their reforming zeal—the dynamics of their creed—aimed to reaffirm and conserve the traditional polity, not to change its fundamental premises."[8]

Another important feature of Confucianism is the low status accorded to the exercise of coercive force, that is to say, the military. This does not mean there were no armies in traditional China; they existed, fought wars, and often shaped political events. But as compared with many periods and places in the Western experience, the military did not occupy high rank in social and political terms. In the later Roman Empire, the role of the military was decisive. In fact, the military was key to the establishment of the modern Western state and to the implementation of eighteenth- and nineteenth-century Western-style imperialism. In China, while there were large armies and frequent wars, the military as an institution never attained the prominence or permanence comparable to that of the civil service either in an organizational sense or as an enduring political force. The military was seen as a tool of policy rather than as an institution that creates or participates in the creation of policy. The status of the military is best expressed in the old saying: "Never make nails out of good iron, never make soldiers out of good men."

It can be argued that China's failure to appreciate the importance of military force as an expression of national interest accounts in part for its victimization at the hands of Western imperialists. Western militaries became highly innovative, while the military in China remained rooted in tradition. Nor did the Chinese military have a role similar to that of Western militaries. "Behind this lay the Confucian disdain for the military," Fairbank and Goldman tell us. "So deep-laid was this dislike that the military were excluded from the standard Confucian list of the four occupational groups or classes—scholar (*shi*), farmer (*nong*), artisan (*gong*), and merchant (*shang*)."⁹

The political role of the military may have been circumscribed throughout China's history, but military organization, strategy, and technical advancements far exceeded those of the West at the same period of time. Military studies such as Sun Zi's *On War*, written in the sixth century B.C.E., continue to influence military thinking today. As is widely known, gunpowder was invented in China in the ninth century and was used against the nomad invaders. But this great breakthrough in military technology had little significance for the tradition-bound political system."¹⁰

In addition to Confucianism, Chinese philosophy was enriched by other schools of thought. Among these was Taoism. This philosophy was contained in the Tao Te Ching, written about 240 B.C.E. While Confucianism was concerned with the individual and society, Taoism was concerned with the individual and the universe. Taoists advocated nonparticipation in social affairs. Man should return to primitive simplicity and seek harmony with natural law. Another early philosophy was that of the Moists, who advocated an all-embracing universal love that would remedy the ills of the world. This philosophy, five centuries before Christ, contained all the moral and ethical doctrines of Christianity except heaven and hell.

During the Qin dynasty (221–206 B.C.E.), a school of philosophy known as Legalism emerged. The Legalists stressed the importance of formal, rigidly authoritarian rules. While this approach did not endure, the notion of standardized rules fused with the more flexible, ethically driven philosophy of Confucianism resulting in a system where rules are made and enforced by conscientious and trustworthy men. Law was thought to be a normative guide to be applied with some degree of flexibility, depending on circumstances. Men were not equal before the law. The social order and traditional values rather than individual privileges had priority and needed protection by the state.

The Legalists believed philosophical disputation to be a waste of time, and to service this idea they set about burning all books. Only the authority of the state is meaningful. Man is evil and must be dealt with by the law and the authority of the state.

Science and Technology

One of the more striking things about traditional China was the disconnect between scientific learning and achievement and the application of those achievements in practical ways. Chinese inventions preceded similar ones by Europeans, in many cases by centuries. China invented gunpowder well before the Europeans did, but the latter made greater practical use of it. To allow discoveries and inventions to influence society by producing change would disrupt the fabric of harmony and stability. The static nature of China's technological development is clearly expressed in a statement by R.H. Tawney: "China ploughed with iron when Europe used wood and continued to plow with iron when Europe used steel."[11]

The long-term stability of China has often drawn the attention of historians. Immanuel C.Y. Hsu observed: "From 1600 to 1800, China's political system, social structure, economic institutions, and intellectual atmosphere remained substantially what they had been during the previous 2,000 years. The polity was a dynasty ruled by an imperial family; the economy was basically agrarian and self-sufficient; the society centered around the gentry; and the dominant ideology was Confucianism."[12] But during the same period, the tradition-bound character of China left it ill-equipped to confront external challenges.

It is instructive to contrast the development of feudalism in Europe with China's experience. The European system was based in part on mounted armored knights who depended upon a Chinese invention, the stirrup. The military utility of knights was ended by another Chinese invention, gunpowder. Why did no similar developmental pattern occur in China? "So deeply civilian was its ethos that the very conception of aristocratic chivalry was perhaps impossible," Joseph Needham suggests.[13] Moreover, institutionalization in the form of bureaucracy occurred early in China, precluding a feudal political pattern like that of Europe. And while, light cavalry like that of the Mongols was militarily superior to the heavy mounted knights of Europe, the military techniques of the Mongols were not those of the Chinese.

Although the Chinese invented the breast-strap harness, which enabled draft animals to pull heavier loads, again it was the Europeans who made significant use of it, not the Chinese. Use of horses, first domesticated on the Eurasian steppe, had a profound effect on European civilization. The horse is more efficient than the ox, and as a result, there was more crop rotation in Europe and a higher nutritional level. The social effects of horse-based development were profound.

One was a marked decrease in the expense of land haulage so that cash-crop produce could travel far more effectively than before; and a considerable technical development in transportation vehicles, notably four-wheeled wagons and carriages with improved pivoting front axles, brakes, and eventually springs. The other was more sociological and involved a proto-urbanization of rural settlement. Since the horse could move so much faster than the ox, the peasant no longer had to live in close proximity to his fields, and thus villages grew at the expense of hamlets, small towns at the expense of villages. Naturally life was more attractive in the larger units: they were more defensible; they could support bigger and better churches, schools, and inns; and commercial facilities could penetrate more easily into them.[14]

The restricted role of the military contributed to China's long-term stability, but also kept the military from serving as a source of innovation and change. Although versed in strategy and tactics, the Chinese military placed little emphasis upon advancing weaponry, which would have encouraged technological development. Moreover, the army was not a good career choice for achieving social status or political influence. The military occupied the lowest rung on the ladder of social prestige. Those engaged in commerce were only slightly higher. Neither the mercantile nor the military mentality had a high place in Chinese civilization. Hence, the fusion of science and technology with the artisanate and commerce was not made. Science was not a matter of private investigation but a state responsibility and monopoly.[15]

The largely unchanging institutional landscape of China could not survive forever. In the end, the imperial system had become effete and largely dysfunctional. With the arrival of the European challenge, China encountered not only aggressive forces intent on imperial conquest but people who entertained different ideas about how society ought to function, ideas that severely challenged those of traditional China. The Portuguese were the first Europeans on the scene when a ship arrived in 1514. Initially, they received the same liberties as the Arabs and the Malays who had already established trade relations with the Chinese. Later, problems arose, which were largely the fault of the Portuguese, although matters improved by 1550 following Portuguese help in dealing with the piracy problem. While relations with foreigners, including trade, were officially discouraged, many Chinese welcomed the opportunity to make money. Government officials were especially active in exploiting unofficial commercial activities. In 1557 a compromise was reached with the Portuguese, who were allowed to establish a permanent residence at Macao.

The Imperial Chinese State

Perhaps the most important reason for the durability of the traditional Chinese system is the essential appropriateness of its ideological foundations. "Because Chinese expectations of what government ought to do, how it ought to be done, and by whom it ought to be done have changed remarkably little in historical times," writes one historian of imperial China, "certain basic governmental principles and practices have persisted from high antiquity down to the present time."[16]

Central to the traditional Chinese system was the institution of the emperor. The imperial institution, the source of all authority in both practical and symbolic terms, developed over the long feudal period from 1200 to 200 B.C.E. Central to this process was the emperor's ability to develop a loyal political and economic elite. In the ancient world the concept of private property was rarely to be found and China was no exception. The absolute authority of the emperor included control of land. The imperial institution was built on the practice of giving land to kinsmen and retainers, thus creating an obligation to the emperor. Not only was such feudal status eventually hereditary, but various offices of royal functionaries also became hereditary. The system was sustained, moreover, by a philosophy justifying its existence, a philosophy predicated on the bonds of family. In a sense, China was one big family with the emperor serving as a father figure. An aristocratic system of leadership that simultaneously served and drew its support from the masses also developed. Rulers and ruled lived in a mutual system of duty and obligation. Professionalization and objectivization of these duties and obligations were slow to emerge, however.

This is not to say that Chinese history was all tranquility and political stability. Dynastic wars occurred and China was often divided into several politically independent parts only to be eventually reunified. According to Fairbank and Goldman, "The sequence of dynasties was due to the inveterate Chinese impulse during a dynastic interregnum toward political reunification. Unity was so strong an ideal because it promised stability, peace and prosperity. Yet unity seemed precariously dependent on historical rhythms. The waxing and waning of regimes, like that of people and families, called for constant attention."[17]

The traditional Chinese system included an effective political structure. Even though wars and political disintegration occurred from time to time, the fundamental elements of the system endured. Sovereignty was vested in an absolute, hereditary monarch whose legitimacy was based on the "mandate of heaven." Heaven was not the abode of a supreme being that "appointed" the ruler, as the European "divine right of kings" idea implied. The Chinese emperor's mandate was rather like the laws of physics; it was a universal principle. A key element of the Chinese system was filial piety, reverence for parents and ancestors. The emperor had a filial duty to heaven which established his mandate. Failure to exercise this filial duty, as manifested by disasters such as floods or droughts, indicated a loss of the heavenly mandate.

The government drew its authority from the emperor. Structurally it was composed of three parts, a sort of three-faced pyramid: the civil administration, the military, and a censorial system that oversaw the operation of the government. Each of these was arranged hierarchically. Each level of government was ordered on a bureaucratic model where officials drew authority from their superior, with all authority ultimately coming from the emperor.

The writ of government authority was without limit and carried the responsibility of defining and maintaining the appropriate patterns of social activity. These patterns were considered to be essentially stable, as promoting progress and growth were not part of the political mission of the state. No citizen or group had rights against the ruler or the government; in fact the notion of rights as it came to be developed in the West did not exist.

The exercise of political authority was in the hands of a gentrified class of virtuous men. To recruit such qualified administrators, the Chinese invented the merit-based civil service system. Recruitment into the civil service was reserved to those with ability as demonstrated by a rigorous exam stressing the Confucian classics and their principles. Nepotism and connections played a lesser role in acquiring a government job. Thus China could be considered to have been ruled by the "best and the brightest."

Missing from the Chinese conception of the state was a territorial dimension. China was not defined by lines on maps or physical markers on the ground, but rather by the extent of Chinese civilization. In fact, the emperor's authority was assumed to extend over the entire world. But this authority was not exercised in practice as the Chinese had little interest in most of the world, which was considered to be populated by barbarians. Areas on the periphery of China were theoretically subject to Chinese rule, although this rule was not exercised directly. Instead, a ritual acknowledgement of the emperor's supreme status was sufficient, an arrangement to be achieved by an annual or more frequent mission to the imperial court acknowledging the supremacy of the emperor and offering tribute.

In the absence of contact with any other state of equal cultural achievement, under the Han and Tang dynasties foreign policy became based on the tribute system, a reciprocal foreign relationship between superior and inferior comparable to the Three Bonds—ruler over minister, father over son, husband over wife—that kept China's domestic society in order. Since presentation of tribute offerings was normally reciprocated by lavish gifts from the emperor, accepting China's supremacy was materially worthwhile. In addition, the tribute system became the institutional setting and indeed cover for foreign trade.[18]

Political History

China's social and political institutions had their origins in the second millennium B.C.E. The first stage of China's history is known as the Shang period. In the transition stage from Neolithic to Shang, from c. 1900 to 1700 B.C.E., important changes occurred, including transformation of chieftanships to regional proto-states. There was also primitive urban development and the introduction of metallurgy.

The early Shang period (1700–1500 B.C.E.), evidence of which was revealed in the inscriptions discovered on the oracle bones, witnessed the development of regional states sharing common culture attributes and institutions. With the establishment of dynastic Shang (1500–1300 B.C.E.) there occurred further urbanization and development of social organizations. Villages became linked for economic reasons; cities were more ceremonial than commercial at this stage. During the middle Shang (1300–1135 B.C.E.) social stratification developed with an aristocracy, craftsmen, and farmers. During the late Shang (1135–1028 B.C.E.) there emerged the concept of China that would endure until modern times. During this period the notion developed that China is the center of civilization with outward moving concentric circles indicating diminishing Chinese cultural influence; barbarians were at the extremities. Power and culture radiated from the center.

China's northwesterly expansion had profound implications for people in that region. Relations between the Chinese and peoples on the frontier were frequently hostile. In order to secure the frontier, the Great Wall was built during the Qin. This was the result of the noncomplementary relationship between the Chinese and the barbarians. It also added to China's sense of insularity. Between 14 and 60 C.E., the Yueh-chi were driven from western China and eventually migrated to Bactria, which is now Afghanistan. There they established the Kushan Empire, a civilization of considerable sophistication that included planned townships and elaborate irrigation systems. This civilization and all its achievements were later destroyed by the Mongols.

By the beginning of the current era as measured by the Christian calender, China had moved further west and had acquired Chinese Turkestan. In 97 C.E., a Chinese military post was located on the Caspian Sea. Never before and never since has a Chinese army been so close to Europe. But because China's ruling elite had no interest in imperial acquisitions, the opportunity for Sinification of that part of the world was forgone. China's potential westward influence was permanently stopped by the advent of Islam. In 751, Muslim armies defeated Chinese forces at the battle of Talas, located in Turkestan north of the Pamir Mountains. From this time onward, Islam was established as the dominant political and spiritual force in Central Asia, and it would expand even further eastward in coming years.

On many occasions, China was in a position to extend its influence, even dominance, to other parts of the world. The human resources, capital, and technology were available to the Chinese at times when potential competitors lacked these capabilities. But for reasons of ideology, the opportunity for conquest was never seriously exercised. The Chinese had no motivation to bring the benefits of their civilization to the rest of the world. There was no religion in need of converts. Imperial grandeur was not to be enhanced by defeating and ruling over subject people. Tributary states were largely left alone, and there was little economic motive to acquire raw materials or markets. Yet, even before the Europeans began crossing the seas, the Chinese possessed the capability to visit distant lands.

During the period 1405–1433, Chinese maritime exploration was greater than before or since. Maritime activity had heretofore been left to the Arabs. Chinese ships traversed the Indian Ocean reaching as far as Africa. But, although Chinese ships were capable of carrying great armed might, the Chinese did not set out in search of imperial gains. They only seemed interested in bringing back curiosities to entertain the court. The Chinese were in a position to dominate the Indian Ocean, but lacked any incentive. Instead they defaulted to the Europeans. As Fairbank and Goldman observe, China did not seize the opportunity to exploit its advantages and ultimately abandoned the enterprise.

Three points are worth noting. First, these official expeditions were not voyages of exploration in the Vasco da Gaman or Columbian sense. They followed established routes of Arab and Chinese trade in the seas east of Africa. Second, the Chinese expeditions were diplomatic, not commercial, much less piratical or colonizing ventures. They exchanged gifts, enrolled tributaries, and brought back geographical information and scientific curiosities such as giraffes, which were touted as auspicious unicorns. Third and most striking, once these voyages ceased in 1433 they were never followed up. Instead, the records of them were destroyed by the vice-president of the War Ministry in about 1479, and Chinese overseas commerce was severely restricted until 1567. In the great age of sail that was just dawning around the globe, Ming China was potentially far in the lead but refused to act on it. It took the Europeans almost another half century even to get started. After 1433, it would be another thirty-seven years before Portuguese explorers on the west coast of Africa got as far south as the Gold Coast, and fifty-nine years before Columbus set sail with three small vessels totaling 450 tons. But the great Chinese voyages had been stopped by Confucian-trained scholar-officials who opposed trade and foreign contact on principle.[19]

Over the centuries, China experienced division and reunification under a number of dynasties. In general, political development was largely the product of indigenous forces. China was free from foreign invasions and was spared the need to accommodate itself to foreign institutions. At times China was ruled by outsiders, notably during the short-lived Mongol (Yuan) dynasty (1280–1368 C.E.) and the Manchu Qing dynasty (1644–1911). The Mongols left an indelible footprint on history. While they contributed little to the development of Europe, the Middle East, and Asia, they left behind vast devastation; in some cases entire civilizations were destroyed. Their military skills were superior to all those who chose to stand in their way. In China, their rule lasted a mere eighty-nine years, but in that short period of time they were able to destroy much that was irreplaceable. The Mongol dynasty collapsed due less to Chinese resistance than to weaknesses in the regime itself. The Mongols were faced with economic problems plus floods, drought, and famine. All signs of these difficulties were taken to mean a loss of the mandate of heaven.

During the Ming dynasty 1368–1644, the imperial system became plagued by corruption. The court had come to be dominated by eunuchs, who acquired considerable political influence. These eunuchs were important officials within the imperial palace organization, and in time they came to be supremely corrupt. Some of them amassed enormous personal fortunes. The purpose of government finance became nothing more than the maintenance of the political and economic status of the ruling elite, and government in general ceased to display any dynamism. This was the time when China withdrew from the maritime world.

Expanding contacts with the West came at a time when China was weakened by political troubles associated with the transition from the Ming to the Qing. Internal rebellions in China allowed the Manchus to expand their influence over neighboring territories. From 1629 to 1638, the Manchus were raiding inside the Great Wall with the Ming unable to contain them. Ming weakness rather than Manchu military prowess led to the fall of the former. Manchus conquered the north first, adding the south forty years later, without the need to use much military force. Nonetheless, there remained much animosity toward the Manchus in the south.

In order to protect themselves, as they were a minority, the Manchus kept half of civil service posts for themselves. One-fourth went to Chinese from the south and one-fourth to the north. This meant that the south, which had a majority of the population, did not have enough government places for all the political elite.

The Manchus were not totally absorbed into mainstream Chinese culture. In fact, they went to some lengths to avoid being absorbed because to do so would have cost them their identity. There were several rules designed to make distinctions between Chinese and Manchus. Intermarriage was not allowed, Manchus were forbidden to wear the Chinese costume, and Chinese men were required to wear the queue.

The Manchus did adopt many aspects of Chinese philosophy and reinforced traditional Confucianism. This ensured them the cooperation of important classes that were highly traditional in their orientation. These classes opposed innovation and thus constituted one of the main obstacles to change and adaptation during a time when China needed to adapt in order to meet the challenges posed by the West. For example, one government act was to make the examination system even more of a traditional exercise and thus more out of touch with the realities of the time. Science was considered a technical skill and inappropriate for the ruling elite and as a result was largely left to foreigners, mainly Jesuits.

Having forgone the opportunity to develop its maritime capabilities, China fell victim to those controlling the seas. Among these were Japanese pirates who eventually became so troublesome that the Chinese government had to bribe the Shogun to suppress them. The pirates' depredations forced coastal populations to move inland in order to escape the threat.

At a time when Western Europe was developing rapidly in science, technology, and industry, China was in precipitous decline. The Manchu regime declined in the nineteenth century due to intellectual stagnation brought on by the domination by a small alien ruling class which was itself dominated by a petrified cultural tradition.

The next phase of China's experience was dealing with Western imperialism, an enterprise that was not only disruptive and frustrating, but would eventually lead to the downfall of the emperor and the formal Confucian system.

2

China and the West

Contacts between the West and China were historically limited by geography and logistics. Not only were the two far apart, there were many obstacles in the form of deserts, mountains, jungles, and rivers restricting the movement of travelers and commerce. Traveling by sea was limited by virtue of distance, intervening landmasses, and the primitive nature of ships and navigation. To the extent there was commerce, it went overland along caravan routes, necessarily restricting the volume and variety of goods and the number of people who could make the journey. A few intrepid adventurers, such as Marco Polo, visited China and brought back to the West information about the mysterious "Orient."

For its part, China had little interest in the world outside East Asia. While it had the ability to expand physically and promote commerce, it lacked the desire. China had a military base on the Caspian Sea in 97 C.E., but, having no imperial ambitions, abandoned the area and forever lost the opportunity to extend Chinese influence westward. China preferred to keep the barbarians out by building walls instead. Islam was on the ascent in Central Asia after the defeat of a Chinese army at the battle of Talas in 751 C.E. In the early fifteenth century, China possessed considerable maritime capability. Chinese ships traversed the Indian Ocean and visited Africa. While the potential for projecting considerable armed might existed, the Chinese were more interested in bringing back curiosities, like wild animals, for the entertainment of the court, and numerous varieties of spices and other goods unique to the regions visited. Lacking a strong economic incentive, the Chinese abdicated their opportunity to dominate areas around the Indian Ocean.

Rapid technological change and political consolidation enabled Western nations to reach out to other parts of the world. They began exploiting China at a time when one dynasty was in decline (the Ming 1368–1644) and about to be replaced with an essentially foreign dynasty, the Manchu or Qing (1644–1911). The first significant contact with Western nations came in 1514 in the form of a Portuguese ship. In addition to Chinese indifference toward and dislike of foreigners, the Portuguese exacerbated the situation by their rambunctious and ill-mannered behavior. With Portuguese help in dealing with the piracy problem, relations improved by 1550, and Portugal was granted permission for a permanent enclave in Macao in 1557. The first voyages made by European explorers, adventurers, and seekers of commercial opportunity soon came to include missionaries seeking to promote Christianity. Jesuit missionaries began arriving in 1582. But suspicious of their intentions, the Chinese government strictly limited Jesuit religious activities. Consequently the Jesuits confined themselves mainly to scholarship and waited patiently for their opportunity to promote "the one true faith." The Chinese were not interested in an alien religion but they found the Jesuits entertaining and useful for their learning. The Chinese were intellectually curious about Western learning, but they considered it to be unimportant and perhaps even dangerous; hence for centuries they tried to limit it to the elite.

In 1604 a succession of Western nations began calling at Chinese ports, interested mainly in commercial activities. The Portuguese were soon followed by the Dutch, and the two immediately came into conflict as the Dutch tried unsuccessfully to drive the Portuguese out of Macao. The Portuguese retaliated by trying to poison the Chinese attitude toward the Dutch, but this was also unsuccessful. In 1636 the British arrived and were granted permanent trading privileges at Canton in 1699.

Restrictions placed on foreigners in the eighteenth century were in part occasioned by the uncivil behavior of sailors. "On the whole, foreign traders in China, who were mostly profit-seeking adventurers and uncouth men of little culture, made a poor show of themselves. Their violent and reckless conduct confirmed the Chinese view of foreigners as barbarians."[1]

Among the restrictions the government tried to implement were confining foreigners to their warehouses; forcing them to winter in Macao; allowing no foreign women; prohibiting the hiring of Chinese servants; prohibiting foreigners from learning Chinese or traveling into the interior of China; requiring Chinese merchants to pay large sums to officials for the privilege of trading with foreigners; limiting trade to Canton and Macao; and preventing Chinese from learning foreign ways. Naturally, the Europeans chafed at these restrictions and used every means at their disposal to change them. They began to chip away at them by imposing on China a series of unequal treaties, usually following punitive military action.

The Chinese sought to perpetuate a system of foreign trade with the Europeans that had been in existence for centuries. Trade was supervised and taxed by officials who were responsible to the imperial court and was assigned to specific ports. "The Chinese attitude toward foreign trade" Hsu explains, "was an outgrowth of their tributary mentality. It postulated that the Middle Kingdom had no need for things foreign, but that the benevolent emperor allowed trade as a mark of favor to foreigners and as a means of retaining their gratitude."[2] Trade was a privilege, not a right, and since it was private, it required no diplomatic relations. No direct contact was permitted between foreign traders and the Chinese government.

From 1760 to 1834, an arrangement known as the *hong*, or trading firm, system was in effect, whereby Chinese merchants acted as intermediaries between foreign traders and China's economy. Officially, the government was anticommercial, allowing trade only because it benefited the elite. Soon after the turn of the nineteenth century, the hong system was becoming inadequate. Commercial pressures were growing so rapidly that private traders, as opposed to companies sponsored by European governments (the British East India Company, for example), became increasingly important.

Europeans tried on several occasions to induce the government to change its restrictive policies and allow greater commercial and diplomatic opportunities. British missions to the imperial government led by George Macartney in 1792 and Lord Amherst in 1816 met with no success. The Chinese claimed they had everything they could possibly need within the borders of China and thus had no need to import the goods of other nations. As a token of their generosity, the Chinese allowed Europeans to export tea, silk, and porcelain, but refused any further expansion of trade. Opium, however, proved to be the lever that would pry open China to foreign penetration.

Opium was grown in India for export to China. This trade grew from 1782 onward and doubled between 1820 and 1830. The basic problem of opium use for the Chinese government was not a moral or public health issue but the fact that the opium import traffic was a drain on the economy; moreover, contraband trade in opium was not being taxed and thus constituted a loss of revenue to the treasury. For the British, revenue from the opium trade financed British imports and helped defray costs of their global imperial endeavors. "Thus the East India Company perfected the technique of growing opium cheaply and abundantly in India, while piously disowning it in China. Legally and officially, it was not involved in the illicit trade."[3]

The Chinese government's efforts to get control of the opium issue inevitably put it on a collision course with foreign interests. Foreign militaries easily defeated Chinese forces, leading to indemnities and concessions granting foreigners more access to China. In 1839 the Chinese destroyed an opium shipment and the British retaliated with armed force after talks had failed. The British sent a military expedition up the Yangzi River, cutting China in half and demonstrating China's military vulnerability. This and related events are known as the Opium War and resulted in the Treaty of Nanking of August 28, 1842. Under this treaty, China was forced to cede the island of Hong Kong to Britain as a permanent Crown Colony. Additional territory on the mainland was acquired under a lease. (The "New Territories" and Hong Kong itself were returned to China in 1997 when the lease ran out.) In addition, the Treaty of Nanking forced China to pay financial indemnities. Five additional ports were opened to trade: Canton (year-round, not just seasonal), Xiamen (Amoy),

Fuzhou (Foochow), Ningbo (Ningpo), and Shanghai. The hong monopoly was abolished, tariffs could not be changed without mutual consent, and most-favored-nation principles were established for commercial relations.

In the years that followed, more treaties were imposed on China granting additional concessions to foreign interests. In 1844 the Treaty of Wangxia included the doctrine of extraterritoriality under which China surrendered judicial control over foreigners. Foreign enclaves had their own legal systems and courts. By this time, the United States had become an active player in China and therefore shared the special legal arrangement.

The Treaty of Whampoa, also in 1844, granted foreigners the right to engage in religious activities. Soon, missionaries were active in promoting Christianity among the Chinese population. Most-favored-nation provisions were extended to cover all contingencies, which meant that any concession obtained by one country was automatically extended to all the other countries.

On October 8, 1856, the *Arrow* incident brought further problems for the Chinese. The *Arrow* was a vessel that, although originally Chinese, at the time was sailing under the British flag. It was attacked and boarded by Chinese authorities, who arrested the crew for piracy. The British, of course, considered this a major affront. The same year, a French missionary was murdered. In response to these and other incidents, French and British warships bombarded Canton on December 28, 1857. The two European countries were joined by the Russians and the Americans, who collectively threatened to march on Peking up the river Beihe from Tianjin, where the foreign troops were stationed, if the government did not relent.

The result of this confrontation was the Treaty of Tianjin (Tientsin) of 1858. Among the provisions was one allowing European diplomats to establish permanent missions in the capital and deal directly with government ministers. Missionaries and other foreigners were permitted to travel to the interior of the country, build churches, and own property. Further indemnities were imposed and tariffs lowered. Opium was legalized and made subject to a regular tax.

In 1870, a massacre occurred at a Catholic church in Tianjin. Antiforeign hostility spread like wildfire as rumors were circulated that foreign missionaries were engaged in evildoings. One such rumor concerned orphanages run by missionaries. The rumor alleged Christian missionaries and their Chinese converts were involved in rituals that required the use of eyes and hearts of orphan children for magical purposes. This led to the massacre of 1870. The problem was exacerbated by the fact that missionaries sometimes paid rewards for orphans, which aroused suspicion. Moreover, some unscrupulous Chinese kidnapped children and sold them to missionaries, claiming them to be orphans.

In 1876, the British established under the Yantai (Chefoo) Convention a supreme court, the jurisdiction of which extended not only to foreigners, who were outside Chinese law, but to Chinese who were involved with foreigners and who wanted protection from their own government. Increasingly, China's political system operated ineffectually.

As the century came to a close, China's situation worsened. There were local rebellions along the borders, especially Xinjiang, Burma, and Indochina. The biggest problem came from Japan, which was actively seeking to extend its imperial grasp at China's expense, eventually including Taiwan and Korea after China's defeat in the Sino-Japanese War of 1894–95. China's nominal suzerainty over Sikkim and Bhutan was surrendered in 1886. Compounding these difficulties, China's population was growing rapidly, leading to a marginal existence for millions of poor peasants. Many moved to the cities in search of economic opportunity, where social and economic problems were exacerbated by limited industrial growth.

By the 1890s, foreign powers had established and were vigorously exploiting their spheres of influence. The United States took exception to this development and called for an Open Door policy, which would allow for fair and equal treatment of all nations without preference by the Chinese government. Actually the Open Door policy had less to do with opposition to the spheres of influence approach than the desire that exploitation of China should be a free for all.

The business of Western imperialism was intensely competitive, and not every European country had the resources to participate in the game. The Portuguese and the Dutch were eclipsed by the British and the French. Toward the end of the nineteenth century, the Russians, Americans, and Japanese had become actively involved. China was not made into a colony of any single foreign power because it was simply too big to be absorbed. Moreover, a kind of balance of power existed among the imperialists, who were suspicious of each other. Although they managed for a time to avoid serious conflict by dividing China into spheres of influence, confrontation was inevitable, largely as a result of Japanese imperial ambitions.

The Taiping Rebellion and Other Uprisings

By the mid-nineteenth century, China was ripe for rebellion. The government was largely ineffective, and corruption was widespread. Foreigners were imposing their will on China at every turn. Western gunboats had cleared the seas of pirates who, forced to change their methods of operation, moved inland to become bandits. As if these afflictions were not bad enough, a series of natural disasters such as the Yellow River flood of 1852 occurred.

The emperor-centered system itself came under serious attack from within. The British practice of selling opium in China demonstrated the weakness of the Chinese government. The *Arrow* incident and other confrontations with foreign interests piled disaster and humiliation one on top of the other. Domestic disturbances and rebellions progressively undermined the integrity of the ruling regime. The most devastating of these upheavals was the Taiping Rebellion, which not only threatened to topple the regime but posed a challenge to foreign interests.

The Taiping Rebellion was a result of the introduction of Christianity into China. Hong Xiuquan was a Chinese convert to Christianity, but he went further than simply embracing the Christian faith. As Jonathan Spence explains, "Some intersection of Hong's own mind and a pulse of the times led him to a literal understanding of elements of this newly encountered religion, so that the Christian texts he read convinced him that he was the younger brother of Jesus."[4] He claimed to communicate with Jesus regularly and to be "imbued by his Father God with special destiny to rid China of the conquering Manchu demon race, and to lead his chosen people to their own Heavenly Paradise."[5] The Christian message was appealing to many in China, and missionaries were busy gaining converts. Europeans, however, did not respond favorably to the idea of an Asian being the brother of or successor to Jesus. Hence, the European missionary community opposed Hong and the followers of his movement, known as the *taiping tianguo* (great kingdom of heavenly peace). Apart from their theology, the Taipings were social reformers who advocated communal ownership of land, equality between the sexes, and an end to characteristically Confucian traditions.

The Taipings fought major battles with the government and at first scored several victories. The Taiping Rebellion lasted from 1850 to 1864, raging over sixteen provinces and destroying more than 600 cities. It is estimated as many as 40 million people died in the process. The Taiping managed to unite against it the Chinese establishment and foreign interests, both of which were threatened by the Taiping crusade. Foreigners had a working relationship with the establishment and a vested interest in keeping it afloat. In the Peking Convention of 1860, more ports were opened to trade and Britain acquired a lease on Kowloon, known as the New Territories. Europeans were busy carrying off Chinese art and other valuables, missionaries were spreading religion, and investors were making money. Together they were able to defeat the Taipings, but not before great expense was incurred and further damage inflicted on the integrity of imperial China. Other disturbances included the Nian Rebellion, lasting from 1851 to 1868 and spreading over eight provinces. There was a rebellion among Muslims in Yunnan Province that continued from 1855 until 1873. In the northwest there was another disturbance, known as the Tongan Rebellion, that lasted from 1863 to 1878.[6]

During the 1860s and 1870s there was some superficial improvement in the political and economic conditions of China. Moreover, British and American diplomats were growing increasingly concerned over China's stability and future viability. By 1868 England and the United States were convinced that revisions in the unequal treaties in China's favor would have a salutary effect. But the other countries active in China as well as special interests—foreign merchants and missionaries—were not supportive. The merchants wanted even more concessions, and there was growing religious and xenophobic friction between these groups and the Chinese people.

Modernization and Reform

During the last half of the nineteenth century, China experienced rapidly accelerating deterioration in its political and economic institutions. The tradition-bound elite frustrated all efforts at reform while foreign interests intensified their exploitation of China. Efforts at reform were thwarted, and financial resources allocated for, among other things, rehabilitation of the military were squandered. China's military forces proved incapable of standing up to any of its foreign adversaries from the first contacts in the sixteenth century up to and including World War II. The feeble efforts to enhance the country's ability to fend off foreign depredations were too few, too late, and essentially halfhearted. China's defeat at the hands of the Japanese demonstrated the failure of the reformers' Self-Strengthening Movement of the late Qing. In Hsu's words, "The limited diplomatic, military, and technological modernization, without corresponding change in institutions and spirit, was incapable of revitalizing the country and transforming it into a modern state. China's loss seemed all but inevitable."[7] Despite its impressive sounding name, the Self-Strengthening Movement pursued a limited agenda. The aim was not to transform China into a modern state but merely to make the necessary adjustments that would allow the privileged elite to perpetuate itself. The only innovations were in the areas of military modernization and suppression of internal dissent.

Reforms were attempted in 1898 (known as the Hundred Days Reform). A new and youthful emperor attempted to change the civil service examination system, improve the general level of education, modernize the military, and develop science. These reforms threatened the status of the elite, whose interests were well cared for by the empress dowager. She saw the emperor's proposals as a threat to her own power and wealth. Accordingly, the emperor was confined to his chambers, and the empress dowager and her cronies drove the country down the road to catastrophe.

Efforts to improve China's ability to meet contemporary challenges were continually frustrated by resistance at the top of the government. The privileged elite couldn't think beyond protecting their own status, ultimately at the expense of the country. Much of the blame for this state of affairs can be laid upon one person, the empress dowager. Empress Dowager Zixi ruled supreme over China for nearly half-a-century, from 1861 to 1908. "To a large degree she must be held responsible for the failure to regenerate the dynasty and modernize the country," Hsu concludes.[8] She had managed to gather into her own hands the reins of power, excluding even the emperor, whom she rendered virtually powerless. She tolerated only minor changes in the system, protecting the antiquated Confucian-based institutions. "The dowager's reform program was essentially a noisy demonstration without much substance or promise of accomplishment. Only three concrete improvements were actually made, namely (1) the abolition of the civil service examinations; (2) the establishment of modern schools; and (3) the sending of students abroad."[9] In the end the Qing rulers failed to deal with the challenges posed by the West.

While the Chinese regime presided with seeming indifference to impending disaster, Meiji leaders in Japan were moving their country in the direction of modernization and introducing reforms in order to increase their ability to compete with the West on its own terms. The Chinese elite was more interested in protecting its disintegrating power and privileges than in promoting national development and protecting the country's integrity. One celebrated example concerns a government allocation of money intended to modernize the navy. Instead of spending it for its intended purpose, the empress dowager and her cronies used it to build a summer palace near Peking. As a result, when the Qing navy met the Japanese fleet in the Sino-Japanese War of 1894–95, the Chinese ships had only one round of ammunition per gun.

The First Sino-Japanese War

Japan was a late entry into the "great game" of imperial competition. Given geographic realities and the fact that Europeans controlled most of the world, Japan's appetite for territory could only be satisfied at China's expense. China's efforts to stop Japanese expansion led to another in a series of military defeats. The dilapidated condition of the Chinese state was revealed in the Sino-Japanese War of 1894–95.

The war was a catastrophe for China, which suffered humiliating military defeat and loss of territory as a consequence. In the Treaty of Shimonoseki of 1895, China acknowledged the independence of Korea (which would be formally annexed by Japan in 1910), Taiwan was ceded to Japan, and commercial and industrial privileges were granted to Japan. Japan was also to receive the Liaodong peninsula in southern Manchuria, but Germany, France, and Russia objected that this would put them at a disadvantage. So Japan was forced to accept a financial indemnity instead, an outcome that greatly rankled Tokyo. "From China's perspective," Fairbank and Goldman write, "Japan's victory in 1895 was not merely a defeat of China by some other civilized power but a real subjection to the powers of darkness represented by the West. . . . By inventing powerful machines this outside world had overwhelmed the order of man and nature that had created civilization and the good life. Chaos was at hand."[10]

The Boxer Rebellion and the Collapse of Imperial China

Chinese conservatives and foreign interests found another common cause in the Boxer Rebellion of 1898. The Boxers, or Society of Righteous Harmony Fists, opposed foreign exploitation of China. They attacked foreign legations, bringing military intervention by, among others, American and Japanese troops. The rebellion produced another settlement favorable to foreign interests. Foreign legations were allowed to have their own military garrisons. Chinese officials were punished and another huge indemnity imposed.

Foreign greed led to a mad scramble to make money from China. One ploy was to impose indemnities on China and then lend the government the money to pay them back at substantial interest. Three years after the 1895 treaty imposed indemnities, a consortium of Franco-Russian and Anglo-German banks loaned China 43.2 million pounds, and China was to repay 102.4 million pounds.

> The total foreign investment in China reached U.S. $788 million in 1902 and U.S. $1,610 million in 1914. The degree of foreign domination is seen in the fact that 84 percent of shipping, 34 percent of cotton-yarn spinning, and 100 percent of iron production was under foreign control in 1907, while 97 percent of railways were foreign-dominated in 1911. The scope of foreign influence was as wide as the modern sector of the Chinese economy, which had been reduced to "semicolonial."[11]

Even more popular than loaning money to pay off indemnities was the building of railroads, which had little to do with China's economic needs or prospects but instead were intended to serve European economic interests. The Russians built a railroad across Manchuria to Vladivostok to advance Russian interests. They retained administrative control of the rail zone, including its security.

Following the Boxer Rebellion, Russia proposed a twelve-article treaty with China that, among other things,

> legalized the occupation of Manchuria by Russian troops disguised as "railway guards." It prohibited China from sending arms to Manchuria, or granting railway or mining concessions to other powers without Russian consent. The culminating insult, however, was the stipulation that China pay for the Russian occupation costs and damages to railway properties of the Chinese Eastern Railway Company, as well as granting Russia the right to construct a line from the said railway to the Great Wall in the direction of Peking.[12]

From 1895 to 1905, the position of European countries, and especially Russia, began to erode and that of Japan strengthened. The European-centered international system based on the balance-of-power concept was starting to come apart, a process that would culminate in August 1914 with the outbreak of World War I. In an effort to shore up their international security position, the British entered into a naval alliance with Japan on January 30, 1902. Both the international situation and domestic politics were increasingly negative for Russia, as became evident in 1905 with the Russo-Japanese War. The war was costly for both countries (the Japanese Navy destroyed the Russian fleet) but the Japanese got the best of it at least in terms of territorial settlements.[13]

The Twenty-one Demands

China's fortunes continued to slide toward the abyss and finally went over the edge in 1912 with the collapse of the emperor-based system. Only the Japanese were in a position to exploit the situation as Europe was soon embroiled in the conflagration of World War I. While Chinese intellectuals attempted to promote nationalistic and patriotic goals, in 1915 Japan issued twenty-one demands which, if fully implemented, would have made China a Japanese colony. The demands can be divided into five groups. The first four dealt with territory and called for Japanese control of Shandong, Manchuria, Inner Mongolia, the southeast coast of China, and the Yangzi valley. The fifth group was the most significant. It would have required employment of Japanese advisors in Chinese political, financial, military, and police administrations, as well as the purchase of at least 50 percent of China's arms from Japan.[14] Needless to say, the Chinese resisted.

The shock of the twenty-one demands generated a search for a new political model in China. Sun Yatsen and other nationalist leaders sought to promote some form of a republic. An intellectual revolution was under way, building upon the abortive efforts at reform during the latter part of the previous century. The earliest of these, the Self-Strengthening Movement, had been sabotaged by the entrenched traditional elite, who saw it as a threat to their privileged status. In the years before 1912, however, there were growing efforts to emulate Western political institutions. The nationalist efforts of Sun and others during the 1920s would bring a further embrace of Westernization. Simultaneously, a new political force appeared on the international scene. The Bolshevik Revolution in Russia afforded China another model. Yet more trials and tribulations lay ahead. Political fragmentation in the form of warlordism, the Second Sino-Japanese War, evolving into World War II, and civil war remained in China's future.

3

Revolution

China's trajectory toward revolution was long and complex. The imperial system began its slide toward collapse sometime in the nineteenth century. One noted historian marks the beginning of the revolutionary process at 1800.[1] A combination of European and Japanese activities undermining the system together with the ruling elite's incompetence finally brought down the age-old Chinese political system in 1912. As early as the 1840s, China had begun to experience severe challenges from outside and a series of internal convulsions. The British had developed the practice of producing opium in India and selling it in China, lucrative for them and debilitating for China. Chinese efforts to control this trade, mainly because of the loss of revenue rather than the deleterious effects on the population, resulted in war. The Chinese lost and were forced to pay indemnities and cede Hong Kong to British control. Other encounters with European imperialism in the years that followed resulted in a series of unequal treaties placing China at a progressively greater disadvantage. Moreover, disturbances and rebellions within China itself further weakened the regime. The rural economy was in serious decline, and urban industrialization did not take up the slack. As the twentieth century dawned, foreign powers continued their efforts to promote their own economic interests at the expense of China's political integrity. A four-power consortium comprising British, French, German, and, eventually, U.S. banks, pressed loans favorable to themselves on China for railroad construction and other industrial enterprises.

The Chinese revolution was more drawn out than others, such as the Russian, for several reasons. For one, alternatives to the existing ideology and political regime were only in their earliest stages of development at the time of the collapse. Moreover, there were only the barest rudiments of a revolutionary movement within China itself. Organizational and ideological efforts to bring substantial changes to China's political and economic systems occurred largely outside of China. Also, there were fewer important leaders in this movement than there were during the Russian experience. The most notable of these leaders, Sun Yatsen, organized the China Renaissance Society in Honolulu in 1894. He later organized another group called the Alliance Society in Tokyo in 1905, which brought together a number of minor revolutionary parties. By this time the movement was beginning to develop a focus, if still an inchoate one. It favored dramatic political change, including expulsion of the Manchus and the establishment of a republican form of government. It called for restoration of the Chinese national state by bringing an end to foreign exploitation. Social and economic changes advocated by Sun's group included an assault on the entrenched elite by means of the equalization of landownership.

The elements of an indigenous revolutionary movement were largely lacking, however. Political ideas that could be employed to question the legitimacy of the regime and to suggest alternatives did not develop out of China's own experience. Also missing was a cadre of activists, the foot soldiers of revolution, to provide the ideological and organizational resources needed to pursue a revolutionary agenda. Instead, both ideological and organizational activities involving Chinese progressives occurred abroad. In the early part of the twentieth century, many recruits for these activities were Chinese students studying in Japan. The numbers of such students grew from 500 in 1902 to 13,000 by 1906. These students, with both the time and the energy, supplied much of the manpower for the revolutionary movement.

Sun's activities, and those of others opposed to the Manchu regime, encountered difficulties even in other countries. The Manchus protested to Tokyo concerning Sun's activities, resulting in his expulsion from Japan, whereupon he took his operation to Indochina. But he wasn't welcome there either. After one year, his newspaper was closed, but his efforts had planted seeds of nationalism among many Chinese students.

Responding to pressure for political change, the Chinese government offered a vague promise of a parliamentary government in 1906. In 1908, another promise was made calling for parliamentary government in nine years. The following year, provincial assemblies were convened. While they had little real power, these assemblies did serve as centers of political agitation. The next year, a Provisional National Assembly was convened with half the delegates elected and half appointed by the throne.

But this was too little, too late. In 1912, the country dissolved into widespread disorder. As the situation degenerated into chaos, the military was called upon to restore order. Yuan Shikai was appointed to head the armed forces and directed to suppress rebellion. While his nominal charge was to save the dynasty, he took advantage of the opportunity to orchestrate events to advance his own power. A transitional government was set up, with Sun becoming the provisional president on January 1, 1912. Slightly over a month later Sun retired in favor of Yuan, who in turn became president. The events of 1912 had less of the character of revolution than of political collapse and a coup d'état. Sun's Alliance Society became the National People's Party, or Kuomintang (KMT), in 1912. In 1913, revolt against Yuan's control ended and on October 6, 1913, he was formally elected Republican China's first president. But Yuan had no interest in promoting democracy and moving the country in a progressive direction. Parliament and the KMT soon no longer served his needs. In November 1913, the KMT was declared illegal, and the parliament was dissolved in January 1914.

Had they not been engaged in the disaster of World War I, the European powers would probably have intervened in China to at least try and stabilize the situation. After August 1914, however, they were so embroiled in a war that eventually was fought on eleven different fronts that they were in no position to influence events in China. Japan had a treaty with Great Britain but did not take an active part in the global conflict. Thus it was free to exploit the situation and to pursue its imperial ambitions. In 1915, Japan made twenty-one demands of China which in effect would have made the latter a colony of the former. This action provoked an intense nationalistic response in China.

Yuan's actions proved to be counterproductive. He did not initiate reforms but instead sought to create a new dynasty with himself as emperor, an action guaranteed to fail and also one opposed by the Europeans. The country began to break up into separate entities, some ruled by warlords, each of whom possessed military forces. Provincial governments asserted their independence from the central government, and non-Chinese people on the borders, such as Mongols and Tibetans, declared their autonomy.

The Chinese army lacked integrity and was incapable of dealing with this chaotic situation. To the extent that it held together at all was due to personal loyalty of men to officers and of officers to Yuan Shikai. The lack of military cohesion and discipline established a pattern that would endure until the final overthrow of the Chiang Kaishek regime after World War II. When Yuan Shikai died in June 1916, the army fragmented into different groups under Yuan's chief commanders. This led to a period of conflict among the petty rulers and warlords lasting from 1916 to 1928. During this period, Confucianism fell out of favor with the younger generation of Chinese. Protests against foreign involvement in the country became more intense as reflected in the works of an invigorated literary movement. Following the successful Bolshevik revolution in Russia, Marxism was introduced to China and found a receptive audience. The Chinese Communist Party (CCP) was established in the 1920s, and the KMT was reorganized to bring it more in line with the increasing popularity of leftist ideas. The old Confucian model of the state emphasizing the dominant role of an enlightened elite fell apart and social disintegration accelerated, as Fairbank and Goldman explain:

> Moreover, local government had customarily been based on decision making not by an indiscriminate show of hands (one man, one vote) but by consensus, as had been the practice in village leadership councils. Even in

the provincial elections of 1909 by a tightly restricted electorate, the persons elected were asked to choose the assemblymen from among their own number by a process of voting that amounted to securing a consensus. If "democracy" in China's two-strata society should try to function by simple majority rule, it would deny the Neo-Confucian faith that disciplined self-cultivation produces men with superior character and worth. Yet, as personal relationships dissipated, this was what modernity seemed to demand.[2]

Social conflicts in turn crippled the agricultural economy and retarded the development of industry. To add to their burdens, people were saddled with an arbitrary and multifarious tax system. Everything from lamps to windows was taxed. During the warlord period, politics became increasingly militarized, a process that had been set in motion in the late nineteenth century. Participation in the army had another consequence. As a result of military service, more people were experiencing social and geographical mobility. By exposing many Chinese to other parts of the country and preaching to them about patriotism, the trend fostered nationalism.

China suffered further humiliation following World War I. At the conference settling postwar accounts, Japan sat with the victors even though it had played no combat role. China was excluded from the conference despite the fact that it was a subject of the proceedings. China sought adjustments in the unequal treaties it had been forced to accept by foreigners, a request that was ignored. China also sought the return of Shandong, which had been given over to Germany in one such treaty. The Peace Conference rejected the first request on the grounds it had no jurisdiction. As regards Shandong, it was given to Japan.

These actions occurred in an intellectual climate that was becoming less and less inclined to accept such insults to China's integrity. A patriotic explosion, especially among Chinese students, began on May 4, 1919. This event came to be known as the May Fourth Movement and is regarded by the Communists as the birth of revolutionary nationalism. On that date, a group of students was arrested for protesting foreign imperialism. The incident provoked an outburst of intellectual and literary activity involving all sorts of modern ideas, including Marxism, women's liberation, peasant liberation, and land reform. Numerous political organizations sprouted up, and mass movements became common.

During the period 1918–1928, China experienced increasing political fragmentation. The government in Beijing was ineffective, warlords ruled and exploited much of the country, and Sun Yatsen's government held control only in the south. In 1921, Sun declared himself president of all China with his capital located in Canton (Guangzhou). He set about trying to reunify the country by force and, in 1922, he launched a military expedition northward which failed due to poor organization. Similar efforts would be undertaken by Sun's successor, Chiang Kaishek, who confronted an additional complication, the existence of Chinese communism.

The Chinese Brand of Communism

Even when communism became available as a revolutionary model, the ideology upon which the Chinese revolutionary movement was based lacked cohesion and a clear sense of purpose. The early revolutionaries were basically nationalists seeking to redress decades of exploitation and decline. Marxism did not appear until 1920 when the first cells were formed in Shanghai. The CCP was officially established in July 1921.

Russia's revolution provided China's revolutionaries with an ideological roadmap that proved to have greater utility in bringing about fundamental change than did the more moderate liberal-democratic ideas originally espoused by the Nationalists of the KMT. Karl Marx's formula called for a spontaneous uprising by an industrial proletariat. An industrial working class existed only in truncated form in China. But the Leninist doctrinal modification of Marx suggested an approach that would enhance the relevance of Marxism to the Chinese context. Whereas Marx claimed the revolution would occur in the most advanced capitalist countries, Lenin advanced the thesis that it would occur in the marginally capitalist countries, those with large numbers of peasants and a backward agricultural economy. Lenin further maintained that the spontaneous uprising envisioned by Marx could be indefinitely postponed through manipulations by the bourgeoisie. If the revolution were to occur, then it would have to be made to happen. To this end he advocated a revolutionary party that would lead the revolution in the name of the workers. This party—the "vanguard of the proletariat"—would consist of a disciplined body of activists who would seize power. Such a party precisely suited the purposes of Mao Zedong, who would use it to mobilize the peasantry and seize power. Leninism did not quite describe China, but it was close enough to allow for the creation of the Chinese Communist Party. Fairbank and Goldman explain how it would work:

> The essential happening was the emergence of a new elite from the peasant society in the person of the activists (cadres) of the CCP organization. The new peasant leadership was self-selected, as ambitious and energetic younger people found opportunity to rise in the new power structure. Unlike the democratic egalitarianism and plural opportunities of the American experience, these new power-holders were adept at the creation of *guanxi* (networks of connections), sycophantic ingratiation with superiors, and

authoritarian exploitation of inferiors in the traditional Chinese style. Intensely political in every act, these nouveaux cadres instinctively sought status, power, and perquisites that set them apart from the masses and entrenched them as a new local elite. Mouthing ideology, playing up their patrons, squeezing public funds as the normal spoils of office, they were seldom constrained by a Confucian concern for the populace nor an educated vision of national needs or the public good.[3]

The Russian revolutionary movement was divided into many factions. They ranged from extreme revolutionary Marxists to more moderate reformers. The Marxists were divided between Mensheviks (meaning the smaller part) and the Bolsheviks (meaning the larger part). Actually it was the other way around, but the labels stuck and the Bolsheviks under Vladimir Ilyich Ulyanov, who later took the name Lenin, succeeded in their revolution, and as a result saw themselves as mentors for others. Moscow enthusiastically supported the revolutionary movement in China. Lacking their own practical revolutionary experience, the Chinese accepted Soviet guidance. In 1924, Sun Yatsen acknowledged this Soviet role and remodeled the KMT along the structural lines of the Communist Party of the Soviet Union. At this stage, the Soviets took the more orthodox Marxist view that China needed to complete the bourgeois phase of its national development before it could experience the socialist revolution. From Moscow's perspective, the KMT was considered the appropriate vehicle for this transition. The Communists were to play a secondary role. This was the strategy followed by China's revolutionaries until Mao took the CCP down an independent course in the 1930s.

The Soviet Union, through the Communist International, or Comintern, sent advisors to China. One of these, Michael Borodin, approached the problem from a traditional Marxist perspective. China had not yet gone through the necessary stages to have a proletarian revolution; it had not completed the capitalist stage yet. So with Borodin's advice, Sun Yatsen declared that Three People's Principles—nationalism, people's livelihood, and democracy—would guide the movement. But Sun was unable to proceed very far with this undertaking, for he died in March 1925.

Sun's successor, Chiang Kaishek, was a man with attributes rather out of character for a Chinese progressive leader. He was, not surprisingly, a military man, but he was also a Christian with strong right-wing political orientations. He found attractive the ideas of fascism as well as the Japanese warrior code or *bushido*. One of his favorite organizations was the YMCA, which he saw as useful for character building. He married into the economically powerful Soong family and thus had connections with the Chinese economic elite. Madame Chiang became a popular figure in the United States, especially among conservatives.

The children of Charlie Soong developed important, and diverse, connections in twentieth-century China. As Sterling Seagrave observes: "Few families since the Borgias have played such a disturbing role in human history. For nearly a century they were key players in events that shaped the history of Asia and the world."[4] Of the three sons, T.V. Soong served in varying capacities in the Nationalist government of Chiang Kaishek. The other two brothers were financiers. T.L. Soong married into a family of New York bankers and T.A. Soong married into a family of San Francisco bankers, thus establishing their connections with the American financial community. The most noteworthy Soong children were the daughters. Soong Ailing, like her brothers, was attracted to money and was "the chief manipulator of the family destiny." She married H.H. Kung, a powerful figure in the world of finance, who served as minister of finance in Chiang's government. Soong Qingling followed a different path. She married Sun Yatsen and after his death became an important, if largely symbolic, figure in the Communist regime, and eventually served as vice chairman of the Standing Committee of the Fifth National People's Congress. The most famous of them all was Soong Meiling, who married Chiang Kaishek. Very popular with Americans, Madame Chiang "was the acknowledged power behind the throne of Nationalist China."[5]

There were many leftists and Communists in the KMT, and Chiang moved against them in March 1926. But he soon became conciliatory because of the greater need to address the warlord problem in the north. In July, he launched the Northern Expedition, which succeeded in overcoming the warlords, after which he established the Nationalist capital at Nanjing. During the Northern Expedition, many warlords, rather than fight, simply joined Chiang's National Revolutionary Army. They were allowed to keep their commands, which seriously weakened the organizational integrity of the Nationalist army. The only thing that kept the army together was personal loyalty among Chiang's commanders, and this loyalty proved to be shallow.

In April 1927, Chiang turned his attention to the Communists. He smashed the working-class movement, including the Communists in Shanghai. One of the problems facing the left in China was the fact that decisions were being made in Moscow that were not necessarily pertinent to China. On the one hand, the Soviet brand of communism did not connect well with China's problems at this time; on the other, the ideology of the KMT became increasingly reactionary. Party purges targeted those interested in reform, leaving in place opportunists and self-servers. The KMT maintained close ties with the rural gentry as a way of protecting against radicalism. The party was essentially an urban-oriented elite alienated from rural China.

Chiang's Nationalist government started out under generally favorable circumstances. Revolutionary enthusiasm had begun to diminish, lessening the internal security problem. The economy was developing favorably during the latter part of the 1920s. Agricultural policies introduced in 1930 showed signs of improving the situation. The condition of government revenues was improving. Infrastructure, particularly communications, was improving, and the government was beginning to establish effective control over the country.

The Nationalists and the Communists had entered into a marriage of convenience. But it was not a union destined to prosper. The main problem was that the Communists, while nominally members of the Nationalist Party, retained their separate identity. As Hsu sums up the situation: "The Nationalists had admitted the Communists as individuals and expected them to accept the KMT leadership and obey its orders, but the Communist Party demanded that its members take orders from itself and form a secret bloc within the KMT. . . . Conflicting orders naturally led to friction which involved the sensitive question of discipline."[6]

But then as the decade of the 1930s progressed, the situation rapidly deteriorated under the impact of the global depression. Cheap, low-tariff imports were undercutting village handicraft industries. The Japanese pressed forward with their imperial agenda by engaging China in the Second Sino-Japanese War, which began with the annexation of more territory in Manchuria. The depressed economic conditions fell heavily on the poor rural peasantry, 25 million of whom suffered from the famine of 1931. As many as 5 million bandits and soldiers preyed on the people. The government staggered under the burden of military expenditures, devoting as much as 85 percent of its budget to the military. In the provinces, warlords, nominally loyal to the central government, supported large armies by taxing the people. Everything from kettles, to bedding, to hemp shoes was taxed. While grain may have been scarce in some areas, there was no shortage of opium, which the warlords forced the peasants to grow because it provided them with a substantial cash return.[7]

With the exception of a few troops trained by the Americans under General Joseph Stilwell, Chinese forces did poorly against the Japanese invaders. The Communists received more credit than the Nationalists for carrying the fight to the enemy. Despite having American supplies and logistical support, Chiang Kaishek preferred to hold back, sure that the Americans would defeat the Japanese, so that he could turn his attention to the inevitable continuation of the struggle with the Communists. The KMT did little to win the support of the people, especially in the rural areas. "Chiang was interested in finding a solution to the agrarian problem only as a way to deprive the Communists of their trump card," writes Lucien Bianco.[8] The Nationalists were interested in little more than remaining in power.

By the time World War II ended in Japan's defeat, the KMT controlled much of the countryside and the major cities. Despite this and substantial American material assistance, the Nationalists were driven off the mainland by the Communists in a vicious civil war that ended with Communist victory in 1949. "In these circumstances, for Jiang Jieshi [Chiang Kaishek] and the Nationalists to lose the civil war was a remarkable achievement," conclude Fairbank and Goldman. "The reasons they lost were both stupidity on the battlefield and incompetence behind the lines."[9] After the end of World War II, however, the Cold War set the United States against communism, which meant continued support for Chiang Kaishek.

The Rise of the CCP

As noted above, during the 1920s the CCP followed the guidance of the Comintern, advice that was not appropriate for China. Based on the Russian experience, and consistent with Marxism, the revolution in China was supposed to be based on the proletariat, the industrial working class. It followed that the CCP had to assist the KMT to achieve the capitalist phase of economic development. From a Marxist perspective, China was still feudal, and in fact the KMT was more representative of landlords than of the peasantry. In the original formulation of Karl Marx, the peasantry could play no role in the revolution. A peasant-based society was feudal and as such precapitalist. The revolution to overthrow capitalism was to be a spontaneous uprising of the proletariat. Lenin modified that doctrine to the extent of giving the peasantry a supportive role, thus acknowledging the large rural population in Russia.

The issue of the appropriateness of the Soviet model to developing countries was raised in the Second Comintern Congress in 1920 by the Indian Communist Ram Mohan Roy. But the Comintern line as it developed would have more to do with Soviet interests in balancing Japan and the West in Asia than it did with promoting revolutionary goals. In August 1932, Mao Zedong advocated a departure from the Russian revolutionary tactic of focusing on urban workers in favor of a rural-based system of guerrilla warfare. Among Mao's key allies in the process of defining the Chinese revolutionary process was Zhou Enlai, who became Red Army Commissar in May 1933, beginning an alliance that would endure until Zhou's death in 1976. By 1936, under Mao's guidance, the CCP had abandoned the Soviet model in favor of a revolution based on a peasant agrarian economy.

In the 1930s, Chiang Kaishek's government was confronted by the Japanese invasion and Communist revolutionary activity. He ignored the first and concentrated on the second. Chiang undertook a series of "bandit suppression campaigns," which were intended to eradicate the Communists. The first, in December 1930, failed, with the Nationalists suffering heavy losses. The second, in February 1931, was an even bigger disaster for Chiang's forces as the Communists captured arms and equipment as well as gaining a number of defectors. In the third campaign, in July 1931, Chiang took personal command but failed anyway, with both sides sustaining heavy losses. The fourth, in April 1933, also failed to dislodge the Communists, who were holed up in Kiangsi Province. In October 1933, Chiang changed tactics. Instead of trying to overwhelm the enemy with his superior numbers, he adopted a strategy of encirclement, blockade, and progressive strangulation. The Communists, faced with eventual annihilation, decided to break out of the encirclement. About 90,000 remnants of the Red Army divided into five corps, left their Kiangsi-Fukien base, and began a year-long trek northward to Yan'an in Shaanxi Province. Attacked all along the way by Chiang's forces, barely a tenth of the original number arrived at their destination. This famous "Long March" lasted from October 1934 to October 1935. Apart from establishing this event as one of the most important iconic experiences in Chinese Communist history, the experience also produced an experienced and battle-hardened leadership.

In 1936, the CCP proposed an alliance with the KMT against Japan. But Chiang rejected the offer, planning instead a sixth bandit suppression campaign. This did not come off. In the famous Xi'an Incident, Chiang was kidnapped by his own generals, who wanted to fight the Japanese rather than the Communists. In December 1936, Chiang agreed to a united front against the Japanese invaders. For their part, the CCP agreed to renounce their objective of overthrowing the KMT government. They also agreed to suspend their program of Sovietization and abolish the Soviet-style government they had established in the areas under their control. Land confiscation and redistribution was also suspended. The name of the Red Army was changed to the Eighth Route Army of the National Revolutionary Army.

With all-out war with Japan under way, the CCP underwent a rectification campaign, a purge that would be repeated many times in the future. The result was the consolidation of Mao's position in the party. Slogans were adopted, a favorite Chinese Communist practice, as shorthand expressions for policy. One such slogan was "oppose dogmatism," which meant that slavish copying of Soviet methods needed to be avoided; by then, adhering to the Soviet line had fallen out of favor with many in the CCP. Additional efforts were made to accommodate and coordinate the influx of large numbers of new members. There were also efforts to better coordinate the activities of various governments under CCP control.

China and World War II

A considerable amount of credit for the ultimate success of the Communist revolution has to go to the Japanese. The Communists would in all probability have failed in the end had it not been for the impact of the war with Japan and Chiang's inept handling of it. The war distracted Chiang, drawing away resources that could have been used to suppress the Communists. Moreover, when the Japanese were defeated, the CCP came into possession of large quantities of arms thanks to the Soviets, who disarmed Japanese forces in Manchuria and North Korea. The Natonalists, in turn, received weapons and advisors from the United States.

The United States and Japan had ambitions in Asia that could not have been more incompatible. "The Americans wanted naval superiority over Japan and the Open Door with an independent China. The Japanese wanted Washington to accept naval parity and Japanese hegemony over China."[10] Despite the clear incompatibility of goals, the United States did little to counter Japanese moves. Washington appeared to think Japan was bluffing or lacked the ability to follow the course it had set for itself.

Flushed with its successes against China in 1894 and Russia in 1905, Japan had grown ever more ambitious. In 1915, Japan presented China with "twenty-one demands" which, if fully implemented, would have established Japanese suzerainty over China. China would have lost control over its foreign relations and international commercial transactions.[11]

The main effort was directed toward Manchuria and the establishment of the puppet regime named Manchukuo by the Japanese. "All the circumstances indicate that it was the Manchurian affair that led Japan to drift away from the alliance with the Anglo-Americans and to choose imperialist expansion."[12] Eventually, Japan's ambitions extended beyond the mainland of Asia and came to include, in the "southern strategy," Southeast Asia.

In the summer of 1931, relations between Chinese farmers and the Japanese in Manchuria deteriorated. The Chinese resented the special status enjoyed by Korean landowners in the area. The latter were protected by Japanese troops. Then in June a Japanese intelligence officer was killed. These developments inflamed Japanese public opinion and encouraged zealots within the army. There was also concern in the army that Japan might be attacked in Manchuria by the Soviet Union. Military action was contemplated to forestall such an eventuality.[13]

The Japanese Kwantung (Guandong) Army and the government in Tokyo were divided on the proper course to take in Manchuria. Hotheads in the army wanted to pursue a vigorous strategy, while the civilian government favored a cautious approach. In September 1931, an emissary was sent by Tokyo to instruct the army commander to exercise greater control over his subordinates. While the emissary was being entertained by army conspirators and before he had delivered his message, an explosion occurred on the tracks of the South Manchurian Railway in Mukden.[14] The Chinese army was blamed, and Japanese troops took action. By the time the emissary met with the army commander, "Mukden was under occupation and the first phase of the conquest of China had begun."[15]

Japan's activities in Manchuria attracted the attention of the League of Nations. The League considered these activities to be inconsistent with the Kellogg-Briand Pact and the League Covenant. Any unilateral action by Japan in Manchuria would not be considered legal.[16] Accordingly, the Lytton Commission was established to report on the situation and recommend solutions. The Commission's report challenged Japan's policy. Japan's response was that the Japan-China problem should be resolved on a bilateral basis. On February 23, 1932, the Japanese government informed the League that it did not consider China an "organized people" and that there was "no unified control of China."[17] The Commission found that Japanese military activities in Manchuria could not be considered legitimate self-defense. Moreover, the creation of Manchukuo was not the product of a "genuine and spontaneous" independence movement but rather was the result of "the activities of Japanese officials, both civil and military."[18] The Commission report was dismissed as little more than an act of white racism.[19] The unacceptability of international involvement in what it considered a matter of national interest eventually led to Japan's departure from the League in 1933.[20]

When it issued its report, the Lytton Commission recognized the complex nature of the Manchurian situation. While Japan was not accused of outright aggression, the Commission asserted that sovereignty over Manchuria rested with China. The suggestion that a special administrative arrangement be developed that could accommodate both Chinese and Japanese interests would have precluded the development of the Japanese client state of Manchukuo.[21]

Up to this time Japan had been pursuing two foreign policy objectives. One was the expansion of Japanese activities in Manchuria. The other was promoting cooperation with other international powers. It had now become clear they could not have both. Despite government sensitivity toward international opinion, the military soon sacrificed all possibility for international cooperation at the altar of continental expansion.[22]

China's ability to deal with the Japanese challenge was diminished by the fact that China itself was politically divided and experiencing severe civil strife. "The Japanese military regarded the Nationalist Chinese challenge as by far the most important and, as Nationalist resistance was more vulnerable to Japanese military force, the Japanese concentrated their military drives against Nationalist armed forces."[23]

The KMT was faced with a dilemma. It lacked the military and political resources to meet the Japanese challenge directly. To do so would likely have provoked further Japanese aggression. Moreover, the internal difficulties posed especially by the Communist insurgency demanded that attention be given to political unification. To deal directly with one while ignoring the other would be to invite either military defeat or political collapse. Efforts by the KMT to suppress the Communists in the interest of national unity were viewed with suspicion by the Japanese. The Japanese reacted to any indication that Chiang was putting his energies into strengthening the political integrity of China as a challenge to their own interests. Should he concentrate his efforts against the Japanese, he would be vulnerable to Communist and warlord challenges. So he tried to appease the Japanese while addressing the problem of internal security. In this effort, he succeeded to the extent of forcing the Communists to retreat in 1936 in the above-mentioned Long March. With their "first internal pacification, then external resistance" approach, Chiang and the Nationalist cause had their priorities reversed. Failure to address the problem of Japanese aggression eventually proved beneficial to the Communists, who established a reputation for defending the homeland. Chiang assumed, correctly as it turned out, that the United States would eventually defeat Japan, so his real problem was the Communists. But by failing to act against the aggressors, Chiang lost the support of the Chinese people.

The Japanese were confident that the Chinese forces could not put up an effective resistance and would capitulate in short order. "Behind this strategy was the deep-seated contempt the Japanese army felt toward China's military capabilities. This lack of understanding of the Chinese people also had irreparable effects on Japan's conduct of the war. Contempt and overconfidence led the Japanese army to engage in a long-drawn-out war essentially unprepared, and no coherent strategic planning was developed."[24]

In the early phases of the struggle against the Japanese invaders, the KMT enjoyed the support of public opinion, which supported measures to oppose Japanese aggression. There was considerably less enthusiasm for the revolutionary goals of Communist ideology. Recognizing this situation to a greater extent than did the KMT, the Communists raised the banner of resistance, substantially enhancing their popularity and allowing them an issue around which they could organize politically. The Nationalists lost additional credibility when other groups besides the Communists showed their willingness to fight the Japanese. Fujian, Canton, and other areas of China were energetic in opposing the Japanese, but the Nationalists failed to exploit this opportunity. Moreover, some non-Communist armies were also effective against the Japanese. But the KMT was unable to achieve a coordinated effort.[25]

The Japanese had no more respect for the Communists than they had for the Nationalists. The Communists were regarded by the Japanese authorities in northern China, mostly veterans of the effort to establish a puppet regime in Manchuria, as bandits to be suppressed. The Communists' ability to win popular support was ignored by the Japanese and certainly produced no corresponding effort by the Japanese authorities to win friends among the Chinese people.[26]

The Communists had another asset. Their ideology offered possible remedies for social and political problems. The Nationalists offered the Communists little competition in this regard. The combination of Nationalist inaction, together with their oppressive methods and Japanese aggression, proved most helpful to the Communists. "Because Chiang made the Chinese Communist movement the pretext for not being able to fight the Japanese, millions of Chinese began to demand a united front. Cooperation with Communism was identified with resistance to Japan."[27]

The Communists were able to capture the spirit of nationalism among the Chinese not only by their willingness to fight the Japanese. The Japanese themselves helped out in several ways. They concentrated their efforts against the KMT and warlord armies, which reduced or eliminated competition for leadership of the Nationalist movement. The policy of terrorizing the populace may have reduced overt resistance to their rule, but by so doing the Japanese encouraged the peasantry to accept Communist leadership. In the final analysis, the Japanese misjudged not only their own capabilities but also the resilience of the Chinese. "Through all dangers and difficulties and turmoil, China maintained its consciousness of being a unified nation. Japan's fatal error was its failure to recognize this fundamental fact."[28]

The People's Republic of China

Following the defeat of the Japanese, the Nationalists and the Communists engaged in a brutal civil war to determine which of them would rule China. The Communists prevailed, and on October 1, 1949, Mao Zedong proclaimed the establishment of the People's Republic of China (PRC). Chiang and the Nationalists were driven to Taiwan. The KMT had never established a system of effective governance. Loyalty to Chiang and the central government was tenuous and based on personal ties to the leader or, more likely, on the possibility of gaining personal wealth by regional commanders and politicians. Chiang also failed to develop a political philosophy appropriate for the times. He tried to employ certain elements of Western political practice while at the same time retaining important features of traditional Confucianism; but the Nationalists failed to mobilize support for either of these elements.[29]

Political systems have a natural tendency to remain conservative; there is a pervasive unwillingness to embrace an altogether new approach. This is true even of revolutions. The French Revolution ended in the tyranny of Napoleon and an abortive effort to restore the monarchy. The Russian Revolution ended in the tyranny of the Stalinist state. The Chinese Revolution ended in the tyranny of Maoism. The French Revolution occurred because of the ineptitude of the ruling class. The Russian Revolution was the direct product of World War I and czarist tyranny. The Chinese Communists have the Japanese to thank for their ultimate success. In each of the three cases, failure to reform and modernize spelled the end of the old regime. In the judgment of Lucien Bianco, "Even an unpopular, conservative government unable or unwilling to tackle China's fundamental problems could easily have maintained itself in power by putting down the forces that were pulling the country apart."[30]

The Nationalists were no more successful on Taiwan than they had been on the mainland. "The Nationalist occupation of Taiwan after 1945 turned out to be a first-class disaster. Instead of being 'liberated,' the Taiwanese Chinese were treated as enemy collaborators; their goods were seized and the economy despoiled by nationalist military and politicians seeking personal loot."[31] The KMT ruled Taiwan for many years not because of newfound skills but because the Taiwanese population was in no position to throw them out. The patronage of the United States also helped perpetuate KMT rule.

Following its accession to power, the CCP began setting up various institutions of government. Underlying this regime would be the pivotal role of the CCP itself. In order to reflect a "united front" coalition approach a Political Consultative Conference was set up in the spring of 1949. This body selected the officials of the new government and enacted organic law. This was followed by the People's Congress, which was to be the highest organ of government. The highest executive organ was the Central People's Governing Council, headed by Mao Zedong and including most members of the Politburo of the CCP. It also had sweeping legislative powers. This body in turn supervised the Government Administrative Council (basically the cabinet), which was headed by Zhou Enlai as premier. It handled the routine matters of government. It also supervised the People's Revolutionary Military Council, which controlled military policy and included both military and civilian members, and supervised the State Planning Committee, which was created in 1952 to draw up and implement the First Five-Year Plan. In the legal category, there was the Supreme People's Court and the People's Prosecutor.

The CCP used other parties for organizational and mobilizational purposes and to give it the appearance of broad representation. It created mass organizations for all areas of life. The experience of the long period of war with the Nationalists, then with the Japanese, and then again with the Nationalists strengthened the cohesiveness of the CCP. Top leaders had all worked together for some time.

The Military Council lasted until 1954 and was the vehicle for consolidation. Under it were six military districts by means of which the army played a key role in the early years of the PRC. The government moved quickly to establish itself at local levels and to press forward with land reform.

4

Maoism

Socialist revolutionary theory has undergone extensive transformation since its introduction in the works of Karl Marx and Friedrich Engels. In their formulation, developed extensively in Marx's analysis of capitalism, the revolution is the result of an inexorable, historically driven economic process. Marx conceived economic history to be divided into discrete stages, from primitive slavery to socialism. At each stage, economic institutions and processes develop toward maturity. When the economic system is fully mature, that is, when it has no potential for further development within its existing structure, a traumatic, violent transformation occurs, pushing the economy to the next developmental stage. At each stage there is a distinct institutional and social pattern that is inevitably conflictive. As Marx and Engels declare in part I of *The Communist Manifesto,* "The history of all hitherto existing society is the history of class struggles."

This process continues until the stage of capitalism is attained, when the most intensive form of class warfare occurs, that between the industrial proletariat and the bourgeoisie. For Marxists, this historical determinism serves to justify what they are really interested in—the liberation of the industrial worker from capitalist exploitation. Profit is what makes the capitalist system function, and this profit can only be generated by exploiting labor. Marx contends that capitalism develops to an ultimate stage when the workers can tolerate their oppressed condition no longer and they rise up spontaneously to seize control of the governing machinery of the state. Having done so, the workers dismantle the capitalist system and establish the next stage, socialism, which is characterized by the dictatorship of the proletariat. The proletariat moves to eliminate class warfare. In the socialist system, all the social and economic inequalities and all exploitation of one class by another would be eradicated. The capitalist exploiters are eliminated, and everyone lives under the conditions of "from each according to his abilities, to each according to his needs." When the perfect condition of the workers' paradise has been achieved, completely free of any exploitation, there will no longer be any need for the state, which exists only to serve the interests of the exploiter; it is "the executive committee of the ruling class." When this condition of social harmony is achieved, the state will wither away and the perfect condition of communism will obtain.

Marx had in mind Western Europe, where his model of revolution was supposed to occur because that was where capitalism was most advanced. The revolution and resulting workers' paradise never came to pass, of course. Capitalists turned out to have more ways of exploiting and suppressing the proletariat than Marx had anticipated. Further refinements in the capitalist system, such as labor unions, kept the day of reckoning and workers' liberation from happening. This led later Marxists to conclude that if there were ever to be a revolution, it would not happen inevitably and spontaneously but must be made to happen. Some even concluded that, for various reasons, the revolution would not occur in the most advanced capitalist countries such as England and Germany. Capitalism could develop to further stages than Marx had expected. Additional opportunities for exploitation came in the form of imperialism, which exported the capitalist system. Revolutionaries could expect more success by plying their craft in those "marginal" capitalist countries, what Lenin referred to as the "weak links" in the capitalist chain. According to Lenin, capitalist countries would eventually get into wars with each other in their intensifying competition for economic colonies. Since the revolution was not determined by the inevitability of economic forces, strategies for making it happen had to be developed. In the late nineteenth century, many different approaches to bringing the revolution to fruition were proposed. Some contended that in the classical Marxist sense capitalism had to mature first. Others favored direct and immediate action. Lenin and the Bolsheviks (later to become the Communist Party of the Soviet Union) prevailed. According to their strategy, the revolution would be brought about, not by the workers themselves, but by the vanguard of the proletariat, the revolutionary party. The party would seize power in the name of the workers. Thanks to World War I and the Germans, Lenin and the Bolsheviks were able to do precisely that in Russia.

Following the Russian Revolution, the Russian approach to revolution and political action was served up as the model for all other potential revolutionaries to follow. Through the medium of the Comintern (Communist International), the Soviets took upon themselves the responsibility of leading others to the promised land of the workers' paradise. Some Russian revolutionaries, such as Lev Bronstein, who adopted the revolutionary sobriquet Leon Trotsky, contended the revolution needed to be a continuing process on an international scale. The Russian experience, to his way of thinking, was but the first phase of a worldwide revolutionary process. The Russian Revolution would ultimately fail if it were not made "permanent" by exporting it.

But in the struggle for power in the new Soviet Union, Trotsky failed to appreciate the ruthlessness of the competition to succeed Lenin, who died in 1924. Josef Djugashvili, or Josef Stalin, as he is known to history, carefully gathered the reins of power into his own hands and marginalized not only

Trotsky but all the other "Old Bolsheviks." Trotsky was exiled to Mexico, where he was murdered on Stalin's orders. Other Old Bolsheviks were put on trial for counterrevolutionary activity in the 1930s and executed, leaving Stalin in undisputed charge of the Soviet Union.

In developing his own revolutionary theory, Stalin put forth the ideas of "socialism in one country" and "capitalist encirclement." The Soviet Union should be made secure since the capitalists, seeing the revolution as a threat, would do everything in their power to overturn it. Defending the "revolution" in this formulation meant promoting the Soviet Union. Communists in all other countries were to be guided in their activities by the interests of the Soviet Union. Once it was no longer threatened by hostile capitalist countries, the Soviet Union could turn its attention to promoting revolutionary activity elsewhere.

Under Stalin, revolutionary tactics had changed completely. Revolution would not take the form of workers' uprisings, or even the seizure of power by revolutionary parties, but instead communism would be spread through the agency of the Soviet Red Army. Stalin, like Lenin, figured capitalist countries would sooner or later begin fighting among themselves. When capitalist wars occurred, the Soviet Union could step in and pick up the spoils. To a large extent Stalin was correct, but he failed to anticipate the German invasion of the Soviet Union in World War II. In the end, however, his method seemed to work as the Soviets gained control of most of central and eastern Europe at the end of the war.

Many Communists in other countries did not warm to taking their cues from Moscow. After the war, the French and Italian Communist parties developed their own nationalistic approaches, and Yugoslavia under Tito departed from Soviet guidance. Another and even more important country to take an independent ideological course was China. The conditions confronting Chinese revolutionaries were a long way from advanced capitalism or even capitalism in its early stages. China was an agrarian society made up mostly of peasants. It would be a long time before China could have a large urban working class. Further modifications in Marxism-Leninism were needed if China were to develop a revolutionary blueprint. Mao departed from Soviet doctrine in the 1930s and took China in a direction little resembling the Leninist model, much less that of Marx. Eventually, China and the Soviet Union came to a complete parting of the ways in 1962.

Mao's inclination to chart a course independent of Soviet doctrine was not solely a product of circumstances surrounding China's revolutionary needs. He later broke with the Soviet Union over the best approach to building socialism and differences regarding foreign policy. This estrangement was exacerbated by his sour personal relationships with Soviet leaders. In the early years of

Mao Zedong

the movement, when the Chinese Communists were taking directions from Moscow, Mao was excluded from the party's leadership by Stalin. Later he felt shabbily treated by both Stalin and Khrushchev. Mao's sense of personal injury at the hands of Soviet leaders had a chilling effect on relations between the two countries.

Little of Marx's revolutionary philosophy remained after Mao's doctrinal refinements. He did keep much of Leninist doctrine, and he added some new components. The core principle of class conflict remained, although the specific classes did not. The doctrine of party supremacy remained, but the idea of party infallibility was compromised by Mao's own ideological role. Most significantly he changed the strategy and tactics of the revolutionary endeavor, making them substantially different from those of the Soviet experience. The major components of Maoist revolutionary philosophy can be divided into five parts: class struggle, the role of force, the nature of revolution, the role of the party, and international relations.

Class Struggle

All Communists have subscribed, in one form or another, to the Marxist doctrine of class struggle. In Marx's original formulation, the class struggle was between the capitalists or bourgeoisie on the one hand and the industrial workers or proletariat on the other. Lenin continued the emphasis on the proletariat but assigned a supportive role to the peasantry, given that the large number of peasants in Russia could hardly be ignored. For Mao the peasantry was central. The challenge he faced was accommodating this reality to Communist doctrine without sacrificing Marx's capitalist development model altogether. The answer was the united front strategy, which nominally created an alliance among the "progressive social forces." These forces included the peasantry, the proletariat, the petty bourgeoisie, and the national bourgeoisie. That this alliance was not particularly Marxian was obscured by the fact that China was fighting an invader—the Japanese. So the united front was tactically, if not theoretically, appropriate under the circumstances.

The modifications made by Mao Zedong to Marxist-Leninist revolutionary doctrine provided a blueprint enabling China to emerge from the chaos and confusion that attended the collapse of the imperial system. Mao crafted a revolutionary philosophy to fit China's circumstances. First, he shifted Marx's stress on the industrial proletariat to the rural peasantry. China's urban working class was small, and it played a very limited role in the revolution, even during the civil war against the Nationalists.

There was little room in Mao's strategy for an emphasis on capitalist development leading to an inevitable workers' uprising. Instead he favored a campaign against the ideological foundations of the traditional Chinese state. "The principal motif of the Maoist style of rebellion" in the words of John King Fairbank," was mobilization of the masses and suppression of the intellectuals who formerly had helped to manage them. In this respect Mao was still a rebel against the Confucianism denounced in the May Fourth Movement."[1] But Mao was not altogether free of connections to China's Confucian past. "Mao Zedong excelled his colleagues in achieving a unity of theory and practice, a major motif in Confucian philosophy."[2]

The Role of Force

One thing all Marxists seem to agree on is that the revolution must necessarily be violent. In the first place, the bourgeoisie will not give up without a fight, and revolutionaries see a cathartic, almost spiritually uplifting experience in political violence. The central role of violence is expressed in Mao's famous statement "Political power grows out of the barrel of a gun. The party controls the gun; the gun must never be allowed to control the party." This statement encompasses several important ideas. First, of course, is the role of violence. Second is the primacy assigned to the party. But Mao elevates the importance of the army, a significant departure from Confucian tradition. The role of military force is also contained in Mao's idea of "people's war." In a frenzy of egalitarianism and to keep the emphasis on the "people," Maoists advocated the elimination of military rank and distinction, thus weakening the potential role for a professional army.

Mao developed a revolutionary technique which, while not altogether original, was appropriate given China's conditions. This was the guerrilla warfare approach which the Chinese Communists honed in the war against Japan, ultimately proving it equally effective against Chiang Kaishek's Nationalist regime. After the revolution had succeeded, efforts to export the techniques used in China to other countries proved largely unsuccessful. Guerrilla warfare methods were effective in Vietnam and Cuba, but elsewhere they failed to achieve revolutionary ends.

The Nature of Revolution

In classical Marxism-Leninism, the revolution is a violent upheaval followed by seizure of power by the proletariat or the proletariat's agent, the party. Mao developed a mobilizational approach that differed significantly from previous theoretical formulations. Mao showed little hesitation in exploiting China's large population for political purposes. This mass line approach energized the population and led to important changes in the entire fabric of Chinese society. But it had its limits and proved expensive. Mao wanted to create a society of perfect equality, where Marx's slogan "from each according to his abilities, to each according to his needs" truly obtained. When the energy of the revolution appeared to be flagging, Mao would call for another mass movement.

For Mao, the revolution is neither the liberation of the working class nor the establishment of the Stalinist bureaucratic state. Mao's idea of revolution is more ideological than institutional. The revolution will be complete when everyone has attained a higher plane of revolutionary enlightenment. This is to come about through the application of the mass line approach in the form of collective organization and behavior. Mao's China was characterized by massive displays of marching, flag waving, and slogan chanting by thousands upon thousands of people. Mao's revolution completely restructured China's social and economic system. Land was first distributed to the cultivators and then collectivized under state control. In Fairbank and Goldman's account, "The whole process of land reform under the CCP had been one in which party cadres supplanted the old remnants of the lower gentry. In vitality they represented a new regime, but in structural terms they penetrated much further into village life, backed by the authority of the party. Where the lower gentry had arisen locally with some degree of spontaneity and autonomy, the CCP cadres achieved their dominance by representing higher authority."[3] The family was attacked; children were encouraged to report on their parents. Farms were collectivized and communes were created. Political education was stressed over practical learning. Technology was denigrated in favor of people power. Economic progress was to be achieved by the Great Leap Forward, launched in 1958, which relied on labor rather than capital and technology. The effort failed, leading Mao to the conclusion that the party and the people were not ready to advance. Another intense application of violent conflict was needed to purge the system of deviation. Hence, he launched the Great Proletarian Cultural Revolution, which lasted from 1966 to 1976 and not only brought ruin to China but discredited Maoist ideology.

The Great Proletarian Cultural Revolution

The Cultural Revolution proved enormously expensive in human terms. It is estimated that as many as 400,000 people died as a result of mistreatment during the Cultural Revolution, for example. In the 1977 trial of the Gang of Four, Mao's wife Jiang Qing and the others were charged with framing and persecuting 700,000 people, of whom 35,000 died. "Many more were physically and mentally crippled, and a great number committed suicide."[4]

In the Sixth Plenary Session of the Eleventh Central Committee held between June 27 and 29, 1981, the Cultural Revolution was criticized and blame was placed on Mao himself. The report stated: "The 'Great Cultural Revolution' from May 1966 to October 1976 caused the most devastating setback and heavy losses to the party, the state, and the people in the history of the People's Republic, and this 'Great Cultural Revolution' was initiated and led by Comrade Mao Zedong."

During the Cultural Revolution, the renewed emphasis on ideological zealotry ("redness") led to a campaign against learning, skills, practical ambition, professionalism, and anything not having to do with politics. There were those who suggested a different approach to China's development. Liu Shaoqi, for example, advocated a "gentle breeze, mild rain" approach, which obviously didn't meet the requirement of the "blooming and contending" of Maoism. For his timidity, Liu was purged. Others, such as Deng Xiaoping, famous for among other things the phrase "it doesn't matter if a cat is black or white, so long as it catches the mouse it's a good cat," was also purged but later rehabilitated. Zhou Enlai, who had the remarkable capacity to survive all the competing political furies, not long before his death, and Mao's, in 1976, proposed the Four Modernizations, which were implemented by Deng Xiaoping. This strategy emphasized production and technology and placed ideology in the background.

The principal engine of the Cultural Revolution, and the most violent, was made up of zealous youth. The first Red Guard group was formed by students at Tsinghua University in 1966 to criticize the university administration's "bourgeois" and "intellectually elitist" policies. Other similar groups began to form, attracting the attention of Mao, who saw them as a vehicle for imparting revolutionary vigor to youth. Mao called on the Red Guards to combat the "Four Olds" throughout the country. The Four Olds were ideas, customs, habits, and culture. In the course of their activities, the Red Guards attacked education that was not clearly political, in effect setting China's technical and scientific learning back a generation. Educators were persecuted, paraded through the streets wearing dunce caps, physically abused, and sometimes killed. The cultures of frontier people were attacked as deviant. Works of art and other relics of China's past were destroyed. Mao used the Red Guards to purge the party itself of factions and individuals who were deemed not sufficiently supportive of Mao's ideas. These ideas were enshrined in the famous "Little Red Book," a collection of excerpts of Mao's speeches and writings from the past.

Initially, the activities of the Red Guards were limited to demonstrations and parades, but soon the movement turned violent. In addition to the educational system, the bureaucracy, the party, and foreign interests were also attacked. Red Guards occupied the foreign ministry and the Soviet embassy. They burned the British embassy and attacked diplomatic personnel.

By 1968 the movement was getting out of control, causing concern even to Mao. Consequently he turned to the military to restore order. This enhanced the political status of the military and especially that of Defense Minister Lin Biao, who replaced Liu Shaoqi as Mao's successor. Lin later attempted to overthrow Mao in a coup but failed and was killed in a plane crash while trying to flee China with his wife and son, who were part of the plot.

The Cultural Revolution had some resonance with China's Confucian tradition, particularly an emphasis on conspiracy. In Mao's view, "capitalist-roaders" were conspiring to undo the gains of the revolution. Maoists also used conspiracy to inspire anxiety and fear in their political enemies. Fairbank and Goldman describe the pattern: "The founder of the Ming dynasty, for example, extirpated his prime minister's conspiracy of 1380 by executing 40,000 people; the Qing Emperor Qian-long feared conspiracy in the 1760s, and the Qing Restoration began with a conspiracy in 1861. Sun Yat-sen indeed pursued conspiracy most of his life. It has been a Chinese specialty in the absence of a 'loyal opposition' based on a distinction between the state power and its policies as in the West."[5]

When the Cultural Revolution had run its course, the central roles of politics and ideology were replaced by a more structured and orderly approach. Moreover, many people returned to the "old ways," and as the revolutionary ideology lost its fervor, many turned to religion. "In addition to the revival of Buddhism and Taoism and a resurgence of Islam, Christianity rapidly gained new converts in the post-Mao era. While officially there were 14 million Christians—10 million Protestants and 4 million Catholics—it is believed that millions more worshipped in underground or 'house churches,' despite the government's harsh repression of any worship outside state auspices."[6]

The Role of the Party

In its Leninist formulation, the party is the central element in the revolutionary process. It performs two primary functions. First, it provides the organization and leadership for the proletariat. Second, it is the infallible interpreter of doctrine. Someone has to decide what doctrinal truth is, and that role belongs to the party and to no one else, including courts and legislatures. One of Mao's major contributions to revolutionary theory and the definition of the role of the party is a major reconfiguration of the Leninist model. This is known as the doctrine of the mass line. According to the "Little Red Book":

> In all the practical work of our Party, all correct leadership is necessarily "from the masses, to the masses." This means: take the ideas of the masses (scattered and unsystematic ideas) and concentrate them (through study turn them into concentrated and systematic ideas), then go to the masses and propagate and explain these ideas until the masses embrace them as their own, hold fast to them and translate them into action, and test the correctness of these ideas in such action. Then once again concentrate ideas from the masses and once again go to the masses so that the ideas are persevered in and carried through. And so on, over and over again in an endless spiral, with the ideas becoming more correct, more vital and richer each time.

Correct thought and action (truth) are buried in the masses, who are not consciously aware of it. Correct thought and action have to be extracted by the party. This idea is clearly expressed in Mao's aphorism "from the masses, to the masses." At any given time, ideology or party doctrine is incomplete and imperfect. The party is thus fallible and can make mistakes. "Closed-doorism" means blindly following doctrine and not being open to new ideas. "Me-tooism" means slavish adherence to current thinking as articulated by party leadership. "Capitalist-roaderism" means backsliding by favoring results rather than the purity of the effort. To avoid these errors requires a periodic rectification campaign to cleanse the party of incorrect thought. Only Mao, it seems, was unaffected by this tendency to stray from the correct ideological path.

Mao's revolutionary mechanics are noteworthy for, among other things, the emphasis on tactics appropriate for a peasant society. While he did not invent it, guerrilla warfare is associated with Mao Zedong. The peasantry is the sea in which the guerrillas operate. It is imperative, therefore, that guerrilla fighters maintain good relations with the peasantry. In his "Three Rules of Discipline" and "Eight Points for Attention" Mao stressed the importance of good relations with the peasantry. These were first stated in 1928 and revised in 1947. The Three Rules are: obey orders in all your actions; don't take a single needle or piece of thread from the masses; and turn in everything captured. The Eight Points are: speak politely; pay fairly for what you buy; return everything you borrow; pay for everything you damage; don't hit or swear at people; don't damage crops; don't take liberties with women; don't ill-treat captives.

The Communists were hardly saints, but the KMT, warlords, and other armed groups were inclined to do the opposite of these injunctions. The Communists' willingness to engage the Japanese, champion the welfare of the peasantry, and employ revolutionary tactics that were effective against the government of the KMT explains their eventual success.

Isolationism

Mao effectively precluded foreign involvement and interference in China's affairs, bringing to an end the self-serving exploitation and meddling that had plagued China during the period of European imperialism. Not surprisingly, however, "China's foreign policy during the Cultural Revolution suffered from the same mindless zealotry as did its domestic politics, for the animus of the time was not only against things old but also against things foreign. Anti-intellectualism was accompanied by xenophobia."[7] During the Cultural Revolution, suspicion of and hostility toward everything foreign was raised to a high level of spiritual intensity.

Throughout most of the period of Mao's ascendancy, China pursued a foreign policy of isolation. Formal relations were maintained with few countries, Albania being a notable exception. Meanwhile, the United States recognized the Nationalist government on Taiwan as the legitimate government of all China. China engaged in little trade even with its immediate neighbors. Beijing did not participate in world organizations like the UN because of U.S. opposition. In 1962, after a long period of decline, relations with the Soviet Union soured even further as a result of the Sino-Indian border war. The

Soviets came to the aid of India. This was a serious turn of events for China since India had consistently supported China's position in world affairs. But China sacrificed friendship in favor of redrawing its western borders. China contended that many of its borders were drawn through a process they called "cartographic aggression" by Western imperial powers.

Mao and Confucianism

In Confucianism, emphasis is placed on ritual to give expression to proper roles and social behavior. The importance of ritual is also found in Maoism through the mass public displays, parades, marches, and so forth. In Confucianism, hostility is to be internalized rather than given expression by displays of deference and such. Expressing hostility leads to disorder which is, of course, the antithesis of that which is "normal." Such expression is discouraged by peer pressure and external involvement to resolve conflicts. Mao sought to "liberate" or channel this hostility and direct it toward public issues as the driving force behind the revolutionary process. The means was ideological motivation conveyed mainly by slogans. The enemies of the state draw ritualized hostility in the form of rectification campaigns, hostility toward capitalist-roaders, and suspicion of "foreign devils."

Mao departed from the Confucian model of harmony by emphasizing struggle. Since communism anticipates a perfect society, the struggle is to achieve that society through ideological purification. Authority in Confucianism exists to maintain the normal, harmonious order of things. Authority for Mao does not exist apart from ideology, not even in the Communist Party, although the party is to guide the revolution along the ideologically correct path. Deviation periodically became so severe, including within the party itself, that Mao embarked on several rectification campaigns, culminating in the Cultural Revolution. While ideological study is the way to correct thought, the traditional role of the teacher is eliminated. The search for truth is no longer a teacher-student relationship, but a collective struggle.

To end the old ways of action and thought and to promote innovation, Mao sought to institutionalize conflict, to harness it to a higher goal. Political and social institutions were not adequate to this task; in fact they were considered counterproductive. Instead of conventional institutions like government or the family, Mao promoted mass demonstrations, rectification campaigns, encounter groups, self-criticism, and the like. The manipulation of aggressive emotions together with political education resulted in mass mobilization. Essentially, the end result was chaos.

Mao's brand of communism is unorthodox in other ways. The centerpiece of Marxism is class struggle, an economically driven confrontation between structural classes: workers and capitalists. For Mao, the key distinction is between ideological friends and ideological enemies. Correct thought is what matters. In extreme cases, ideological rehabilitation is not possible; landlords and capitalists must ultimately be eliminated. For those who are not thus tainted (workers, peasants, and soldiers) the task is avoiding ideological deviation. The bourgeoisie is not so much an evil class as bourgeois thinking is an ideological germ. Manifestations of this germ include reference to economic growth, professional growth, and expertise.

The Post-Mao Era

Mao's ideology did not long survive his death in 1976. A group including Mao's wife, Jiang Qing, and three others, former Shanghai cultural affairs officer Zhang Chunqiao, former newspaper editor Yao Wenyuan, and former security official and labor organizer Wang Hongwen, collectively known as the "Gang of Four," attempted to perpetuate the radical line. Opposing the radical Maoists were moderates led by Zhou Enlai. Zhou, who died eight months before Mao in 1976, was an important link between the Maoist and post-Maoist periods in China's history. Zhou had a knack for not becoming a victim of the power struggles that occurred, especially over the question of Mao's successor. Liu Shaoqi, Lin Biao, and the Gang of Four all lost in these struggles, and Deng Xiaoping was temporarily eclipsed. But Zhou managed to remain above it all. Not only that, but he articulated a moderate approach (the Four Modernizations) which anticipated the reforms of the late 1970s.

The radicals gained temporary control following Mao's death. But they encountered popular opposition, and the Gang of Four was arrested a month later. They were tried and convicted in a show trial. Jiang and Zhang were each sentenced to death, although their sentences were later commuted to life in prison. The other two were given long prison sentences.

5

China After Mao

Mao's efforts and those of his followers to realize the system he had envisioned ultimately ended in failure. Toward the end, Mao had come to the conclusion that the vitality had gone out of the revolution and the quest for socialist perfection had turned into backsliding toward capitalism and the revival of exploitation. His solution to this situation was the Great Proletarian Cultural Revolution, which ultimately not only failed to revive revolutionary enthusiasm but proved to be a major disaster. Rather than reviving ideological fervor, it produced a political climate where a less radical approach was favored over ideological frenzy. Other than the "Gang of Four" and the other adherents to Maoism, most people, including the national leadership, favored political stability and economic growth. When Mao died in 1976, China embarked on a course fundamentally different from that prevailing since 1949. As one historian wrote, "So fundamental and far-reaching have been the social and economic changes in China in the last decade that if Chairman Mao were to return for a visit, he would be stunned beyond belief by what he would see. Communist ideology is largely ignored and irrelevant. The entrepreneurial spirit fills the air, and the new religion is money."[1]

Important deviations from the Maoist model had previously been put forth in Zhou Enlai's Four Modernizations. Zhou, who died just months before Mao, managed to avoid getting caught up in the power struggles that claimed the careers, and lives, of others such as Liu Shaoqi and Lin Biao. His political survival may be attributable to the fact that he was never designated as Mao's heir. Zhou's protégé, Deng Xiaoping, himself twice temporarily purged, was able to carry the more pragmatic approach to fruition. Deng was one of the Long March survivors who, in the course of the war against Japan and later the civil war, established sound political skills, if not military genius.[2] These skills would serve him well as he later assumed control of China's destiny. Deng's policies included economic development as determined by empirical results rather than an emphasis on ideology. In the party conference of December 1978 (Third Plenum, Eleventh Central Committee), the rise of Deng Xiaoping as the paramount leader was made evident and his modernization strategy confirmed.[3]

Among the most important actions taken in the post-Mao era was the opening of China not only to the world economy but to foreign ideas. China remained suspicious of the outside world, however. The "beware of foreign devils" attitude would take time to overcome. Initially it was hoped, naïvely as it turned out, that foreign science and technology could be imported and converted into economic progress while foreign culture, values, and political ideas could be kept out.

During the late 1970s and early 1980s, the government tried in various ways to discourage the adoption of foreign ways. To prevent "spiritual pollution," censorship of the media was vigorously pursued. There were even efforts to restrict the rapid expansion of electronic communication. But radio, television, and the spread of computer technology could only be slowed, not stopped.

Traditional values and standards of behavior were further undermined by foreign students and tourists, who poured into China while Chinese students in large numbers went abroad to study. This made it increasingly difficult to keep foreign ideas out. Electronic media, and especially the Internet, made intellectual isolation impossible. The "infection" of foreign ideas culminated in the Tiananmen incident in 1989 when youthful protesters demanded democratic political reform and an end to corruption.[4]

China's leaders were faced with the need to rationalize the new social, economic, and political realities. The challenges of the late twentieth century required, among other things, a rearranging of ideological priorities. Classical Marxism was obsolete, and revolutionary doctrines had become not only irrelevant but undesirable under contemporary conditions. Building "socialism with Chinese characteristics" could not be achieved relying on the ideas of nineteenth-century theorists, who had envisaged socialism being built on the basis of highly developed capitalism, nor by following the examples of other socialist countries.[5] The party elders were not about to relinquish their hold on political power, however. There would be political and economic modernization but with definite limitations.

The Chinese Communists continue to embrace the Leninist conception of the overriding dominance of the party, but the party's revolutionary mission is hardly to be found in contemporary political discourse. The party transformed "from an ascetic, revolutionary organization to an elitist political instrument, no longer committed to world revolution, international brotherhood, national liberation, and the Communist utopia, but to the perpetuation of its dictatorial power and the enrichment of its members and families."[6] The success of the new policy approach soon became evident. China's economy has grown often by double-digit figures, so fast indeed that the government eventually was obliged to put on the brakes lest the economy overheat and inflation run out of control. Barring any political disasters or major economic reverses, China's economy could conceivably overtake even that of the United States. "By A.D. 2020 the Chinese economy could be the largest on earth," writes Hsu. "Politically, the government is searching for a unifying philosophy to replace the bankrupt Communism and seems inclined to a mixture of traditional Confucianism, nationalism, patriotism, and a touch of Great Chinaism that subtly resembles the Middle Kingdom concept."[7] Economic change has had far-reaching effects. Traditional practices have eroded under the impact of the quest for material gain. Even the bedrock of traditional society, the family, has been affected. Parents' ability to determine their children's marriage partners and career choices has diminished. The younger generation is now more assertive in deciding for itself and is less inclined to attach importance to family values and traditions.[8]

In response to these trends, there was a neo-Confucian revival in the post-Deng period. The ruling elite found some traditional ideas more compatible with their own views than those of the neo-leftists and liberals. As described by Merle Goldman:

> These neo-Confucianists were seeking ways to achieve modernization without the corrupting influences of Westernization. They argued the former could be achieved relying on Chinese history and values, specifically on Confucianism. Instead of China's Confucian tradition blocking modernization, as preached by the May Fourth intellectuals, Maoist radicals, and liberal party reformers and intellectuals in the 1980s, the neo-Confucians contended Confucianism was conducive to modernization. They referred to the dynamism of Japan and South Korea both having strong Confucian elements. They asserted that a revived neo-Confucianism would provide the intellectual and cultural underpinnings for China's rapid economic development, while helping China avoid the immorality and individualism of Western capitalism.[9]

The Military

In the traditional Confucian system, the status of the military was low. This notion continued with the Communists, who viewed the military as an extension of the people, not a separate institutional entity. Given the social leveling implicit in communist doctrine, various attempts were made from time to time to avoid conferring military rank on officers according to status. This egalitarianism presents problems for a system of command; the role of officers becomes ambiguous. To complicate the role of the military in contemporary China, the CCP's experience in gaining power involved guerrilla warfare tactics. To be effective these tactics require a close relationship between the military and the people as expressed in Mao's famous "three rules of discipline" and "eight points for attention."[10] China's military doctrine continued to stress mass mobilization in the form of "people's war." Material aspects of warfare such as modernization of weapons were deemphasized in favor of manpower.

The Chinese Red Army was founded in 1927 and became the tool of the Communist quest for power. The engine of the revolution was, of course, the party. As Mao said: "Political power grows out of the barrel of a gun; the party controls the gun." This doctrine worked fine until the People's Republic was established and China found itself involved in military relationships with other countries. The experience of the Korean War suggested that China's military doctrine and especially its armaments were inadequate to meet the needs of a state in the mid-twentieth century.

Even after the Korean War experience, military modernization remained controversial, and when China invaded Vietnam in 1989 to teach it a "lesson," the limitations of China's military capacity became evident. Since then, reorganization and improvement of weapon systems have been main features of public policy, and expenditures on the military have steadily increased since the 1980s. Still, China is no match for the major powers and would have difficulty holding its own against Taiwan. In March 2007, the government announced an 18 percent increase in military spending. This would place the regular budget for the military at $44.94 billion, which is about a third of the actual amount if all military-related expenditures are included. This is considerably less than the $623 billion the United States planned to spend over the same time period. Moreover, this latter figure did not include special appropriations to finance operations in Iraq and Afghanistan.

China began working on the acquisition of nuclear technology in the mid-1950s. Until the Sino-Soviet split in 1962, China received technical assistance from the Soviet Union, although this assistance did not include nuclear weapons technology. On October 16, 1964, China tested a small (22 kiloton) nuclear device. Three years later it had achieved a 3.3 megaton hydrogen device. A missile delivery system was tested in the late 1960s. By the early 1980s, China was deploying nuclear weapons, including a sea-launch capability. Maoist rhetoric described nuclear weapons as "paper tigers," and the Chinese criticized the Soviets for being unnecessarily frightened of the possibility of nuclear war. Mao at one point declared that socialism could be built on the ashes of nuclear destruction. This led the Soviet Union to suggest to the United States a joint preemptive attack to prevent China from bringing about a nuclear Armageddon. Of course, this attack never happened. China's possession of nuclear weapons complicated American foreign policy and very likely served as an important deterrent to any aggressive military actions to achieve "regime change" in China. The end of American military involvement in Vietnam opened the door to normalization of relations between the United States and China. From the U.S. perspective, "playing the China card" would serve the purpose of isolating the Soviet Union.

The Party

During the ascendancy of Mao's political ideology, institutional development had been deemphasized. "Politics in Command" was the slogan. Those who suggested that emphasis should be placed on administrative mechanisms, or procedures, or substantive goals, especially economic targets, were chastised for "careerism" or "bureaucratism," or "capitalist-roadism." The political universe was defined in terms of the pursuit of ideological purity. Even the party did not escape criticism; it came under attack during the Cultural Revolution. This radical ideological approach came to an end during the late 1970s. Beginning with Zhou Enlai's Four Modernizations, China embarked on a path more in line with conventional political development, that is, institutions, policies, and procedures. This process accelerated under the regime of Deng Xiaoping and has continued ever since. While there are outward manifestations of a modern, and democratic, political system, actual power remains in the hands of the party. In the 1982 constitution of the People's Republic, legislative, executive, and judicial organs of government are laid out as well as the other accoutrements of modern government such as civil rights.

China inherited certain practical and theoretical approaches from the Soviet Union. Among these was the priority assigned to doctrine. Marxism-Leninism-Mao Zedong Thought constituted a kind of secular theology from which all truth derives. As with any such fundamental doctrine, the basic problem is interpreting its meaning. Since truth is not self-evident, somebody has to determine what it is. In the Soviet model, this took the form of party supremacy. Whatever the CPSU determined correct interpretation of doctrine to be was, by definition, correct. In the Chinese experience, Mao played a unique ideological role. Although later considered to have made mistakes himself, Mao's "thought" was superior to ordinary party doctrine, which was supposed to be guided by occasional ideological pronouncements put forth by Mao. Mao's ideological role undermined the Leninist party infallibility idea. With Mao, the party did not necessarily have a monopoly on determining the correct line. The status of the party was further weakened by the attacks on it during the Cultural Revolution. Following the demise of Maoism, party leaders have, more or less, reestablished the political dominance of the party, although doctrinal orthodoxy has all but disappeared. Hence, the rationale for the party's dominance has become increasingly dubious.

The disintegration of the Soviet Union raised questions regarding the theoretical foundations of the state as defined by communist doctrine, forcing China to reassess the situation. The status of communism and the role of the Chinese

Leaders of the Chinese Communist Party

Mao Zedong	Chairman	1943–1976
Hua Guofeng	Chairman	1976–1981
Hu Yaobang	Chairman	1981–1982
	General Secretary	1982–1987
Zhao Ziyang	General Secretary	1987–1989
Jiang Zemin	General Secretary	1989–2002
Hu Jintao	General Secretary	2002–

Communist Party became increasingly ambiguous. To shore up its status, the party pursued two courses of action. Among the basic decisions taken by the party, the most immediate was a commitment to never voluntarily abdicate its monopoly of power as the Soviets had done, and "the media were instructed to play up the specter of disorder and chaos in the Soviet Union as a warning to the Chinese people should they think of following the Soviet course." The second commitment was to economic development and improvement in the quality of life. "Thus, the authorities promised economic prosperity and political stability as long as they were in control."[11] The legitimacy of the party's political dominance thus was predicated on its ability to maintain political stability and promote economic prosperity, which, it would seem, amounts to a return to Confucian basics.

The Legislative Branch

It is common in modern constitutional systems for the legislative body to occupy the position of superior authority. The British parliament is supreme, and the Congress is mentioned first in the U.S. Constitution to secure its place as the source of law. China is no exception. The supreme government organ is the National People's Congress (NPC). The main function of the NPC, as with most legislatures, is to serve as the constitutional source of law and public policy. Additionally, it has the authority to appoint, recall, or remove from office top executive and judicial officials. Upon recommendation of the president of the People's Republic, the NPC designates, and may remove, the premier and other members of the State Council. It also elects the president of the Supreme People's Court and the chief procurator (prosecutor) of the Supreme People's Procuratorate. It also has the authority to amend the constitution.[12]

One of the biggest problems in China is that the constitution declares that government institutions are designed to serve the Communist Party. All ministers heading various parts of the executive branch are not only members of the CCP but are also members of the Party Central Committee, which means the State Council and the party executive apparatus are made up of the same people. The dynamics of politics do not involve interaction between the government and political parties, but occur within the top levels of the Communist Party.[13]

Another problem with the "party-government bureaucratic machine" has been the party's control and 'intervention' in matters of government policy," complicated by the fact that the party "has become increasingly more corrupt, and its members too often subvert Party directives."[14]

In order to address the problem of the party-government interlocking relationship, a 1987 constitutional change created two types of cadres under separate management systems: "political civil servants appointed for a fixed term of service and administrative civil servants with tenure, but managed through state civil service laws."[15]

Actual authority in the Chinese system is fragmented, and the system is often thought to have too many political members to work effectively. In Kenneth Lieberthal's analysis, "The simple point is that the officials of any given office have a number of bosses in different places. In this sense the Chinese polity can be considered one of 'fragmented authoritarianism.' It becomes important in these circumstances to determine which of these bosses have priority over others."[16]

The NPC has nominal control over the executive branch in that it chooses both the president and the vice-president. The term of office of the president and vice-president of the People's Republic of China is the same as that of the National People's Congress. Under the 1982 constitution, these officials are limited to two consecutive terms. Since 1993, the president has also been the general secretary of the CCP. Jiang Zemin's successor, Hu Jintao, became general secretary in late 2002 and president of China in March 2003. The "fifth generation" is scheduled to come into power in 2012–13, with Xi Jinping, Hu's vice president and first secretary of the CCP's Central Secretariat, widely expected to come out on top.

When the NPC is not in session, there is a Standing Committee that acts on behalf of the NPC. While the Standing Committee is elected by the NPC, it is this committee that has the power to conduct elections of the deputies of the NPC and to convene the NPC sessions. Since the NPC meets once a year at most, the Standing Committee exercises a great deal of influence over the functions of the legislature.[17] Members of the Standing Committee of the National People's Congress are elected for terms corresponding to those of the Congress. It remains in power until a new Standing Committee is selected by a newly chosen National People's Congress. The chairman and vice-chairman of the Standing Committee are, like their counterparts, premier and vice-premier, limited to two consecutive terms.

The National People's Congress has established a number of committees that focus on different issue areas. The special committees examine, discuss, and draw up relevant bills and draft resolutions. They are under the direction of the Standing Committee of the NPC when the Congress is not in session. Lieberthal describes the system in *Governing China*:

> [T]he 1982 constitution gives the Standing Committee the powers and functions normally possessed by the NPC itself, to serve as an interim national congress when the NPC is not in session. The Standing Committee now supervises a new system of parliamentary committees on nationalities, law, finance and economics, public health, education, foreign affairs, overseas Chinese, and any other areas deemed necessary. When the NPC is not in session, the Standing Committee can enact and amend decrees and laws in civil and criminal affairs, including those affecting the structure of the central government. It can annul any administrative regulations and decisions of the central government, and it has the power to interpret the constitution. In order that the Standing Committee be an independent body, its members are not permitted to hold posts in any branch of the central government.[18]

The Executive Branch

The cabinet, or the State Council, is the highest executive organ, and has functional administrative authority over ministries and commissions.[19] The State Council is composed of the premier, vice-premier, and heads of national ministries and commissions. The number of executive offices has increased over the years, ranging from thirty to over one hundred. Members of the State Council serve terms that are the same as those of members of the National People's Congress. The premier, vice-premiers, and state councilors are limited to two consecutive terms. There is also within the State Council an independent audit agency, under the supervision of the premier. Its function is to audit the revenues and expenditures of the various ministries both at the central and provincial levels. This agency is intended to monitor and check the vast Chinese bureaucracy.[20]

At the provincial and local levels, the constitution provides for people's congresses and people's governments. These are directly under the central government and include counties, cities, municipal districts, townships, nationality townships, and towns. The organization of local people's congresses and local people's governments at different levels is determined by the central government. There are also self-government organs established in autonomous regions, autonomous prefectures, and autonomous counties. These deal mainly with minority populations. The organization and working procedures of organs of self-government are prescribed by law in accordance with the basic principles laid down in Sections V and VI of Chapter Three of the constitution.

There are twenty-two provinces, five autonomous regions, and four municipalities—Beijing, Shanghai, Tianjin, and Chongqing—that make up the various levels of government under the central government.[21] Constitutional power lies in the people's congresses at the province and autonomous region, city and county levels, and deputies at these levels are elected indirectly. Again to quote Lieberthal's description: "These bodies have six main responsibilities: to enact local statutes according to local conditions; to ensure the observance and implementation of the state constitution, the statutes, and the administrative rules; to approve plans for economic development and budgets at the county level and above; to elect or recall governors, mayors, and chiefs for the counties and townships; to elect and recall judges and procurators; to maintain public order."[22]

The commune system, an important experiment in collectivization during the Maoist period, was replaced by the 1983 adoption of the township-collective-household system.[23] Village committees bridge the gap between local villagers and township organizations and are considered to be a mass organization rather than a governmental organ. These local committees are responsible for "road and bridge repairs, nurseries and homes for the aged, cultural and recreational activities, public order and security and provide an informational bridge between the township and village."[24]

The power and influence of local leaders remains largely intact. But at this level, there is widespread corruption not only by officials but by members of their families, who have taken advantage of economic liberalization to enrich themselves. They often delay if not ignore altogether orders from Beijing. This problem extends also to the military, which is involved in all manner of business enterprises.[25]

The Legal System

China's legal system has fluctuated between the Confucian model (with communist modifications), which stresses proper social norms governing behavior, social pressure to ensure conformity, and emphasis on a ritualized form of persuasion, and a more formalistic model familiar to people in the West. This model involves codification of rules and their application through well-defined structures and procedures. The first was employed following the Communist takeover in 1949; beginning in 1954 the more formal approach was introduced. The period of the 1958 Great Leap Forward through the 1966–76 Cultural Revolution involved the return of the Confucian or "extrajudicial" model. A new constitution introduced in 1978 marked the beginning of the end of Maoism and the return of the formal legal model.[26]

China resisted the need to modernize its legal system until circumstances forced it to do so. Under pressure from economic changes and the nineteenth-century version of globalization, imperialism, China's legal institutions proved increasingly inadequate. Throughout most of its history, ethical criteria governed relationships rather than formal legal ones. In order to deal with world trade and Western laws, China adopted written law modeled on the Japanese system, which itself was borrowed from Europe. The proximity of Japan and the trade relationship between the two nations led the Chinese to send students to Japan for legal training. A legal system independent of foreign precedents was not adopted until 1949, and that one was based on Maoist-communist ideas.

The Chinese legal system today is an amalgam of three legal traditions that have been intertwined over the past one hundred years. The first is the informal system made up of Confucian ideas and practices that deemphasize law codes, structure, and procedure in favor of ideology and political guidance. The second system is the formal legal system essentially forced on China beginning in the nineteenth century by Western nations. The third system is the Maoist-communist system that is ideologically driven and stresses "people's" justice. In the informal system, emphasis is placed on mediation for resolution of conflicts and disputes. This process worked well and allowed China to exist for long periods of time without a codified law. Confucian theory held that society must take care of its own and discouraged litigation. Taking no legal action was seen as the correct path. Under Confucianism, the function of the law is to protect society, not the individual. Litigation and pursuance of individual need was considered an embarrassing excess and routinely discouraged. "Except for very serious cases, the traditional settlement of a dispute was one of informality, compromise, and face-saving for everyone involved. Disputes were settled largely through mediation by elders in a family, clan, or village, with consultation all around."[27] Under the Communist regime there has been a similar emphasis on mediation involving party organizations and street, neighborhood, or workplace committees.

From the Han dynasty onward, the Chinese legal system combined both the "societal" and the "jural" models in various combinations and degrees.

> In the traditional Chinese legal system, Confucian virtues were expressed in terms of law and backed up with punishments that could be quite severe. China's dynastic government continued, at least rhetorically, to regard the law as a supplement to rule by virtuous example, proper organization and

care of the people, and moral instruction. But in the concrete practice of government, hard decisions had to be made regarding the proper use of moral suasion and criminal punishment. Should preventive and punitive techniques be used in tandem or in sequence? If in sequence, then what is the proper sequence of their employment? On what basis should the ruler decide which approach to take toward deviant behavior?[28]

The formal court system in operation under the constitution is made up of the Supreme Court, the Higher People's Court, the Intermediate People's Court, and the Basic People's Court. Special courts exist for maritime, railway, and military law. Very rarely is a case referred to the Supreme Court unless it has special significance for the entire country. Instead, the Supreme Court is designed to oversee the lower courts and instill leadership.

The People's Court hears cases of first instance that may involve a life sentence, an appeal of mediation, an appeal of mediation from the informal courts, and cases involving foreigners. Higher Courts hear appeals, major criminal cases that affect an entire province, or appeals from the Procuratorate.

The informal courts handle the majority of cases through mediation. The idea is that "the teachings of proper behavior and the controlling of law-breaking run a parallel course through formal and informal methods."[29] This system relies on the public security and mediation committees. Citizens are expected both to intervene in any conflict without being asked and to report to local police any possible criminal or potentially criminal behavior. Litigation is seen as expressing overt individual characteristics and is not perceived as just or attractive; therefore mediation plays a big role in informal courts. All outcomes may be appealed at the higher courts; however, this happens infrequently. The informal justice system relies on local police for support.

In practice, however, when it comes to civil cases, "Chinese courts continuously face the problem of enforcement and execution of court decisions. It has become a regular feature in the Supreme People's Court's annual reports to the NPC that judgments on economic cases are often too difficult to enforce."[30] As James C.F. Wang explains the problem: "[T]oo often there is interference by local leaders and/or party officials under the accepted practice of 'local protectionism.' Local protectionism, or preferential treatment, in civil judgments by local courts has been an entrenched traditional practice simply because of institutional dependency of the local courts on the support of the local political power base for the court's budget, personnel, and housing facilities."[31]

The Chinese government has always taken the approach that lawbreakers can generally be rehabilitated. Prisoners can be made useful to society through a reform process based on useful labor. Only those who cannot be rehabilitated or who have committed serious crimes such as murder or drug trafficking are dealt with harshly. Care is taken to settle them back into society when they complete their terms. Accounts of former political prisoners and by Western human rights groups contest this image, as they describe labor reform camps as being characterized by unsafe and unsanitary working and living conditions, arbitrary brutality, and the naked pursuit of profit.[32]

Chinese criminologists and the law itself assume that lawbreakers have the potential for rehabilitation and to become good citizens. It is further assumed in the legal philosophy that the social, cultural, and economic milieu of the People's Republic provides the necessary resources for individuals to develop a healthy sense of morality and self-discipline. Only those who cannot be rehabilitated face the ultimate penalty. Execution, in theory at least, is reserved for those who commit the worst offenses and are considered to display "complete and utter alienation from human society," and education and reform for those "who, although having taken a wrong turn in life, were considered capable of responding positively to the concentrated efforts of the state and society to bring them back into the fold and give them a new life by including them in collective work and study."[33]

The role of law in China differs in many respects from practices in the West. It does not serve to protect personal rights of the people against the state or the party. There is also little sense of judicial independence or an emphasis on judicial integrity in the administration of justice.[34]

Professionals formally trained in law are a new addition to China's political structure. Administration of the law was in the hands of officials during most of China's history. During the period of Maoist communism, the law as an established and codified body of rules did not really exist. Instead rules were determined by political realities of the moment, leading to highly unpredictable situations. This has changed rapidly in recent years as economic realities and especially international involvement have demanded greater transparency and predictability in legal relationships.

The judicial system employs a hybrid of the accusatorial system that is common in much of the world. (The adversarial system found in the United States, where lawyers contend before juries, is uncommon.) The Chinese system can be described as inquisitorial in that judges take an active part in legal proceedings. Judicial officers are elected or appointed by the state. Standing committees elect the vice-presidents, presiding judges, and deputy judges at all court levels. The standing committees do not prosecute the cases but can influence the outcome of the trial. Confucian ideals encourage a confession by the accused and in a trial, it is the sentence that is argued rather than the guilt of the party. People's assessors assist in the proceedings and may even act as judge in some instances. The assessor is a layperson who can be elected by the public once he or she has reached the age of twenty-three.

Lawyers in China during the early post-Mao period primarily served the interests of the state. Their relationship with their clients was merely to advise them about the law, not in any way to plead their case. Loyalty of the lawyer lies solely with the court, and private legal practice has not been permitted in China until recently. Additionally, it is a criminal offense for the lawyer to protect the client in any way other than to plead for leniency. Formal law schools were introduced in China for three years in the 1950s then discontinued until 1979, when formal training was reintroduced with law students being sent to Japan for instruction in international law. Today the demand for lawyers is growing rapidly and is met by a growing number of law schools. By the late 1990s, the number of lawyers had grown to over 90,000, but most had limited formal legal training. Since 1992 the Ministry of Justice has required a license examination for those individuals who want to qualify for legal practice as a lawyer. The total number of law firms staffed by licensed lawyers has grown, but only about 10 percent of them are financially independent of the government. The government aims to train as many as 150,000 lawyers.[35]

Before reforms were introduced in the 1970s, the public security organ (police) had considerable discretionary power to arrest and incarcerate individuals for criminal acts, and of course it still does. But, at least nominally, separation among the different legal organs was clarified in 1979: the public security organ is to investigate crimes and detain criminals, the Procuratorate approves arrests and prosecutes criminal cases, and the courts try them.

During the first years of the PRC (1949–1953), formal organs of criminal justice existed but were essentially nonfunctional. The extrajudicial model prevailed whereby revolutionary justice was dispensed by administrative agencies or by the people themselves under party leadership. From 1954 through 1957, the legal system switched to the formal or jural model. A constitution was adopted (1954), some laws were written, and class struggle was deemphasized. From 1957 through 1960, the formal model was attacked as bourgeois, and the extrajudicial model returned to favor. From 1961 through 1963 there was a return to the formal model and then from 1964 through 1977 there occurred the nearly complete domination of the extrajudicial model. Since then, the formal model has been ascendant.[36]

Nevertheless, China is a considerable distance from a fully institutionalized legal system, although it is moving in that direction. Access to the system remains limited, and it is far from transparent. The judiciary is not independent of interference from other government agencies. The role of legal professionals, especially private attorneys, is limited, making not only criminal justice but commercial legal issues unpredictable and erratic. Influence peddling by leading party and government officials, rather than formal procedures, remains the name of the game. All things considered, however, the situation is improving.

6

Contemporary Issues

Since the end of the period of radical politics that marked the Mao Zedong era, China has confronted a range of policy issues that were products of either neglect or conformity to the revolutionary agenda of Maoism. In addition to the problems stemming from the failed policies of the Maoist period, China is further challenged by the fact that the world changed dramatically during and after the reign of Mao's ideology, leaving China further behind in such important areas as technology, economic institutions, and political infrastructure. As a result, China's present-day policy challenges are complex and daunting. In some areas, there has been commendable progress, while in others the country continues to be bedeviled by difficulties.

The reality of meeting demands for public services is exacerbated by the fact that China has the largest population of any country in the world today—about four times the population of the United States. Meeting the needs of so many people is difficult enough. Despite the country's large landmass—China is about the same size as the United States—the population is not evenly distributed. Most of the population is concentrated in about one-third of the country's space. Moreover, the heaviest population occurs in areas of the country that are most agriculturally productive. The human pressure on the land is thus considerable.

With its large population and restricted developmental experience, providing the public services the country needs is a great challenge. Political development and public policy are further complicated by factors other than sheer numbers. These include ethnic diversity, gender values, generational changes, and the need to provide for the elderly, handicapped, unemployed, and the like.

Population

China's population is currently estimated at over 1.3 billion, most of whom are ethnically classified as Han. Other ethnic groups are concentrated along the western and northern borders. About two-thirds of the population is concentrated in the eastern one-third of the country. In the coastal areas, there are large urban centers and most nonagricultural economic activity takes place here. The high population density of China's cities has resulted in the usual urban phenomena: congestion, pollution, crime, and other social problems. The eastern third of the country is also where the best farmland is to be found. Taking agricultural resources out of production and turning them into highways, factories, and houses not only aggrieves the peasants who are forced off the land; but also impacts the country's ability to feed the population. Eastern China is where the classical Confucian culture developed. As one moves further away from this area, the less pronounced the signs of traditional Chinese civilization. The result over the last century has been rural-urban and sociocultural tensions.

The interior two-thirds of the country is sparsely populated in comparison, although there has been substantial growth in recent years. The economic development of minority groups along the frontier has lagged behind that of industrial-urban China. Areas where Kazakhs, Tajiks, Kirgiz, Uigurs, Mongols, Tibetans, and other groups reside have from time to time presented problems of separatism, a sensitive issue even today. These people are not fully integrated into the national fabric of the country. Many of them have been little touched by the modern economy and continue to try and sustain themselves by nomadic practices and pastoral lifestyles. This traditional lifestyle is now nearly impossible to sustain in China or anywhere else because of the encroaching demands of modern society, including national security.

There are several dimensions to the demographic process of transition from a society that is primarily rural-agricultural to one that is urban-industrial. As societies experience economic modernization, the rural-agricultural model becomes obsolescent. With mechanization and improved farming techniques, agriculture becomes more productive. The amount of physical labor needed to produce a particular crop declines, resulting in a "surplus" rural population. People are thus "pushed" from the countryside to the cities in search of alternative sources of livelihood. The redundancy of rural populations is exacerbated by improved living conditions. More children survive infancy and life expectancy increases thanks to better diet and health care. Rural populations are stressed by their disengagement from the mainstream of socioeconomic development. In addition to those driven from the land, where for cultural reasons they would prefer to remain, many leave to seek employment in the cities. Younger people with weaker connections to the rural lifestyle may be attracted to the opportunities seen to be available in the city. Thus they are "pulled" to the urban areas. While such migrants provide the manpower needed for industrialization, the new arrivals generally lack the skills needed for occupational advancement, and housing and other amenities are not always available in the amounts needed. A result is often unemployment or underemployment and urban slums and the political and social stress that these produce.

The "surplus" labor population has been a boon to Chinese and foreign entrepreneurs and foreign consumers seeking cheap labor. Another population issue of increasing significance in today's China is the growing gap between the rich and the poor. China's economic growth has been phenomenal, but it has produced inequities. Those with energy, enterprise, connections, and good luck have prospered while many in the rural population and the lower ranks of the urban working class have been left out. A particularly acute problem involves urban workers in state-owned factories that are obsolete and incapable of making a profit. The government has shut some of them down and sold others, but there are risks of creating unemployment should profitability be pursued more energetically. In any event, the "iron rice bowl" of socialist job security is becoming a thing of the past. The growing numbers of people with poor economic prospects, or those who see themselves as being deprived of rewards available to others, pose potentially serious political problems.

One approach to the numbers issue employed by China and other countries, such as India, has been to try and limit growth through family planning. China's population policy is the most draconian example of its type in the world. To slow population growth, China in the late 1970s adopted a highly controversial one-child-per-family program (rural families could request permission to have a second child). The policy reduced the growth rate but has, among other things, created the "little emperor syndrome." Chinese families have always preferred male children in order to carry on the family line, to care for the elderly, and in agricultural areas, to work the land. In the traditional male-dominated society, it is the males who produce wealth for the family. The preference for boys exacerbates the problem of female infanticide, a practice that has existed in China for centuries. With modern technology, such as ultrasound, parents can determine the gender of a fetus and if it is not what they want, the mother can undergo an abortion. Some parents abandon female babies, which results in a large population of orphans, a substantial percentage of whom are girls. Many are adopted by Western families.

Families that conform to the one-child policy are rewarded with better jobs and housing, educational opportunities, and other economic incentives. Failure to adhere to the one-child rule can lead to the loss of these rewards. All manner of contraceptives are available, as is abortion. The campaign has included a heavy dose of propaganda such as the ubiquitous billboards extolling the virtues of the happy family with one child. Three decades on, however, the success of the one-child campaign, in combination with improved health care and life expectancy, have resulted in an aging population that will increasingly require social support. The policy is widely expected to be modified within the next few years.

Education

At or near the top of every country's public policy agenda is the need to educate the people. Education is not only the mechanism for transmitting traditions and values to future generations, it also provides the skills necessary for modern society to function. Fortunately, learning has always been highly valued in China. The Confucian tradition of the veneration of scholars led to a system that put the government in the hands of capable people. Under the imperial system, education and learning were highly valued. In fact, the learned man, the sage, occupied the pinnacle of social status. These men of letters were recruited by examination and were basically in charge of running the country. China was well served by this process except for the fact that education did not evolve with the changing conditions and demands facing the country. The examinations for recruitment into government service were geared to the ancient Classics, which meant that scholarship was always looking backward and its proponents were fundamentally conservative. This scholarship also accepted as a given the static social order and the centrality of authority in the form of the emperor. The dialectical interaction among different schools of thought, whether products of religious sectarianism or the dynamic tension between ecclesiastical and secular authority, was simply not a part of the Chinese intellectual universe.[1]

In the nineteenth century, the education system had lost its vibrancy, and education did not extend to the general public. While it served China well for centuries, at the start of the twentieth century, China's educational system was woefully inadequate. The subject matter was tradition bound, and there were growing problems in terms of quality and quantity. As Fairbank and Goldman report: "A nation of 400 million people had produced annually before 1949 only some 185,000 college graduates; and as the population rapidly increased after that date, the proportion of highly educated personnel did not improve. College graduates comprised somewhere around 1 percent of the population. How could one hope to create a modern country with that proportion of trained personnel?"[2]

The Communists set a goal of a people's school in every village. But this proved to be unattainable. Education in newly developing countries presents several dilemmas. First, expanding education requires money, something always in short supply, which means limiting investment in other priorities. Second, educational development is a bottom-up process; primary education is logically first. But primary schools require teachers who must have secondary education. Secondary education requires faculty who are the products of universities and colleges. Third, those advancing up the educational ladder have expanding expectations that are difficult to satisfy in an underdeveloped economy.[3]

Now China finds itself meeting the challenges of the early twenty-first century with woefully inadequate educational resources. Part of this state of affairs is the result of China's status as an "underdeveloped" country throughout most of the twentieth century, a time when the West experienced rapid intellectual growth. The backwardness of China's institutions, including educational, meant that China fell further and further behind advanced countries in the West, and Japan as well, in providing the necessary skills for modern industrial society. Education, other than the political variety, was never a high priority during Mao's time, and problems with education were compounded by the depredations of the Cultural Revolution when education in particular was severely set back.

The post-Maoist embrace of modernization entailed a major commitment to improving education in general, and science and technology education in particular. Vocational and higher education was expanded, with a variety of institutions and financing schemes, and the tradition of competitive entrance exams was revived. Despite the dramatic improvement in China's higher education system, high prestige still attaches to a degree from an elite Western university.

Economic Policy

During the period in which the ideas of Mao Zedong prevailed, China lurched from one economic disaster to another. In 1958, Mao launched the Great Leap Forward. Mao had concluded that the revolutionary transformation of China had been proceeding so well during its first decade that the communist model of national development could be accelerated. The idea was that, rather than relying on the conventional (Western) tools of economic development such as technology, investment capital, market development, and industrialization, China would exploit its main economic resource, its people. Mao rejected conventional statistical measures of economic growth in favor of abstract goals of socialist purity. Tools to this end included communization of agriculture, state ownership of practically everything, central planning, and even an assault on the family.

Mao also rejected the Soviet model of economic development, which emphasized a top-down approach. The Soviets stressed the importance of concentrating on heavy industry first, largely at the expense of agriculture. Once steel and other basic industries were developed, then medium and light industry could follow. This meant that consumer goods industry had the lowest priority. Mao's Great Leap called for small-scale industry at the village level. Peasants would make the tools they needed in local foundries. Mobilization of labor was the key.

The result was inadequate supplies of nearly everything, and much of what was produced in the local industries was of shoddy quality. The government deluded itself into thinking the strategy was a success largely because it continued to receive rosy reports from the field. Bureaucrats reported that quotas were met and often exceeded. They had little choice but to offer false claims because to expose failure would have been received with displeasure by the top leaders. But in the end it became clear that the Great Leap Forward was a catastrophe falling most heavily on the common people. Some 20 to 30 million people lost their lives due to malnutrition and famine.[4] Natural droughts and floods in this period contributed to this high death toll.

A second and even greater disaster occurred beginning in the mid-1960s. At that time, Mao formed the opinion that the spirit of the revolution had begun to flag and that strong medicine was necessary to get it back on track. The country had become too concerned about material things. Bureaucracy was too content with the comforts of office. Even the Chinese Communist Party had lost its way. The answer was the Great Proletarian Cultural Revolution. Educational, political, economic, and other institutions came in for attack, mainly by Mao's new revolutionary foot soldiers, the Red Guards, made up mainly of students. After ten years of effort, the Red Guards managed to set China's developmental trajectory back decades. The disaster ended only with Mao's death in 1976.

In December 1978, Deng Xiaoping presented a reform program to the Communist Party's Eleventh Central Committee Plenum. This program was based on the Four Modernizations first introduced by Deng's mentor Zhou Enlai in 1975. The proposal called for change in the agricultural system by introducing a contract responsibility system. Farmers had to sell to the state a certain quota, while the rest of their production could be sold on the open market. Investment credits and other resources were also made available to farmers.

Individually owned businesses in cities were to be revived. After some hesitation, the number of small businesses increased rapidly. It was an important psychological transition for Chinese to move away from the idea of job security provided by state enterprises to the uncertainty, but greater opportunity, available with "free" enterprise. As a result, entrepreneurial activities, especially in the service sector, have expanded rapidly. It has

Zhou Enlai's protégé Deng Xiaoping (1904–1997), although not formally head of the Chinese Communist Party, became China's leader in 1978 and embarked on a course of economic reform and modernization.

become fashionable, and not ideologically objectionable, to make money and even get rich.

State-owned enterprises (SOEs) were allowed to assume greater responsibility for decisions affecting the operation of their business. Profits were no longer turned over to the state. Instead they were taxed, and what was left over could be reinvested in the plant or handed out as bonuses to spur worker efficiency. Those enterprises that could not attain profitability were supposed to go out of business. But this would have resulted in destabilizing levels of unemployment, so many of the enterprises continued to operate at a loss or were merged into larger SOEs.

The price system, which had been determined by the state, was reformed. Introducing a market mechanism driven by supply and demand proved difficult. Some commodities that had formerly been set at low government-determined prices rose sharply under market conditions. Other problems such as hoarding, speculation, corruption, shortages, and bribery attended the process of economic liberalization. Economic growth was uneven, resulting in regional disparities. Coastal provinces, and the people living in them, prospered more rapidly than did the interior provinces.

By the late 1980s, China's economy had developed a number of ailments. There were serious inflationary pressures and a trade imbalance favorable to China, which caused complaints from trading partners. The violent suppression of the protesters in Tiananmen Square in 1989 led to economic sanctions by other countries. As these problems were eventually overcome, a different kind of concern emerged—too rapid economic growth. But now that China's economy was increasingly integrated into the world economy, it was vulnerable to external economic shocks, and one came with the Asian financial crisis of 1997–98. An economic stimulus program restabilized the situation, and China entered the twenty-first century experiencing continued expansion. Whether that same stimulative remedy will be sufficient to carry China through the global financial crisis that began in 2007, engulfing China's major trading partners, remains to be seen.

There are other problems, too, especially with the United States, which has continually pressured Beijing to realign its currency, which Washington considers undervalued. In recent years, a host of products made in China, from drywall to dog food to toys, were discovered to be contaminated. The United States blocked imports of such products and demanded better quality control on the part of Chinese exporters. The Chinese government, desiring to maintain good trade relations with the United States, sought ways to mitigate the problems. Nonetheless, the magnitude of Chinese manufacturing for the American market, the corruption problem and weak oversight infrastructure, and the slump in global demand due to difficult economic conditions, present continuing challenges.

The Minority Question

The minority population of China is a small percentage of the total, but there are as many as fifty-five officially recognized groups. Even though the populations of these groups are small, the importance attached to minorities by the government is considerable. As June Dreyer observes, minorities receive considerable attention for several reasons. First, minorities live on the borders, particularly in the northwest, with members of the same population group living on the other side of the borders. This often raises touchy political issues. Second, minority areas have less population density than southeast China, where most people are Han Chinese. The latter have been encouraged to move into minority areas in significant numbers, causing some social friction. Third, some of these areas are resource rich and are being exploited for the benefit of all China. Fourth, Beijing wants the minority populations to be contented so that it can be claimed that the Chinese model of social relations is successful. Finally, there is tourism, which has become a significant new commercial opportunity in China.[5] An indication of the volatility of the minority issue occurred in 2008 when China was preparing for the Olympics. Worldwide protests at the treatment of Tibetans caused considerable embarrassment to the Chinese government.

Initially, China's approach to the minority issue was to assume it would disappear with the achievement of the ideal communist state. Until the late 1950s, programs were in place to accommodate cultural and linguistic variations with the intention of "reforming" social conditions. With the beginning of the Great Leap Forward in the late 1950s, there emerged the policy that progress toward the goals of the revolution had to be accelerated. Cultural practices of minorities were viewed with less tolerance. Uniformity was the goal of the Great Leap, which had the effect of further alienating minorities from the mainstream culture. The Great Leap was a great disaster not only for minorities but for all of China. Policies that followed the Great Leap returned to a more moderate approach to accommodating China's minorities.

The Cultural Revolution ushered in a return to political orthodoxy, which for minorities meant the pursuit of policies designed to assimilate them into the mainstream. The radical Red Guards had little sympathy for cultural and linguistic differences. Many government officials who had taken a soft line toward minorities were purged. The Cultural Revolution was another disaster for China and resulted not only in the moderation of policies toward minorities but in all areas of public policy.

With the ascendancy of Deng Xiaoping, the emphasis on prosperity marginalized minorities because they lived in areas of China that did not produce immediate economic growth; as noted, the areas of economic potential tend to be along the coast. The income gap between the minorities far in the interior and the mainly Han Chinese along the coast increased considerably. Government policy sought to end pastoral lifestyles and turn the people practicing them to conventional, sedentary economic pursuits. The breakup of the Soviet Union allowed for more cross-border contacts between Kazakhs, Kirgiz, and other Muslim minority peoples of Central Asia, increasing political sensitivities—a matter further exacerbated by the American "war on terror." To gain China's cooperation in this undertaking, the United States had to turn a blind eye to

China's dealings with resistance movements in the frontier areas, although Washington continues to raise "human rights" issues.

Despite the twists and turns in public policy and the political status of minorities, the underlying issues remain pretty much as they have always been. "Minorities who were content to be part of the Chinese empire have not been disruptive under the PRC. Those who were unhappy continue to be so. Neither pluralist nor assimilationist policies have succeeded in solving the nationalities problem."[6]

Foreign Relations

China began to end its isolationism in the early 1970s, even before the death of Mao. With the end of the Vietnam War and the highly symbolic visit to China by President Richard Nixon, China and the United States began the process of normalizing relations. Full diplomatic relations were established on January 1, 1979, followed by rapid expansion of commercial, technological, sports, and cultural relations. A major sticking point was the status of Taiwan. Washington and Beijing had heretofore agreed there was only one China; the disagreement had been over which government, Beijing or Taipei, was the legal one. By accepting the legitimacy of the Beijing government, the Americans had in effect declared the matter to be an internal Chinese one. The United States would not accept reunification by force, however, and continued to maintain economic, political, and even military relations with Taiwan.

Throughout the 1970s, China moved to restore relations with other countries. Embassies were reopened, diplomacy resumed, and trade expanded rapidly. In October 1971, Beijing joined the UN and took over from Taiwan China's permanent seat on the Security Council. Similarly, in 1980 it assumed membership in the World Bank and the International Monetary Fund. Finally, after 15 years of arduous negotiations over the opening up of its economy, China was admitted to the World Trade Organization in 2001.

Over the last two decades, China has confronted changing international realities. For one, the United States is now the only superpower, and both China and Russia have an interest in limiting its global hegemony. The long rift in Sino-Soviet relations was healed by Mikhail Gorbachev and Deng Xiaoping, although the Chinese leader was skeptical of Gorbachev's political liberalization and the centrifugal forces it was unleashing. The bloody suppression of the democracy demonstation in Tiananmen Square, not long after Gorbachev's visit to Beijing, had a chilling effect on China's efforts at developing "normal" formal relations. But eventually the Soviet Union collapsed and both countries pursued a more pragmatic course.

President Richard Nixon meets Mao Zedong in Beijing.

The main regional problem in recent years has been North Korea's nuclear program and concern about the country's unpredictable leader. When the Bush administration threatened to effect "regime change" upon Pyongyang, China played a pivotal role in the "Six-Party Talks" that eventually resulted in defusing the crisis, at least temporarily. In the case of Iran's perceived determination to become a nuclear power, China has been slow to support international efforts to constrain the Islamic regime, with which it has signed major oil and gas deals. The Taiwan issue surfaces from time to time, especially when there is talk of Taiwanese independence. Japan's moves to elevate its international security profile encourage China's suspicions of a revival of Japanese imperialism. But it is China's own dynamism that promises to have by far the greatest impact on the region in the twenty-first century.

II

Korea

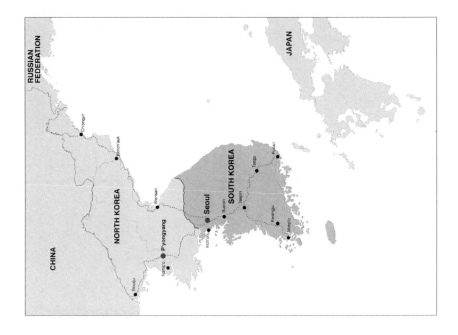

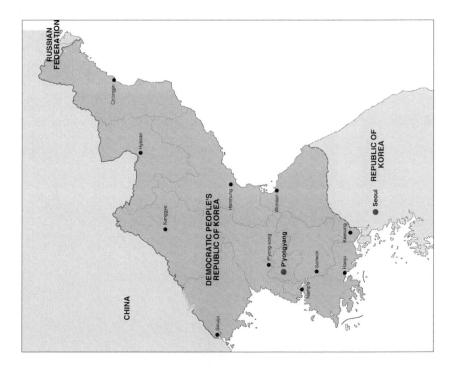

7

In the Shadow of China

Korea, like its neighbor China, has been host to human habitation for millennia. It is estimated that there have been people on the Korean peninsula at least since the Paleolithic period, or for about 60,000 years. The earliest communities were hunter-gatherers; later, rice cultivation entered by way of China. In the Late Neolithic period (9000–8000 B.C.E.) there began a regional trade system which brought about the importation of technology into the region. Populations grew, and people began to migrate to other parts of East Asia. Continuous settlements eventually appeared, making possible the development of economic and political institutions. These early peoples are the ancestors of today's Koreans.

Archeological evidence also suggests that the establishment of communal life led to the formation of social groups based on a clan structure. The social rituals associated with these clans included the use of the totem to promote social solidarity as well as for spiritual purposes.[1] Evidence of totem-based rituals has been found in the area that began as a chiefdom and became the kingdom of Silla. With increasing social sophistication, trade relations were expanded. As the population grew, clans developed into tribes, which took on specific territorial identities. Spiritual traditions included the idea that all living things have a soul and that the soul of man is immortal.

The social order continued to change during the Bronze Age (approximately 3200–1200 B.C.E.), as reflected in the fact that the specific geometric designs used in pottery up to this time had begun to disappear. Technology introduced from China spread throughout the peninsula, but the process was uneven. Some regions achieved higher levels of development than did others. Artifacts from this period suggest rice cultivation was expanding throughout the region, which reflects growing agricultural and technological exchange with China.

During the Bronze Age, Korean society became stratified and burial tombs came into use, signifying that certain members of society held greater status and no doubt political power. The first cohesive and permanent political units to emerge in the region took the form of walled towns that functioned as city-states.[2] These communities were ruled by chieftains who oversaw agricultural production and other social activities. These city-states were territorially small, but they served as important centers of cultural development. The amalgamation of these city-states led to larger social organizations, creating the need for expanded economic and political institutions. But economic and political development also meant a growing disparity between rich and poor.

By the fourth century B.C.E., friction had developed between Korea and China. One of the largest of the Korean city-states, Old Choson, came into conflict with the northern Chinese state of Yan. At the beginning of the Iron Age, Korean city-states bonded together into a confederated kingdom, elevating the authority of the rulers even more. Technological innovation meant better farming tools, which led to greater food production and population growth. Korean development, however, did not keep pace with that of China, and by the third century B.C.E., Old Choson came under Chinese rule.

Agriculture remained the most important economic activity in Korea during the Iron Age. Production was mainly at the village level with little regional interaction. Social development included a system of stratification with freemen, slaves, and a ruling class. Freemen may have owned individual plots of land for agricultural use but, most likely, they also worked in the fields on a communal basis. They were not allowed to bear arms as this was reserved for the privileged classes, and they were heavily taxed and forced to provide labor service to the state.[3] The elite most likely lived in walled cities with several people sharing power simultaneously. Eventually, the ruling class adopted the Chinese word *wang*, or king, signifying a sole ruler for the kingdom. During the early stages of kingship, the role of king may have alternated between two or more royal families, finally giving way to hereditary succession.

China's Continuing Dominance

China continued to expand its control into the peninsula during the centuries that followed and eventually came to dominate the northwestern part of Korea. Chinese cultural and intellectual influence spread throughout Northeast Asia as evidenced by pottery designs originating in China that have been found in Korea, Manchuria, Japan, and Mongolia. Once Han China gained control of the region, important political changes were set in motion. The Chinese allowed considerable local autonomy, but the influence of Chinese culture was substantial. One consequence of this influence was the emergence in Korea of a new ruling elite with a distinctly Chinese orientation. The system that prevailed during the Old Chosen period gave way to a new one patterned after the Chinese model.[4] Other areas of East Asia also came under the influence of the Han dynasty, and a tributary system developed in which the subject states acknowledged the supremacy of imperial China but in practice were largely left to their own devices. Ceremonial garb and grants of office were presented to the Han as a show of submission to the dynasty.

The rise of the confederated kingdoms in Korea posed a potential threat to Chinese supremacy. Initially, three Korean kingdoms (Koguryo, Silla, and Paekche) were most powerful and fought frequently over territory. "Each of the three kingdoms had relations with China, that led to the percolating yet pervasive influence of Sinic civilization upon Korean society and its values."[5] Chinese intellectual influence was especially profound through Confucianism and Buddhism.

The kingdom of Puyo, in Manchuria, provided a buffer between China and the Korean kingdoms to the south. Eventually, Puyo sought an alliance with the more powerful Chinese empire, and ambassadors were sent to the Chinese court in 49 C.E. This alliance lasted approximately 300 years, during which Puyo remained isolated. It was eventually incorporated into China. Population growth and the appetite for more territory put China and Korea in intermittent conflict over several centuries.

During the Silla period, 57 B.C.E. to 935 C.E., Koreans were commercially active throughout East Asia, and their mastery of navigation allowed them to pursue trade interests as far away as the East Indies. But the contradictions between Korean culture and imported Chinese institutions created stress and weakened the Silla kingdom, which fell in 936. Among the problems facing Korea at the time were peasant rebellions, conflicts among the ruling elite, and economic difficulties. Toward the end of the period, Korea's first dynasty, the Koryo, introduced significant changes, including the sponsorship of Buddhism and the expanded role of Confucianism.

During the Koryo period (918–1392), Korea was beset with problems and threats from many quarters. Northern tribes were a constant threat. In 1231, Korea came under Mongol domination. Despite the brevity of the period of their rule, the Mongols left behind a significant legacy that, in Korea, included cultural influences. The Mongols recruited Koreans in their failed efforts to invade Japan. The Koreans, like the Chinese, suffered at the hands of Japanese pirates, who preyed upon coastal communities.

Reflecting the political ideology of China, authority in the Korean system was believed to have been bestowed by the gods and was put into practice by the elites in the kingdom. This divine origin meant that the law coincided with religious thought and punishments under the law were carried out during religious ceremonies. Very little actual structure existed in the legal system within the kingdoms. The law's main purpose was to regulate the social order. Offenses included murder, thievery, female adultery, and jealousy. The law supported respect for individual life and property and showed a fierce regard for the patriarchal family system that existed at the time.[6] Eventually, the institution of kingship moved away from functioning in both religious and political capacities. The king focused on the governance of the state rather than supervising religious festivals. Religious practice was based on animism, which had evolved from even more primitive forms. More complex religious practice required elites schooled in the religious belief system, elites that were able to supplicate and curry favor with the gods rather than just paying homage to them.

The Pervasive Influence of Confucianism

In 1392, a new Korean dynasty was established, with its capital at Seoul, and took the name of the ancient kingdom of Choson (also known as the Yi). This new dynastic system was based almost completely on the principles of Confucianism imported from China. "The influence of Confucianism on Korea's traditional culture was both profound and pervasive," writes Young Whan Kihl.[7] Under the Yi dynasty (1392–1910), Korea was governed by Confucian scholar-officials who stressed ability, virtue, scholarship, and education. There ensued a phase of intellectual accomplishments which, unfortunately, was ended by the same forces that brought it about, Confucian values and practices. In time, the ruling elite succumbed to corruption and political dysfunction. In Korea, as in China, Confucian ideology failed to adapt to the requirements of the time.[8]

Although outward manifestations of Confucianism are not necessarily easy to find in Korea or other parts of East Asia today, this ancient philosophy is still evident in subtle ways. For example, "leaders are still depicted as patriarchal figures and the state is still ideally seen as the extreme of one's family."[9] Moreover, "the Korean tendency to form and treasure affective networks derives from a world view deeply rooted in Korea's history, tradition, and philosophy, namely, Confucianism."[10]

The Confucian emphasis on close personal relationships is manifested today in the importance of blood ties, school ties, and regional ties. "Korean businessmen are (in-)famous for the way in which they are family based. Most of the largest *chaebols* (conglomerates), including the most internationally competitive such as Samsung, Hyundai, and LG, are still controlled by members of the founder's family, usually brothers, sons, nephews, and grandsons."[11]

Asians in general and Koreans in particular place alot of importance on participating in social networks and gatherings such as weddings, funerals, alumni meetings, and other social group activities.[12] These socially interactive activities are augmented by the practice of gift giving. These rituals enhance the sense of interpersonal solidarity and interdependence.

Isolation and Domination

China saw itself as the "Middle Kingdom," meaning that it was the center of the universe with areas outside being regarded as progressively inferior the farther away they were from the center. Peoples beyond those on China's periphery, which were considered tributary states, were regarded as barbarians. Those having tributary status included Korea, Japan, Tibet, Vietnam, and Nepal, among others. Tributary status was maintained by sending missions to the imperial court to show acceptance of the dominance of the emperor, at least symbolically. While maintaining the missions was an expensive proposition, there were advantages. The acceptance of the tribute missions formed a kind of legitimization of the rule of foreign kings and raised their prestige. China also offered protection in times of invasion and aid in times of natural disasters. In return for the tribute, luxury articles were bestowed on the tributary ambassadors by the emperor. The missions traveling to China not only served as an important cultural link, but also facilitated expanded trade with the Middle Kingdom. For the Chinese emperor, the tributary system promoted the myth of his universal overlordship and helped shield China from barbarian attacks.[13] During the Yi dynasty, in addition to the three annual regular tribute missions to the Ming court, and the later four to the Qing dynasty, a number of smaller embassies were dispatched.[14]

By the middle of the nineteenth century, European nations were running roughshod over China, defeating the feckless Chinese military in punitive battles, extracting concessions, and imposing unequal treaties. In the face of these developments, the Yi king determined that the only way to avoid a similar fate and keep the Europeans at bay was not to modernize the state but to reinvigorate Confucianism and embrace a policy of isolationism. Isolation was also pursued by both China and Japan, but it was a major cause of the fall of the imperial system in China and was abandoned by Japan in favor of Westernization. For Korea, isolationism would prove to be almost as big a disaster as it was for China.

Japan played a more important role in transforming Korea than did Western nations, which saw little opportunity there. On three separate occasions, Japan pressured Korea to open treaty negotiations, but in each instance the conservative Korean rulers rejected the requests. Korea's vulnerability to outside pressure grew when in 1871 Japan extracted from China a concession to the effect that Korea had no special status vis-à-vis China; that is, the tributary status was ended. Henceforth, Korea would be regarded as a state possessing sovereignty, to be treated as an equal by other states. Nominally, Korea was under Chinese protection as a corollary of the tributary system. When actually threatened, however, China was unable to defend itself, much less its tributary states.[15]

Western imperialism forced many parts of the world to confront the realities of modernization, no matter how reluctant they were to do so. Korea's ability to resist modernization was encouraged by the fact that most Europeans took little interest in the peninsula, so they did not press their advantage as forcefully as they did in China. Unlike Japan, the Korean government did not pursue a modernization agenda. There was only a small group of "innovators" who favored new approaches; basically the country was in the hands of the Confucian traditionalists. "Old Korea entered the twentieth century world with its death throes already underway."[16]

The Western challenge to Asia enhanced the sense of common identity among the peoples of the region. This identity was partly territorial but more particularly cultural. Among those with a sense of "Asianism," China, Japan, and Korea shared a common cultural and racial heritage.[17] For Koreans, this sense of solidarity was strained by Japan's developing imperial ambitions in which Korea was to play an important part. Despite this challenge, there were advocates of Asian solidarity, even in Korea, who accepted Japanese rule as preferable to Western domination.[18] In today's world, there are proponents of a similar "New Asianism" who consider closer links with China to be preferable to reliance on and the close embrace of the United States.[19]

At the dawn of the era of Western imperialism, Korea, like China, was in a state of institutional deterioration. Political factionalism and clan rivalries prevailed despite a high degree of ethnic and cultural homogeneity. Lack of communication and transportation infrastructures together with the geographical contrast between the mountainous north and the relatively flatter south exacerbated the divisions. To meet the Western challenge required social solidarity, political development, and technological advancement. Korea possessed none of these.

The condition of the population was poor. Agriculture was backward and unproductive. Disease and infant mortality were rampant. Education lagged while the rich exploited the poor. The rapacity of landlords and the corruption of officials left the masses of the peasantry in deplorable condition.[20]

Korea was thus ripe for the picking. Itself enfeebled and with only the worthless friendship of China, it fell to Japanese domination.

8

Korea and Imperialism

Throughout its history, Korea has been dominated by outside forces. The proximity of Korea to China and the overwhelming influence of the latter meant that Korea would not be able to develop an exclusively independent civilization. For centuries, Korea maintained a tributary status toward China, a satisfactory arrangement in that China did not seek to physically annex Korea, which allowed Korea to merely acknowledge China's nominal preeminence. The magnitude of Chinese cultural and economic achievements meant that smaller neighbors like Korea would inevitably and substantially be affected by them. But China was not the only foreign influence that would come to bear on Korea's development.

Korea's Vulnerable Geographic Position

The first significant foreign influence was felt in the twelfth century. At that time, Korea, like most of Asia and a large part of the Middle East and even Europe, fell victim to Mongolian invaders. Korea was subject to the short-lived Mongol (Yuan) dynasty, which ruled China for less than a century. Mongol influences outside of East Asia were of little lasting consequence, except that the Mongols were masters of the art of devastation, leaving behind them a trail of ruined civilizations.

The next foreign power to set its sights on Korea was Japan. In 1592, the Japanese Shogun Hideyoshi challenged China's dominant position on the peninsula. In that year he embarked with more than 100,000 troops from the Japanese southern island of Kyushu and engaged Chinese forces in Korea. While the Japanese won battles, they were unable to win the war. Aided by Korean naval successes against the Japanese, the Chinese were able to confine the Japanese to the southern tip of the peninsula. Three years of negotiation failed to produce an agreement, so Hideyoshi tried again in 1597, an undertaking no more successful than the first. The results of these wars were a devastated Korea, a seriously weakened Ming China, and a Japan left with the bitter taste of failure. The Japanese would not try to gain control of Korea again until the nineteenth century, when they embarked on an undertaking to dominate all of East Asia in a manner patterned after Western-style imperialism.

Korea's exposure to modernizing influences from Europe was indirect. In 630 a Korean envoy to the Chinese court returned home with books and artifacts from Europe, including an astronomy book, which influenced the Koreans considerably. A short time later, Christian literature was brought into Korea from China. When the first Catholic priest arrived in 1794, Koreans were already familiar with the outlines of Christian doctrine.[1]

Although the United States was not the first and by no means the most active Western nation in Korea, it was the first to sign a formal treaty with Korea. Following the American Civil War, American interest in Asia expanded. The driving forces behind this interest were missionaries, who wanted to bring the benefits of Christianity to what they perceived as the spiritually depraved people of Asia, and commercial interests, which saw mass market opportunities. In May 1882, a treaty was signed that immediately ran into opposition in both countries. Koreans saw it as an assault on their tradition, while Americans were becoming concerned about the "yellow peril" following the entry of large numbers of Chinese laborers into California.[2]

Korea attracted little interest among Western European imperialists because it offered limited commercial opportunities. The main strategic contest over Korea was between China and Japan. For its part, China's position continued to deteriorate as it succumbed to repeated depredations at the hands of various European countries. The ambitions and capabilities of Japan, on the other hand, were another matter. In a few short decades Japan transformed itself from a provincial backwater to a major player on the international stage.

At the turn of the century, future prospects for both China and Korea were grim. China had lost a war with Japan in the mid-1890s, and Russia would lose another in 1905. Although Korea was not a combatant in these wars, it was a loser because Japan's ambition was to gain territory at Korea's expense. To make matters worse, the Korean economy was in bad shape. Most Koreans were poor peasant laborers with little prospect of improving their living conditions. Even those who made up the small elite class were in an insecure position. Industry and commerce had not developed, and there was little trade except for the export of rice and the import of Japanese goods. Education was available to only a few, and even for them it was scanty in both quantity and quality. As disease was endemic and medical services woefully inadequate, public health suffered. Public security was minimal; the ill-trained and ill-equipped police could not even provide protection against banditry. Infrastructure had not kept pace with demand, and as a result transport and communication facilities were inadequate or nonexistent.[3]

Japan's Annexation of Korea

Japan ended China's nominal influence over Korea with the First Sino-Japanese War of 1894–1895 and formal annexation in 1910. The Japanese then set about systematically exploiting the resources of the peninsula and oppressing its people. In the centuries-long and worldwide experience with imperialism, Western nations differed in the extent to which they contributed to, or detracted from, the development of their possessions. The impact of Spain was substantial. As a consequence of Spanish (and to a lesser extent Portuguese) imperialism, most people in Central and South America now speak Spanish or Portuguese and practice Catholicism. For their part, the British may have made the most positive impact of all imperialists as they left behind important political institutions and practices, especially in South Asia. Parliamentary government, the legal system, bureaucratic practices, and military organization are legacies of British rule in India and Pakistan. The French, Dutch, and others also made their mark in areas of politics and economics. While always maintaining their superiority, most Europeans were restrained in the extent of their oppression of subject peoples (although this was not the case with Belgian actions in Africa). The Japanese were different. They had a self-aggrandizing agenda and showed little sensitivity toward the people they conquered. "Japanese agents went through the peninsula, seizing properties on military authorization. Koreans were roughly treated and were denied access to any areas the Japanese declared 'off limits.'"[4] They tried to suppress, if not eradicate altogether, Korean culture by banning the teaching of Korean literature, and the use of the Korean language in schools was forbidden at any level. Education was conducted in Japanese, although not all Koreans had access to it. The Japanese also engaged in merciless economic exploitation. As a result, even today there is an abiding dislike and distrust of Japan among older Koreans and other people in East Asia. In these circumstances, "Koreans were less able than some other colonial peoples to grant the legitimacy to colonial rule. This did not mean that Koreans always and in all places resisted the Japanese—they did not—but it did mean that the Japanese had perhaps a more difficult time imposing and sustaining their rule in Korea than did most European powers in their colonies."[5] As the memories of Japanese rule fade into history, younger Asians display diminishing animosity toward Japan.

Korea Under Japanese Rule

Colonial regimes never fully integrate with the subject society. There is always a gap between the rulers and the ruled. Even when colonial administrators try to engage the indigenous population, these administrators are still an alien presence. Most, of course, do not try to "go native" but energetically attempt to retain their national identity and modes of behavior. This was certainly true of the Japanese. As Bruce Cumings writes: "The colonial state stood above Korean society, exercising authoritative and coercive control. It possessed connections to only the fringe Korean upper class and colonial parvenus—aristocrats, landlords, bureaucrats—and even those ties were tenuous at best, designed to co-opt and thwart dissent, not to provide meaningful participation in the affairs of state. In general, the Japanese sought to strengthen central bureaucratic power in Korea as a means of shifting the balance of forces and providing the wherewithal to mobilize and extract resources on an unprecedented scale."[6]

Among the institutional changes introduced by the Japanese was a legal code identical to that practiced in Japan. This system was not designed for Koreans, however, as they were essentially frozen out of it. Legal professionals were almost all Japanese, and the process mainly served the interests of the Japanese. The legal system, and especially law enforcement, was an important tool enabling Japan to control the Korean population and to advance Japan's exploitative agenda.[7]

As they did elsewhere in their Asian empire, the Japanese used conquered territory to provide a destination for Japanese immigrants. Thousands of Japanese, mostly poor farmers themselves, went to Korea "to make their fortune at the expense of the inhabitants, whom they contemptuously treated as inferiors."[8] Favored by the colonial administration, these immigrants expropriated land or set themselves up in commercial ventures from which the locals were excluded. Some well-off Koreans were able to cooperate with the Japanese and thus to survive as a rural elite.

The Japanese immigrants lost their privileged status when Japan lost World War II. The sudden collapse of the Japanese army left the immigrants in peril. Many returned to Japan, while those unable to do so suffered the consequences of retribution at the hands of their former colonial subjects. For those in areas liberated by the Soviet Red Army, this often meant transfer to the Soviet Union as slave labor. Tens of thousands of these unfortunates were never heard from again. One scheme employed by the Soviets was to inculcate Marxism into the Japanese with the intention of sending them back as "fifth columnists" to Japan in hopes they would promote the communist agenda.

During their thirty-five-year reign in Korea, the Japanese built industries and the transportation infrastructure to facilitate Korea's linkage to the Japanese economy. Korea's traditional isolation from outside contact was broken, but it remained limited to links with Japan. When the war ended with Japan's defeat, Korea was liberated, but it also faced economic calamity because the economy had been essentially run by and for the Japanese. Political partition of the peninsula by the United States and the Soviet Union only made matters worse. It took decades for the South Korean economy to revive, and the North Korean economy, while it started off promisingly, eventually went into sharp decline.

Japanese rule did not change the social system; rather it perpetuated it and kept intact Korea's traditional elite hierarchy based on a landed aristocracy. European colonial rulers often engaged local elites who, to show their gratitude and retain their status, served as the political tools of the occupiers. The French in Vietnam retained a social structure similar to that in Korea.[9] The British in India were little interested in rearranging the social system and relied heavily on local elites. They did, however, seek to end some Indian practices that they found objectionable, such as widow burning.

The Japanese, by contrast, were merciless in exploiting the Koreans. Not only did they take every advantage of the people in Korea itself, but many Koreans were taken as labor to Japan. Those who suffered this fate worked in mines and in other jobs generally avoided by the Japanese themselves. As many as 70 percent of the workers in the mines were Koreans. The day's work began early and lasted late, as long as twelve hours. There was a high accident rate owing to the poor working conditions and the cumulative exhaustion of the miners. Toward the end of the war, Japanese industry was stretched to the limit as the country struggled against overwhelming odds. As the war machine was ground down, life became even more miserable for the Koreans, who were forced to work harder and in return received a diminishing supply of staples for their survival. "After a few years of squeezing labor out of people who were working for a pittance under wretched conditions, they discarded them and brought new people in.[10] Korean women were coerced or tricked into brothels where they became "comfort women" for Japanese soldiers. A very high proportion of these victims did not survive their brutal treatment, but some who did have given horrifying testimony about their ordeal.

Before the Japanese occupation, the material existence of the ordinary Korean was modest at best. Under the Japanese it became even worse. Koreans were stripped of their limited landholdings. Laws affording some protection regarding working conditions were abolished during the war, putting workers at the complete mercy of the state. "In place of free labor contracting, a military command system was substituted so that capital and labor would 'sincerely unite' to serve the war. Japanese mines used little machine power, thus human labor was in great demand."[11]

In Korea itself, conditions were little better. As the end drew near, the Japanese stripped the country of anything of value. "They sacked warehouses and sold the contents, whether food, oil, cloth, or whatever. They sold factories, homes, furnishings—anything that they could not carry back to Japan. In their rush to liquidate their assets, the Japanese nearly ruined the South Korean economy. In a few weeks, they printed some three billion yen against an estimated five billion yen in circulation on August 15."[12]

9

Partition and War

Japan and Korea are not only geographically close, they share a common cultural tradition. Their Confucian heritage gives them a shared outlook, especially on social values and the central role of the family. Yet their historical relationship has been abrasive. The Japanese look with condescension toward the Koreans, and the Koreans harbor undisguised hostility toward the Japanese. This problem continues largely because of Japan's unwillingness to make amends for past behavior. The Japanese often refuse to apologize for their imperial activities and even deny they committed any war crimes.

While relations between the two have never been warm, today's problems began over a century ago, when Japan embarked on its imperialistic conquests. In 1905, Japan invaded and occupied the Korean peninsula in the context of its war with Russia. Had the Japanese not added Korea to their growing colonial empire, the Korean War probably would not have occurred. The responsibility for creating conditions that led to the Korean War lies with the Japanese. "The origins of the conflict ran deep into the colonial period. The Japanese sowed the wind; Koreans reaped a whirlwind."[1]

Japan formally annexed Korea in 1910 and continued its imperialistic actions in the 1930s with the addition of Chinese territory. The Second Sino-Japanese War (1937–1945) marked the beginning of World War II in Asia. In seeking to expand its "Greater East Asia Co-Prosperity Sphere," Japan made a serious strategic mistake. In 1941, it sought to secure its growing Asian empire against American interference by attempting, unsuccessfully as it turned out, to neutralize the American Pacific fleet operating out of Pearl Harbor in Hawaii. In their surprise attack on Pearl Harbor on December 7 (December 8 in Japan), several battleships were damaged or destroyed, but the real targets, aircraft carriers, were not in port and therefore escaped the attack.

The bombing of Pearl Harbor produced the opposite effect of what the Japanese were aiming for. Rather than being discouraged from involvement, the United States, which had been resisting entering the wars in Europe and Asia, was galvanized into action. American resources were mobilized to provide the war-making materiel not only for the European theater but to begin rolling back and destroying the Japanese empire. By making an implacable enemy of the United States, Japan brought doom upon itself. Japan surrendered on August 15, 1945, and formally on September 2, 1945.

Great Power Diplomacy

With the defeat of Japan, Korea was liberated from colonial rule. For Korea, however, that was not the end of the story of suffering and war, but the beginning of a new chapter. Realizing the war would end eventually with an anticipated victory, the allies had been making preparations for dealing with postwar Asia.

The future of Japan's Asian empire was discussed at several allied conferences. In the December 1, 1943, Cairo Declaration, the United States, Great Britain, and China announced their intention to return all lands that Japan had acquired since World War I. This meant Manchuria and Taiwan would be returned to China. Although Japan would be expelled from Korea, the independence of the peninsula would have to wait. Instead there would be a temporary trusteeship of Korea for an undetermined amount of time in order to ensure the future freedom of the nation.

In 1945, an allied conference (which excluded China but included the Soviet Union) was held at Yalta in the Soviet Crimea at which the status of Korea was addressed. It was decided that Korea would be administered by an interim government under international jurisdiction until such time as the Koreans were able to govern themselves. The conferees wanted to avoid single-power occupation and administration of Korea, and they wanted to keep Korea intact as a single political unit. The mechanism to achieve this end involved discussion of a trusteeship. The Yalta conference ended in early February 1945 and it was announced that important compromises between the Western allies and the Soviet Union had been achieved at the conference. The Yalta Agreement soon came under criticism in the United States for being too generous to the Soviets.[2]

By the time the Korean War erupted five years later (June 1950), Yalta was regarded by many, especially American conservatives, as a dismal failure. The postwar behavior of the Soviet Union was not in keeping with the spirit of cooperation that had, at least nominally, existed during World War II. Thus, the reaction of the U.S. government to problems rising out of the Yalta agreement was to place the blame on betrayals by the Soviet Union and its desire to expand communism into satellite territories, actions that could lead to another war. The Cold War confrontation extended into Asia when Mao Zedong's Communists took control of the Chinese government and Chiang Kaishek's Nationalist regime fled China to Taiwan. The Soviets had initially supported the Nationalist government, but with the defeat of Japan, Stalin seized the opportunity to help Mao install a Communist regime in the country.[3]

It was assumed an interim occupation of Korea in some form would be sufficient during a period of transition. The Japanese occupation had not prepared the Koreans for self-government. Accordingly, Korea was partitioned at the 38th parallel in 1945. It can be argued that the outbreak of the Korean War in 1950 occurred as a consequence of the failure of Japan to develop Korea politically.[4]

In 1942, President Franklin D. Roosevelt had approved a State Department initiated policy to create an international trusteeship for Korea. This initiative acknowledged that the region had been at the center of great power struggles throughout history and was still considered to be a key strategic location. Seeking international support in 1943, the United States met with China and New Zealand to create a plan for development. After tentative backing by China and Britain, the United States proposed it to the Soviet Union, which approved it. However, there was little additional support for the trusteeship idea, especially among Koreans, and it was eventually dropped.

Roosevelt attended the November 1943 Cairo Conference with the intention of gaining formal approval from Allied members for a trusteeship arrangement. Winston Churchill of Britain and Chiang Kaishek of China formally approved the trusteeship idea, and it was included in the Cairo Declaration, "which promised the liquidation of the Japanese Empire" and referenced Allied intentions to assist Korea in forming a "free and independent" nation.[5] Immediately after the Cairo Conference, Roosevelt met with Josef Stalin in Tehran; they discussed the trusteeship, and Stalin reiterated the Soviet Union's endorsement.

Roosevelt's advisors encouraged the president to seek Soviet involvement in the Pacific war, hoping to end the conflict without an invasion of the Japanese homeland. At the Yalta meeting with Churchill and Stalin, Roosevelt formally requested Soviet involvement in the Pacific. On February 8, in a private meeting between Roosevelt and Stalin, it was decided that a four-way trusteeship of Korea should last approximately thirty to forty years, and both orally agreed that no foreign troops would be stationed on the peninsula; nor should there be a postwar occupation. Because the meeting was designed mainly to involve the Soviets in the Pacific war and neither side expected a rapid end to the war, specific details about the trusteeship arrangement were not discussed. Despite warnings from his political advisors, Roosevelt remained optimistic and continued to believe in the establishment of postwar peaceful international cooperation with Soviet support. His death on April 12 ended any expectation of friendly U.S.-Soviet relations. Once Soviet territorial ambitions became evident and a new president came into office, the fate of Korea was caught up in an ideological Cold War.[6]

The death of President Roosevelt did not deflect the trajectory of American policy with respect to an international organization. The new president,

Harry Truman, went ahead with the planned international conference in San Francisco, which was intended to create a peaceful world body. In 1945, nations from around the world met to discuss the possibility of founding what is now the United Nations. Highly suspicious of Stalin and his push for hegemony in Europe, Truman and his advisors suspected that the Soviets also intended to conquer Asia. The methods the Soviets employed to expand their powers have been described as follows:

> Even before the German surrender was signed at Reims in May 1945, the Soviet Union began the policy of creating satellite states on its borders. Old-time Communist agitators, deserters, expatriates, exiles, escaped prisoners, and apprentice conspirators began to find their way to power. Some emerged from resistance ranks, where they had served courageously during part of the war years, or were sent back from the Soviet Union to their former homes to organize or strengthen Communist cadres in key government ministries. In some cases, they reached power directly; often they infiltrated labor or agrarian regimes and ultimately eliminated or won over those who initially opposed them.[7]

Truman's first meeting with the allies was at Potsdam from July 17 to August 2, 1945. On arriving at the conference, Truman received word that the United States had completed testing of a nuclear bomb. Secretary of State James F. Byrnes and Truman had decided that the use of this weapon in Japan would end the war early and, ultimately, save countless lives. Without divulging this knowledge, they steered the conference away from talk of a trusteeship for Korea, refusing to discuss the matter or have it entered into the conference record. Baum and Matray assert that this was the last attempt by the United States to avert war in Korea and come to a peaceful agreement with the Soviet Union to rebuild the region.[8]

An atomic bomb was dropped on Hiroshima on August 5, 1945, and another on Nagasaki on the eighth. Two days later the Soviet Union entered the Pacific War and the Red Army moved into the northern portion of Korea. Accords were drawn up and agreed on by both the United States and the USSR. Concerning the liberation of Korea, the Truman administration proposed a temporary division of the peninsula along the 38th parallel without any real reason to expect that the Soviets would accept it given their superior military position. But Stalin agreed to the plan, thus allowing the United States to send troops into the South.[9] The United States refused to reveal any details about the coordination of the occupation, and very little negotiating occurred. Tensions in the region mounted as occupation forces moved into the divided peninsula.

The use of nuclear weapons, while still controversial even today, brought the war against Japan to an end without the need for an invasion of the main islands, an event that would have likely been horrifically costly. Some problems remained, however. As it turned out, the involvement of the Soviet Union was not really necessary. But they were involved and the United States had to scramble to avoid having the Soviets occupy all of Korea, which they were in a position to do. "A month after Korea was nearly conceded to the Russians at Potsdam," writes Bruce Cumings, "the United States was sponsoring a rush into Korea and had acquired, so it seemed, a commitment to defend at least a part of Korea against Soviet encroachments or a Soviet inspired regime."[10]

In a short period of time, Korea had gone from colonial occupation by the Japanese to partition and occupation by two different powers. The Japanese occupation and subsequent partition of Korea were devastating. "In the process, railroad, road, and sea networks were severed, trailing off into wilderness or emptied of purpose. The Japanese defeat thus destroyed an integral and delicate structure that had linked metropole to periphery."[11]

South Korean political leaders were altogether opposed to socialism, communism, and the idea of a trusteeship arrangement that included the Soviets. Public demonstrations in the South sparked an uprising against any agreement that was produced by Moscow and the United States, and the Koreans began seeking alternative options via a joint committee. There were various proposals, including the creation of internal Korean working groups, encompassing members from the right and left that would meet under the auspices of the occupying powers to decide Korea's own fate. The United States and the Soviet Union, however, were never able to agree on the ground rules for such a meeting. The joint committee approach was suspended on May 8, 1946.

In August 1947, the United States returned to the original trusteeship agreement proposed in the Cairo Declaration and sought Soviet approval for a four-power conference. The Soviets opposed the idea, leaving the door open for the Truman administration to take the issue to the newly formed United Nations Security Council. Armed with the Soviet rejection of the most recent proposal, Secretary of State George C. Marshall and Warren R. Austin, U.S. representative to the UN, received approval for the installation of a provisional democratic government in Korea on November 14, 1948. Ninety days after the new interim government was installed, American and Soviet troops could be recalled. In addition to these provisions, the United Nations Temporary Commission on Korea (UNTCOK) was created to monitor elections and promote self-determination on the peninsula. The Commission was made up of eleven UN member states, nine of which came from democratic, capitalist countries. Soviet resistance to monitored elections in the region forced UNTCOK to reevaluate the process and proceed with elections in the southern part of the peninsula only. Aware of further rifts within the region and a lack of legitimacy if elections were only held in the South, moderate Kim Kyusik opposed regional elections and created the "National Independence Federation," advocating a North/South conference to resolve the turmoil. Around the same time, North Korea announced that it was on the verge of approving a governmental system for the whole of Korea and issued statements warning the South of American intervention and manipulation. Political dissent erupted in the South in opposition to UNTCOK-monitored elections, and the committee returned to the UN, arguing that separate elections would only further divide the two Koreas.

Despite occasional American suggestions, there is a very good possibility that Korea would not have accepted trusteeship had it been offered. Historians have indicated that Kim Il Sung, appointed in 1946 as the chairman of the North Korean Communist Party and later elevated to supreme military commander, would have balked at the idea of a Korea run under democracy. Initially trained in a Korean battalion of the Soviet Red Army, Kim was familiar with the tenets of communism and, more importantly, had made several important allies when fighting with the Soviets. Some accounts indicate that Kim was chosen by Stalin for the role of chairman, and new interpretations hypothesize that it was Kim who actually requested Soviet occupation of the peninsula and encouraged Stalin to later enter the war.[12]

With occupation forces on either side of the parallel, both Stalin and Truman were concerned about the possibility of military actions, and both wanted to avert another war. Truman and the State Department revived negotiations for trusteeship of Korea, but this time the Soviets were hesitant to sign any formal agreement. Early clashes between North and South Korea indicated that if civil war were to break out in the region, the entire peninsula would fall to communism, an outcome that the United States was unwilling to tolerate, but not well prepared to prevent. "Had there been no foreign occupation in 1945," says Cumings, "the People's Republic and its committees would have won control of the peninsula in a matter of months."[13]

Toward the end of 1945, movement toward two separate regimes began, with the earliest initiatives occurring in the South. According to Cumings, "It was only in the aftermath of the results of southern policies that the north began to follow suit. We could argue, of course, that a separate northern regime was inevitable. But the sequence remains undeniable: the south moved first."[14]

In December 1945, U.S. Secretary of State James F. Byrnes attended the Council of Foreign Ministers meeting in Moscow, where he promoted the idea of trusteeship for a ten-year period and also suggested removing the 38th parallel as a dividing line. Soviet foreign minister V. M. Molotov concurred with the idea but requested additional time to review the proposal. Molotov proposed creating a joint committee to design and incorporate Korean principles into the new governing system in addition to developing the infrastructure in the region. Without lifting the 38th parallel barrier, both parties agreed that formal reunification of the peninsula was key and established a plan of action for self-determination in the region. Although sounding altruistic, both the great powers, their public statements notwithstanding, were intent upon realizing their own ideological outcomes on the peninsula, and they encouraged activities that continued to divide Korea. Given the strategic importance of the peninsula to both the United States and the Soviet Union, neither would allow the entire peninsula to fall to an unsympathetic government, either North or South. Adding to the tension was the Soviet declaration, in 1946, that a worldwide struggle between communism and capitalism had been renewed.[15] This statement widened the rift between the former allies and intensified efforts by both parties to construct a sympathetic governing system in Korea. The rhetorical war that was emerging between the two ideologies soon eliminated any possibility of achieving Korean reunification in any form.

Military Occupation

The first Soviet troops to arrive in Korea were a desperate lot. They were poorly clothed, poorly equipped, and were expected to live off the land, which meant taking things from the Koreans, who themselves were not in very good shape. The departure of the Japanese and the devastation they left behind exacerbated conditions for both Koreans and the Soviet occupiers. "Somewhat ameliorating the situation was the fact that the Russians expressed very little of the racial prejudice with which Americans denigrated the 'Gooks' in the south."[16] Not only were the Americans ignorant of the culture and conditions of Korea, they had no plan to deal with the situation after the defeat of Japan. The U.S. command at first suggested that the Japanese continue to govern until other arrangements could be made. Korean outrage at this idea prompted a rapid change of plans.[17]

A U.S.-educated nationalist leader (and a Christian convert) named Syngman Rhee, recommended by Chiang Kaishek as a capable leader, was flown to Korea on General Douglas MacArthur's own plane. The Soviets, meanwhile, installed Kim Il Sung as head of the Provisional People's Committee.

The Soviets' treatment of the Koreans was much better than that which they experienced under the Japanese. Still, the Soviets had an agenda. Russian-language instruction was compulsory starting in the fifth grade. All upper-level government officials had to be fluent in Russian, a practical matter since they had to deal with their Soviet occupiers. The Soviets sought to combine Korean culture and national pride with the universalism of communist doctrine. "In effect its message to the Korean people—in the south, as far as it could reach them, as well as in the north—was: be Korean, but in the Russified communist way."[18]

Fearing another possible war, American military leaders were less than enthusiastic about the prospect of defending South Korea from the communists, but Truman was apprehensive that any evacuation of military forces would cause his administration and the United States to lose prestige and international credibility. The international community had just approved the formation of the United Nations, and the United States felt a need to take a leadership role in the Security Council. The rebuilding of Japan and Europe had not yet begun, and the United States faced the need to play a major role in the reconstruction process. Owing to wholesale economic devastation caused by World War II, European allies were growing weaker as the United States and the Soviet Union were emerging as superpowers. In order to increase the strategic role of the United States, Truman felt it necessary to retain the prestige and credibility accorded by the international community.

On March 5, 1946, Winston Churchill made his famous "iron curtain" speech in Fulton, Missouri. This was the first public indication that Western leaders thought the Soviet Union posed a threat and needed containing. The strategy of containment would later be articulated by George F. Kennan and would serve as the foundation of American security policy, and indeed that of all Western states, until the demise of the Soviet Union in the 1990s.

The United States took the matter of Korea to the United Nations, where it was thought two interim governments could function in the country until a unified form of government could be agreed upon. Noting the imminent Communist takeover of Czechoslovakia and fearing Soviet expansionism, the UN voted in favor of restricted elections in Korea.

South Korean leaders, led by President Syngman Rhee, were opposed to the two government idea, even if it were only temporary, and continued to seek a North-South Conference, traveling to the North Korean capital of Pyongyang through late April. Open to the idea of reunification under almost any form of government, the South only requested that the North not "advocate a dictatorship, nationalization of all industries, the establishment of foreign military bases or less than free elections."[19]

In areas along the 38th parallel, some Americans observed that the Russians seemed to get along better with the Koreans than did the Americans. The Soviets apparently went so far as to allow Korean officers to command Russian troops. For their part, the Americans often behaved as if they were colonial overlords by, among other things, retaining Korean servants. As noted above, most Americans referred to Koreans with the pejorative term "gooks."

Accordingly, in the observation of one American, "Russian-Korean relations generally seemed cordial, whereas Korean villagers were 'sullen, surly, and aloof' toward Americans."[20]

The American occupation was ill-starred from the beginning. Robert Oliver gives several reasons for the overall failure of the U.S. Army Military Government in Korea. First, the Americans were not prepared for it; they had been planning on a different outcome. In contrast to the extensive planning and preparation for the occupation of Japan, the United States not only lacked contingency plans, but it did not have the people to carry them out even if plans had existed.

Second, American troops and especially their commander were combat veterans still stationed in nearby Okinawa. While other American troops returned home, these men were sent to Korea, thus generating some resentment. Their commander, General John R. Hodge, was ill-suited to the task of civil administrator. "He had no knowledge of Korean culture or of how in many respects it differed from American ways. He had neither the temperament, the tact, nor the sensitivity suited for political management."[21]

Third, the alliance with the Soviet Union during the war left the United States psychologically unprepared to deal with postwar Communist aggressiveness. Policies did not exist for dealing with Communist subversion or with more overt Soviet actions until the late 1940s and the full articulation of the containment doctrine. Failure to anticipate the threat allowed a situation to develop "guaranteeing for the Communists freedom to organize, to evangelize, and to infiltrate into every branch of government and into all aspects of the society."[22]

Fourth, Koreans and Americans did not understand, and came to resent, each other. For their part, Koreans expected liberation from Japanese rule to mean independence. Instead they got another foreign ruler and a divided country. Americans had no particular fondness for Korea, which had been part of the Japanese empire, and was thought to share some of Japan's war guilt. Moreover, the Americans were not comfortable in the role of rulers.[23]

Fifth, Koreans had always been suspicious of foreigners, and their thirty-five-year experience as a colony of Japan exacerbated their hostility toward foreign domination. No matter how benevolent the American occupation, and it was not always so, Koreans did not welcome it and resisted at every turn, making the Americans' task that much more difficult.[24]

Sixth, Communist activities in Korea were widespread, creating political instability. When the Communists succeeded in taking control of China, the prospects for further Communist successes appeared good. In the face of this opportunity, the Soviet Union intensified its efforts to promote the cause of revolution in Asia.[25]

The Korean War

Of all the modern wars in which the United States has been a participant, the Korean War has proved to be one of the least celebrated. With some exceptions, the heroic sacrifices of American forces in Korea have not been popularized in films to the extent that those of World War II have. Nor have there been books touting the involvement of the "greatest generation" in the Korean conflict. In fact, the war has been something of an embarrassment. American forces did not acquit themselves as well as might have been expected given the record of their accomplishments in the defeat of Germany and Japan. The Korean War itself ended in stalemate and could only in a technical sense be declared a victory. The North Korean effort to take over the entire peninsula by force had been stopped, but the Communists still controlled the North. China's international stature had been enhanced by their involvement in driving the UN forces out of North Korea.

In the conventional political view, the Korean War, a product of Cold War ideology, was an obvious manifestation of Soviet expansionist ambitions. According to this line of reasoning, the Soviets had been encouraged by Secretary of State Dean Acheson's statement before the National Press Club on January 12, 1950, that left Korea outside the American security perimeter in East Asia. Based on this articulation of American security policy and the fact that President Truman had withdrawn American troops from Korea the previous year, Stalin saw an opportunity to enhance Soviet geopolitical interests. According to Samuel S. Kim, Stalin saw Korea as presenting multiple opportunities. Gaining the Korean peninsula would extend the Soviet security perimeter outward. Japan would become further isolated, and American resolve to support it would be tested. China would be pushed further into the Soviet orbit, and American military resources would need to be sent to Asia, thus creating further potential opportunities for Soviet action in Europe.[26]

In the broad strategic sense, the United States was unprepared for developments in Asia. The containment doctrine, which was evolving by 1948, envisioned two threats to the United States. One was a surprise attack on the United States itself, a prospect that was made more real later when the Soviets acquired nuclear weapons. A more likely threat was thought to be a conventional military assault against Western Europe. "Nothing in America's behavior would have led policymakers in Moscow or Pyongyang, North Korea's capital, to expect more than a diplomatic protest when North Korean troops crossed the 38th parallel," writes Henry Kissinger.[27] They were even more surprised when the United States reacted to the invasion by mobilizing troops in Korea because Washington had done nothing following the Communist takeover of China.

What the Communists had failed to appreciate was the crusading tendency that underlay American foreign policy.[28] In the view of many countries, America acts erratically and sometimes even irrationally. The United States does not always act in ways consistent with its stated strategic views. It sometimes sees itself as on a mission to correct a moral wrong. In the event, Truman sent American troops into action two days after the North Korean invasion. In Kissinger's succinct summary, "America thus found itself in a limited war for which it had no doctrine and in defense of a distant country in which it had declared it had no strategic interest."[29]

At 4:00 in the morning, Sunday, June 25, 1950, North Korean troops advanced toward the South. The Korean War had begun. American members of the Korean Military Advisory Group (KMAG) were confident that South Korea was prepared to deal with threats to its security. Brigadier General William L. Roberts, who was ending his tour as commander of KMAG, remarked in an interview that the Repubic of Korea (ROK) had "the best damn army outside the United States."[30] In fact:

> The ROK had eight divisions. Except for those fighting guerrillas in the South, they were armed with American M-1 rifles. The guerrilla fighters had to make do with old Japanese Model 99's. The ROK had machine guns, of course, and some mortars, mostly small. They had five battalions of field artillery to back up the infantry divisions, all with the old, short range Model M-3 105mm howitzer, which the United States had junked.
>
> The best damn army outside the United States had no tanks, no medium artillery, no 4.2-inch mortars, no recoilless rifles. They had no spare parts for their transport. They had not even one combat aircraft.[31]

The South Koreans were quickly overwhelmed. "The best damn army outside the United States had not merely been defeated. It had been destroyed."[32] The United States quickly responded with the few forces available in an attempt to stem the North Korean tide. Among the first to arrive was Task Force Smith, which took up a blocking position. At first the Americans inflicted heavy damage on the advancing North Korean forces. But supply and communication problems, and especially an inability to deal effectively with North Korean tanks, forced Smith's group into a disorderly withdrawal. MacArthur had referred to Task Force Smith as "an arrogant display of strength, sent to Korea to give the Communists pause."[33] As it turned out, Task Force Smith delayed the North Korean advance for only seven hours.

With a few exceptions, the war was a grinding affair. The North Koreans enjoyed initial success and almost pushed U.S. and South Korean forces off the peninsula, leaving them bottled up in the extreme south in the Pusan salient.

Fortunately for the American and ROK forces, the North Korean advance was largely used up and the salient held. Meanwhile, substantial UN assistance was pouring in. By the end of August 1950, the North Koreans were outmanned and outgunned. The UN forces had uncontested control of the sea and air and held a six-to-one advantage in tanks. But this was a limited war which meant essentially that "victory" was simply denying the enemy its goals. President Truman stated in 1951 that the fighting was "to resist an outrageous aggression in Korea." He went further and said "we must conduct our military activities so as to ensure the security of our forces." Expending lives and treasure on such a military operation generates little support, however. Henry Kissinger observes that, fighting a war to "resist" aggression and keep our forces "secure" is strategically vacuous.[34]

In a brilliant stroke, MacArthur devised a flanking maneuver involving an amphibious landing up the Korean west coast at Inchon.[35] This effectively cut off the North Korean forces, and they began a precipitous retreat. UN forces pursued them back across the 38th parallel and approached the Chinese border. Fearing an attack on China itself, the Chinese sent "volunteers," who successfully pushed UN forces back to and beyond the 38th parallel.[36] A new offensive in the spring of 1951 pushed the enemy back, liberating Seoul and crossing the 38th parallel again.

Armistice

In June 1951 the Communists called for armistice talks. Major offensive operations were stopped in the hope the Communists might be induced to end the war. Negotiations dragged out, however, as the Chinese took advantage of the opportunity to inflict casualties, especially on U.S. forces. During the period of negotiations at Panmunjom, American forces suffered more casualties than they had during the entire preceding year of the war. Eventually, the Communists reached the end of their physical abilities and an armistice was achieved in 1953.[37] Technically, however, the war is still on. There has been no peace treaty, and both sides continue to meet at Panmunjom.

The war lasted for thirty-seven months. American casualties numbered 36,940 dead, 92,134 wounded, 3,737 missing in action, and 4,439 prisoners of war. South Korea lost an estimated 400,000 troops plus a large number of civilian casualties. North Korean and Chinese losses may have been as high as 2 million. Physical destruction was extensive. American bombing of North Korea "left almost nothing standing anywhere in the country."[38]

Americans consider the Korean War to be proof of the Communists' intention to take over the world. North Koreans consider U.S. participation in the war and the continuing American military presence in the South as a continuation of the Western imperialist intervention in Asia. Suspicions and hostility continue today, and with North Korea's determined development of its nuclear weapons program and intermittent provocations, the situation has grown worse.

The war put an indefinite end to any possibility of Korean reunification. Occasionally, such as during the 1990s "sunshine" period of South Korean president Kim Dae Jung, relations softened only for hostility to resurface. Despite continued political indoctrination and enforcement of communist values, reinforced by nearly complete censorship, North Koreans are becoming aware of the disparities between the North and the South. Black market sales of Chinese radios and cell phones and the increased accessibility of South Korean television broadcasts have increased the flow of outside information into the North.[39] In addition, more North Koreans have been crossing the border; initially in desperate attempts to escape the widespread famine in the region; more recently, to find jobs in China. The movements have been exposing North Koreans to the world beyond their borders.[40] Andrei Lankov indicates that mobile cell phone use is sporadic, still illegal, and subject to periodic crackdowns.[41] However, people in the northern mountains have been able to use cell phones to make calls to China and South Korea, adding to the exposure to outside influences.

In addition, some limited market reforms have been adopted, perhaps as a necessity to combat the economic collapse and extreme famines that wiped out the reserves of food and left many of North Koreans starving in the 1990s and reportedly again in 2011. While not embracing capitalism by any substantive definition, these reforms do open up markets within North Korea, and encourage restricted trade with China and South Korea. Park notes that "multi-purpose markets for consumers . . . [which legalize] black markets," market management, and attitudes toward open markets are all becoming more positive and widely accepted in the region.[42] Both Park And Lankov are cautiously hopeful that such small steps will eventually gain momentum.[43]

If nothing else, the inflow of information has made the population in the North realize how drastically different their lifestyle and economies are compared to those in the South. Bruce Cumings writes that very few nations in the world remain as homogenous as the Korean peninsula, despite the ideological differences of democracy and communism.[44] And although dialect differences have emerged in both the North and the South, the language has remained the same, which enhances the chances for reunification, or at least some measure of eventual reconciliation.

North Korea agreed to allow a few South Korean businesses to build in an industrial complex approximately 1.5 miles north of the Demilitarized Zone (DMZ). In 2002, North Korea and the Hyundai Asan Corporation signed an agreement to lease land for fifty years in Gaeseong, estimating that South Korea would invest approximately one million dollars in start-up costs to develop over 16,000 acres. This type of initiative offers an example of a "win-win" arrangement, with South Korean firms gaining access to a low-wage labor force and 40,000 North Korean workers (2010) gaining employment in technologically advanced enterprises.

10

Korea and the Cold War

Korea became a pivot point at the very beginning of the Cold War as the United States and the Soviet Union confronted each other at the 38th parallel. Korea was the first arena in which U.S. military forces were engaged in operations pursuant to the containment doctrine. The Korean War was unpopular in that it did not result in a clear-cut "victory," something that Americans had come to expect following the unconditional surrender environment of World War II. Communism had been contained, however; the more ambitious idea that it could be rolled back was not seriously entertained by Washington.

Following the armistice in 1953, relations between North and South Korea remained sour, with only occasional indications that there might be reunification some day. As part of the stand-off, American forces remained in Korea to ensure against further aggression. Korea had been thrust violently onto the world stage and it was not well prepared to fend for itself in the mid-twentieth century.

> We find in Korea, perhaps until the mid-1960s, but certainly in 1945, a society that had produced no vibrant commercial class; an ethos so suffused with Confucian doctrine that it could place no blessing on capitalist pursuits; a colonial period perceived to have constituted an imposition of alien capitalist forms from without, and, perhaps, less clearly perceived but no less important, an experience in which a strong and foreign state intruded and substituted itself for "natural" processes. We can perceive how wrenching this experience was, and how compressed in time; structure became a graft onto a foreign body, ideology appeared lacking in all subtlety, and assumptions emerged with no complexity. In other words, in ideology as in reality, Korea has been a harsh battleground where great and modern forces have clashed with naked abandon.[1]

Syngman Rhee, 1875–1965

Korea's involvement in the Cold War and the longstanding relationship between Korea and the United States are intimately tied to the career of Syngman Rhee (who had changed his name from Yi Seungman). Syngman Rhee was born on March 26, 1875, into a poor *yangban* (gentry) family.[2]

The family's financial circumstances did not improve over time, but Rhee received an important break when he was twenty years old. He began a classical Chinese education at the Paejae (boys') missionary institution in preparation for government service. During this time, Rhee joined the Independence Club and the Debating Society founded by the U.S.-educated reformer So Chae-pil, who had returned to Korea after Japan ended Chinese rule over the peninsula in the wake of the 1894–95 war. Initially, it drew a large number of "opportunistic reform politicians of pro-Western and pro-Japanese backgrounds,"[3] but because of its open enrollment, many ordinary citizens of Seoul soon joined. When Chae-pil was expelled from Korea again in May 1898, new leadership emerged, including Rhee, who eventually "figured prominently as a leader among younger members of the Club."[4] The Club was developing into a citizens' assembly and "began to initiate direct social and political programs"[5] that promoted popular education through a debating forum and newspaper publications.

The Club had three main goals: (1) to promote Korean independence, condemn foreign interference, and oppose economic concessions that limited or restricted Korean success in the capitalist market; (2) to promote the self-strengthening movement by building schools and increasing industrial production; and (3) to increase citizen participation in politics while limiting autocratic power. Considering it subversive, the government of Korea ordered the dissolution of the Club and arrested seventeen members on November 4, 1898. The Club members organized campaigns and daily demonstrations calling for the release of their comrades. The government ordered the Imperial Association, an organization of peddlers, to attack the demonstrators. After a bloody battle, the government backed off and rescinded the dissolution of the Club. The government took a different direction and reconstituted a Privy Council, which incorporated members from the Club and the Imperial Association, effectively creating Korea's "first attempted modern legislative assembly."[6] Despite being a minority within the Council, Club members succeeded in passing legislation that recalled So Chae-pil and other exiled leaders and appointed them to "positions of responsibility in the government."[7] On December 26 the Club was again dissolved and the leaders were imprisoned "or otherwise punished."[8] (Rhee had earlier been imprisoned and tortured in 1897.)[9]

Rhee converted to Christianity while in jail, moved to the United States after his release, and eventually earned degrees from George Washington University, Harvard, and Princeton. In 1909, he formed the Korean National Association in order to lobby for "foreign assistance for the Korean independence movement."[10] At the same time, other exiled Koreans created a loose international network of activists. Rhee received a Ph.D. in theology from Princeton in 1910.[11]

Syngman Rhee

He returned to Korea the same year only to confront the fact that his country had been annexed as a colony of Japan. He again became involved in political activities and, as a result, was forced to flee the country for a second time. Rhee moved to Hawaii, where he directed the Korean Christian Institute, living in exile for the next thirty-five years.[12] During this time Rhee "organized Korean immigrants in Hawaii and on the West Coast and inculcated them and their children with Korean nationalism. The immigrants in turn gave Rhee financial and moral support in his fight for independence."[13]

For the first decade following its annexation of Korea on August 22, 1910, Japan banned political organizations and the right of assembly, and placed restrictions on Korean businesses. Under the Company Law (1911), the formation of private and public corporations required government approval.[14] Japanese repression encouraged the development of a nationalist reaction among Koreans. This nationalism was augmented by returning Korean students who had studied in Japan. They had not only been exposed to a variety of political ideas but had become nationally sensitive due to the discrimination they had experienced.[15] When Woodrow Wilson presented his fourteen points for peace following World War I, Korean nationals "were quick to seize upon Wilson's principles as proof of major power interest in the plight of oppressed nations the world over."[16] The Korean National Association was determined to send Rhee to the Versailles Peace Conference in order to plead for international assistance in achieving Korean independence. However, Japan refused to issue a passport to Rhee. The nationalist movement was now limited mainly to religious moderates who had taken up the cause. Most of the political radicals had been jailed or exiled.

On the occasion of the funeral of Korean Emperor Kojong, scheduled for March 3, 1919, activists planned demonstrations in hopes of igniting nationalist sentiments among the mourners expected in Seoul. Activists gathered in the city on March 1 and announced Korean independence, surprising the Japanese and local police forces. Inspired by the gathering, over a million participants demonstrated over the next few months. In response, the Japanese escalated their repression with arrests and beatings of activists. More importantly, the demonstrations and subsequent civilian abuses unified the independence movement.

Nationalists attempted to create a "government in exile" with a provisional government of the Republic of Korea. On April 9, 1919, "in order to establish its legitimacy, [the republic] elected as its ministers the absent leaders of all established independence groups abroad."[17] Syngman Rhee was elected president and "traveled yearly to Shanghai to attend the annual conventions of the government-in-exile."[18]

Once Japan was defeated in 1945, Rhee began actively lobbying the United States to become Korea's postcolonial leader. He criticized U.S. advocacy of the partitioning of Korea rather than promoting unification. "Rhee had a messianic belief that he was destined to reunite Korea under an anticommunist banner."[19] Despite the criticisms, the United States, with some reservations, accepted the leadership of Rhee, in large part because of his anticommunist stance. On October 20, 1945, despite the fact that he was seventy and had spent thirty-five years in exile, the Americans "presented Syngman Rhee to the Korean public with great fanfare."[20] As Bruce Cumings summed it up: "Rhee's manipulation of southern politics must be judged a marvel. In the past his presence had been noted within the nationalist movement and the Korean Provisional Government; but all along he had really been involved with but one movement, and that was the Syngman Rhee movement."[21]

U.S. maneuvers to find a more moderate candidate to lead the newly formed Republic of Korea (ROK) failed, and Rhee was elected president on August 15, 1948. The ROK claimed legitimacy over the entire peninsula. On September 9 the North announced the founding of the Democratic

People's Republic of Korea (DPRK) with Kim Il Sung as premier. The DPRK, too, claimed authority over the entire peninsula. Late in 1948, the Soviets began to withdraw from North Korea, and the Americans followed suit by removing troops from the South, effectively setting the scene for a civil war.

Left on his own, Rhee quickly established a National Security Law (NSL), which enabled him to prosecute Communists. It is estimated that by 1950, over 60,000 South Koreans were in prison and 60–80 percent of those were in violation of the NSL. Prisoners included assemblymen who had overridden Rhee's veto on land reform and opposition forces hoping to win the next elections. By February 1951, Colonel "Tiger" Kim had massacred an entire village of 500 people for "allegedly harboring communist guerillas."[22]

Despite U.S. backing of Rhee, he was a disappointment for Americans and a source of embarrassment because of allegations of corruption and the executions of political prisoners. The South Korean army was ill-equipped and untrained in comparison to the North Korean army. American and Soviet attempts at creating a trusteeship for the region failed, in part due to Rhee and Kim's quest for unification each on his own terms.[23]

The Rhee regime's dictatorial and corrupt rule eventually undermined its legitimacy.[24] When President Rhee found it difficult to win reelection in the National Assembly, he coerced the Assembly into passing a constitutional amendment allowing for a direct popular election in contrast to the 1948 constitution, which called for presidential elections via the National Assembly. "Although a constitutional amendment legalized Rhee's retention of the Presidency, legality, and therefore legitimacy, itself became less meaningful."[25]

In 1954, Rhee retained the presidency by eliminating the two-term limit for presidential tenure and packing the assembly with his political party members.[26] Assassinations and illnesses kept rivals at bay and in March 1960 Rhee claimed reelection with 90 percent of the vote.

Then, on April 11, 1960, the body of a boy was found dumped in the bay of Masan. He was believed to have been killed for demonstrating against the elections. Public opposition to the regime erupted. As many as 30,000 university and high school students marched on the presidential palace and were met with deadly force by the police. Casualties included 130 students killed and over 1,000 wounded.

In response to the violence against the students, 300 university professors called for the resignation of Rhee. In addition, the United States condemned the regime as oppressive and corrupt. Eventually, the Martial Law Command refused orders to continue firing on demonstrators.[27] On April 26, Syngman Rhee resigned from office and in May he returned to Hawaii.

A postmortem of Rhee's political career led one source to conclude: "Rhee's early liberalism does not seem to have evolved much in the succeeding fifty years and was clearly anachronistic by 1948. His ambition for personal power was also in sharp conflict with the political system he had been forced to adopt as the price for continued American support after 1948: an elective democracy with various constitutional safeguards against arbitrary executive power."[28] In contrast, others contend that the United States not only allowed repression but supported it. "When observers criticize the continuous autocratic harshness with which the ROK has dealt with the left wing and with communists over the past fifty years, they should remember that the United States has been tacitly supportive of and complicit in it since the founding of the system. Such measures were thought justifiable, given the threat posed by the regime to the north."[29]

U.S.–South Korean Relations

Beginning with the confrontation with the Soviet Union in Western Europe, the United States developed the doctrine of containment and associated policies to implement it. Among these was an alliance system to counter the threat of Soviet aggression. Eventually, this United States alliance system consisted of two types of alliances. There were multilateral alliances such as NATO, and bilateral alliances such as the one with South Korea. These alliances were intended to do several things. One was to pool resources since no country in Europe or elsewhere could expect to withstand a determined Soviet assault. The second purpose was to serve as a link between alliance members and the United States. Typically, the idea was that an attack on one would be an attack on all. Thus the United States committed itself to the defense of alliance members. Third was to develop a common military doctrine allowing for the integration of forces. To this end the United States provided training for alliance members. Fourth, the alliances served as a conduit for American military assistance. In this way Korea and other alliance members received American military equipment and the training resources to learn how to use them. Fifth, the alliances made possible the stationing of American forces abroad. At the peak of the Cold War the United States had substantial military forces in countries from England to Japan.

Some of the multilateral alliances proved insubstantial and on occasion produced the wrong results. The Central Treaty Organization (CENTO), originally called the Baghdad Pact, was ineffective in producing a common position vis-à-vis the Soviet Union. The Southeast Asia Treaty Organization (SEATO) was of little use during the Vietnam War, although some of its members did send token forces. In the case of Pakistan, which was a member of both CENTO and SEATO, American military assistance was not used to secure the northern border against Soviet aggression as intended. Instead, the Pakistanis used American arms to conduct war with India. In the event, Pakistan lost these engagements, resulting, after a 1971 encounter, in the loss of the east wing of the country, which became the independent country of Bangladesh.

Whereas SEATO and CENTO no longer exist, the bilateral alliances with South Korea and Japan continue to thrive. These two alliances were the centerpieces of American East Asia strategy. The Korean and Japanese militaries continue to be equipped with American arms, and American troops are still stationed in both countries.

For Japan, the alliance was highly profitable, as it benefited economically from both the Korean and Vietnam wars. This economic benefit went a long way toward rehabilitating the Japanese economy and allowing it to challenge even the American economy. Militarily, however, Japan resisted American pressure to enhance its military capabilities and activities.

For Korea, the alliance has been a matter of survival. Without American intervention, North Korea would have reunified the peninsula in 1950. Since then, the United States has been an important partner in resisting North Korean adventurism. Any military effort on the part of North Korea to alter the political configuration of the peninsula would amount to suicide for the Pyongyang regime.

Since the end of the Cold War, the strategic situation in East Asia has changed completely. The position of the United States is now defined in terms of the war on terror and threats posed by rogue states. North Korea is one of the latter and was referred to ominously by the Bush administration. "Regime change" is an unlikely scenario for Washington, however, as long as the North is shielded by China. Pyongyang's nuclear program and missile technology have alarmed Japan, which has set about elevating its own strategic profile.

South Korea seems not to fear an invasion from the North despite several provocative attacks, but would consider American military operations to bring about regime change there a disaster. The immediate effect of such an action would be a large number of refugees leaving North Korea for the South and also for China. But when President Bush began pressuring North Korea, including the threat of economic sanctions, South Korean president

Kim Dae-Jung, advocate of a "sunshine policy" favoring engagement with the North, and his successor, Roh Moo-Hyun, opposed the strategy. They argued that isolating the Pyongyang regime internationally and imposing sanctions would be counterproductive. Instead they favored dialogue and an energetic search for a peaceful solution to the nuclear issue—an approach that has not been effective so far.

11

The Hermit Kingdom

The partition of Korea is the last remaining unresolved major legacy of World War II. Divided Germany was reunified following the fall of the Soviet Union. North and South Vietnam, following the failed effort by the United States to stem the tide of communism, were reunited and are under the control of Hanoi. The situation in Korea derives from a lengthy history beginning with the Japanese annexation of the peninsula in 1910 and its subsequent "liberation" following Japan's defeat in World War II. Partition was not what the victors had in mind, of course. The United States and the Soviet Union, wartime allies, had agreed that liberated territories would only be occupied as long as it would take to clear out the Japanese, or in the case of Germany, the Nazis. The liberated territories would have their independence and national integrity restored, it was hoped, in short order. But the Soviet Union, ever disingenuous, had other plans. The Soviets wanted to extend the Communist revolution, and the Red Army's occupation of Eastern Europe at the end of the war presented them with a golden opportunity. There was less of a need for Soviet troops in Vietnam and in Korea as the local Communists there were strong enough to promote the cause of revolution on their own.

Kim Il Sung, 1912–1994

The postwar history of North Korea was defined by the career of Kim Il Sung, who ran the country with an iron hand until his death in 1994. The early life of Kim, born Kim Song Ju, is shrouded in mystery and embellished by the cult of personality that came to characterize his rule. It is known that he was born on April 15, 1912, in the city of Mangyongdae, near Pyongyang. However, discrepancies exist as to the background of his parents, with one report indicating that his father was a schoolteacher and revolutionary leader who chose to move the family to eastern Manchuria because of the Japanese occupation.[1] In China, Kim Il Sung joined the Communist Youth League in 1926, attended the Whampoa Military Academy, and later, in 1931, organized guerrilla resistance cells to fight the Japanese when they invaded Manchuria.

A different biography claims that his parents were very religious Presbyterians who moved to Manchuria to open an herb pharmacy.[2] After only eight years of schooling, two of which were in Manchuria, Kim was briefly jailed in the early 1930s for participation in guerrilla activities with the Chinese Communists and subsequently expelled from China. Much of Kim's early history has been obscured by official North Korean hagiography. Nonetheless, Kim was involved in guerrilla activities, as evidenced by the Japanese posting a reward for his capture.

Forced to retreat from Manchuria, Kim crossed the border and made his way to a Soviet military camp. He fought for the Soviet Red Army during World War II as a commander of one of the two Korean units, but his actual rank is unknown. Korean reports claim that he returned home as a colonel; it is more likely, however, that he was only a captain or major in the Soviet ranks. He married a Korean woman and fathered two sons, one of whom was Kim Jong Il, his future successor. During his time in the Red Army, Kim became well known to the Soviet officers. But when Soviet troops invaded Korea in 1945 to accept the surrender of Japanese troops, Kim and his 88th Brigade were not with them. Stalin considered another group of Koreans who had closer connections with the Soviet Union to be a better choice to assist in liberation. Kim entered Korea a month later.[3] Contrary to the official biography, Kim was neither the personal choice of Stalin to lead Korea nor did he and his group fight their way into Korea to liberate their country from the Japanese.[4] The Soviet troops that liberated Korea were hardened veterans from the war against Germany.[5]

Despite his connection to the Soviet Union, Kim's development of military forces was not exclusively a result of Soviet efforts but instead grew out of Korean resistance to the Japanese occupation in China and Manchuria.[6] His record in the resistance "was formidable compared to that of other Koreans in 1945; and he had the Japanese police records to document it. In addition, he had an armed contingent of several hundred guerrillas under his control." Other Korean exile leaders had small groups of supporters and few had arms. "This was Kim Il Sung's most important advantage."[7]

Sometime in 1945 or 1946, Kim Song Ju changed his name to Kim Il Sung, in honor of an uncle who had fought and disappeared in the 1919 revolution.[8] Accounts maintain that Kim initially remained a humble man, one who was described as coming from a family of "hard-working ordinary people."[9] When he took over the leadership of North Korea, however, Kim's past was molded to fit that of a great leader. He was lavished with gifts and retained five palaces and countless guesthouses. Slowly, he became cut off from the common people and was surrounded by servants and bodyguards, forbidding the uninvited from his presence. It is suggested that he traveled with a cadre of doctors, each assigned to evaluate a different part of his body, and that a special institute was created in the capital of Pyongyang to research his health in an attempt to slow the aging process.

Kim Il Sung

He cultivated the adoration he received from his people and was known as *suryong*, or Great Leader, within his country. Thousands of monuments were built to honor him, creating what Don Oberdorfer refers to as an "impermeable and absolutist state that many have compared to a religious cult."[10] Dissent was not tolerated, and those who chose to criticize any aspect of his regime were sent to one of the twelve prisons camps located in remote areas throughout North Korea. The cult of personality is a political phenomenon found in various places around the world at various times. But that of Kim Il Sung does have a certain East Asian, Confucian quality about it. "With the possible exception of Japan and its imperial family, North Korea has been unique in East Asia in literalizing the filial piety of nationalism in the family of the leader, in effect making Kim Il Sung the universal patriarch."[11] In addition to his personal qualities, Kim could claim leadership because of his family lineage. Given this tradition, it followed that Kim's son Kim Jong Il would inherit his father's political position.

Political Reforms

In order to broaden the base of support for the new Communist order, especially among the lower classes, social reform was given the highest priority.

At the top of the list was land reform. "The North Korean land reform was achieved in a less violent manner than that in China and North Vietnam." This was attested to by official American sources.[12] "Land reform was something the regime emerging in South Korea after liberation pursued slowly, and with great reluctance, until after the Korean War. North Korea, on the other hand, carried out land reform throughout the northern zone quickly and decisively in the spring of 1946."[13]

The government gained additional support from the rural population by its emphasis on education and literacy, an effective approach given the East Asian reverence for learning. Apart from the agricultural working class, the regime cultivated favor among the industrial proletariat through worker-friendly labor laws and a social insurance program. The foundations of industrialization had been established during the Japanese occupation. Reform efforts also addressed women's rights, an issue on the agendas of both the Soviet and Chinese revolutions. There was also an emphasis on generational change. In the Confucian tradition, age carries a high degree of social status, a cultural aspect particularly strong in Korea. Like their Chinese counterparts, the North Koreans sought to elevate the status of young people by including them to a greater extent in public life.[14]

The peasants' honeymoon with the new regime did not last long, however. The government established an effective system of tax collection. This undermined the traditional rural method of avoiding taxes by underreporting production. Peasants were also required to perform labor on construction projects, in mines, and in factories.[15] Despite some grumbling, however, the countryside in North Korea was much more tranquil than that in the South.

North Korea, like China and Vietnam, embraced an ideology that stressed ideas over material conditions. But "this humanistic and voluntaristic emphasis was even more pronounced in Korea than in the other two East Asian communist revolutions, which may reflect the fact that Korea had long been more orthodox in its Confucianism than Vietnam or China."[16] Unlike Soviet East European satellites, where state socialism was an essentially alien doctrine imposed from outside, for Korea, and other East Asian countries, communism wedded with nationalism was an effective vehicle for liberation from colonialism and achievement of national development. Charles K. Armstrong contends that the Soviets did not have plans in place to establish communist regimes in East Asia until well after World War II was over. Rather, their primary goal was to ensure that Japan would never reestablish control of Korea.[17]

In economic and political terms, North Korea started off with significant advantages over the South. The Japanese had stressed industrial development in the northern region because of the availability of natural resources. As a result, many North Koreans possessed modern technical skills. They were also better organized and had a sense of direction.[18]

By 1950, North Korea had reversed the economic slide that followed the end of Japanese rule. "It was a remarkable achievement, especially in contrast to South Korea, whose industrial output still lagged far behind that of the North."[19] Centrally planned economies such as those of the Soviet Union, China, and North Korea have an advantage in overcoming initial economic difficulties. In all three cases, when the communist regimes were first established, economic conditions were poor. By mobilizing and directing resources, they were able to achieve significant economic progress, at least early on. But after the command economy model delivered its results, eventually, the dead hand of stagnation would set it. In the Soviet Union people said, "We pretend to work and the state pretends to pay us." In China it was the "iron rice bowl" concept whereby people could expect a minimum standard of living but lacked any incentive to be more productive. The role of money, prices, and markets was absent from centrally planned economies, thus removing the main forces for growth and expansion. Moreover, any pursuit of private economic initiative could attract harsh punishment.

The initial improving economic situation in North Korea was one of the factors that lead Kim to contemplate reunifying the peninsula by force. There are discrepancies in the evidence as to whose decision it was to invade South Korea. North Korea guards its documents from this period of time very closely. The fall of the Soviet Union allowed access to Soviet archival materials, but there is very little that is not ambiguous about the Korean War. Harry Summers claims North Korea initiated the invasion. North Korea carefully approached Stalin with the idea, and Kim insisted that the invasion would only take a few days to complete. Given the poor state of security in the South, such a feat seemed plausible at the time.

Kim was careful to lay out a North Korean agenda without blindly following the advice of the Soviets or the Chinese. Kim met with both Stalin and Mao Zedong, but the substance of their conversations and decisions remains unknown. Most historians take the position that Stalin initiated the decision to invade South Korea. This may be true, but it was also the most convenient assumption in that blaming Moscow for all communist activities fit American Cold War ideology. Regardless of who provoked whom, North Korean troops invaded the South on June 25, 1950, and had captured Seoul within forty-eight hours. North Korean historiography blames South Korea, asserting that it was the South that crossed the 38th parallel and invaded the Communist country first.

Chapter 9 deals with the Korean War in detail. Suffice it to say here, North Korea failed in its efforts to reunify the peninsula. The United States, under

UN auspices, succeeded to the extent of frustrating North Korean, and Soviet, ambitions. But the war was very unpopular in the United States because there was no clear victory, something Americans had become accustomed to during World War II. Moreover, the war was a catastrophe for Koreans. It did have considerable strategic significance, as it demonstrated to Stalin that the United States and the West would not stand idly by while the Soviet Union expanded its empire. But the stalemate would leave the North locked into its intransigent position for decades to come, and ultimately a geographical and ideological isolate.[20] Only Japan was a net gainer, as it enjoyed substantial economic benefits from the war, as it did later with the Vietnam War. Wars are prodigious consumers of goods and materials, and the Japanese were only too eager to supply them.

Kim Jong Il, 1941–2011

If little is known about the childhood of Kim Il Sung, next to nothing is known about his son and heir. Subject to spin-doctors and government propagandists, Kim Jong Il remains an eccentric enigma to the outside world. North Korean official accounts state that he was born on Mount Paekdu, the birthplace of Tangun, the "mythic father of the Korean people. More objective sources say the younger Kim was born . . . in a Russian military camp in the [Russian] Far East."[21] Kim returned to Korea when he was three but was then evacuated to China five years later when the Korean War began. Kim's mother delivered a daughter and later there was another son who died in a drowning accident. Kim's mother herself died while giving birth to a stillborn child.[22] In the 1960s, Kim Il Sung remarried and fathered two sons and two daughters.

Kim Jong Il attended and graduated from Kim Il Sung University in 1964 and "went to work in the Central Committee of the Workers Party, with special responsibility for films, theater, and art, which became his lifelong passion."[23] He became notorious for his kidnapping of South Korean actress Choi Eun Hee and her ex-husband Shin Sang-ok from Hong Kong in 1978. The couple tape-recorded Kim admitting to the abduction. He claimed he had kidnapped the couple in order to improve the North Korean film industry. Shin was imprisoned for four years for attempted escape but was later reunited with his former wife and produced motion pictures for the "Dear Leader" until the pair escaped to Vienna in 1986. Despite North Korea's poverty, stories persist that Kim throws extravagant parties, drinks substantial amounts of expensive liquor, and lavishes expensive gifts on his friends.[24] Bruce Cumings warns that these statements could be fabrications created in Seoul to undermine the Communist regime.[25]

Kim was named the successor to his father in October 1980 and was given the name "Dear Leader." He was assigned senior posts in the Politburo, the Military Commission, and the Party Secretariat.[26] But long before this time he was widely expected by North Koreans to succeed his father. Kim's grooming for leadership was carefully planned, and he became involved in party organization work in 1973.[27] His picture was displayed alongside his father's, and he was meticulously primed for future responsibilities by the party. Kim Jong Il became the "sole successor to the Great Leader" in July 1994.[28] By contrast, Kim Jong Il's third son and chosen heir, Kim Jong Un, was almost completely unknown to the public before 2009. Given the heir's relative youth and unexperience, it is widely expected that his uncle, Jang Sung Taek, will provide guidance.

North Korea's Development Prospects

As described by Marcus Noland, "contemporary North Korea is a wild mélange of an authoritarian Confucian dynasty, a Stalinist state, and a religious cult, complete with its own theology, *juche*."[29] *Juche*, the core doctrine of Kim Il Sung's ideology, enshrines the values of national independence, self-reliance, and self-sufficiency. While there have been periods when the estrangement between the two Koreas appeared to be abating, *juche* reinforces intransigence, and there is little prospect of genuine reconciliation until there are important political changes in the North. The departure of Kim Jong Il could conceivably result in regime change, but that may not necessarily be a happy occasion. Given the dilapidated state of North Korea, should political control collapse, not only would chaos result but there would likely be a mass exodus of refugees, especially to the South. Seoul is more worried about such a probability than it is of an armed assault from the North.

Poor economic conditions are exacerbated by North Korea's emphasis on expanding its military capability. "It is common knowledge that North Korea's economic collapse in the 1990s was the inevitable result of Pyongyang's massive expenditures on military preparedness and the demise of Soviet aid and trade."[30]

The collapse of the Soviet Union was a special blow to North Korea. In the early 1990s, trade between Russia and North Korea dropped sharply from $2.35 billion in 1990 to $222 million in 1993. The Russians also "ended transfers of military equipment and technology to Pyongyang, cultural and scientific ties were abandoned, the intergovernmental commission on economic and scientific cooperation ceased operations, and even direct flights were cancelled. In response, Pyongyang refused to repay a four billion ruble loan."[31] These developments effectively ended any hope Pyongyang may have entertained of reunifying the peninsula on its own terms.

China has maintained closer relations with North Korea than has any other country, including the Soviet Union. But North Korea's status vis-à-vis China has deteriorated. China is North Korea's most important economic partner, and it provides North Korea with most of its basic necessities. Clearly, North Korea's own economic development prospects are not good. It runs a substantial trade deficit with China because it "does not have high value products to export," and what it does have to export is losing its competitiveness in the Chinese market.[32]

The regional picture is complicated by the fact that there has been a significant movement of people around the area. Despite tight restrictions on travel, some hundreds of thousands of North Korean refugees have fled to China. Chinese-Korean illegal migrant workers have gone to South Korea. South Korean officials, business executives, and even some tourists have gone to North Korea.

Authoritarian regimes typically restrict public access to information. The ruling elites do not want people to have knowledge about how good things are abroad and how bad things are at home. "North Koreans who had been overseas were forced to remain silent about their experiences, and a number of people who made references to the higher living standards of other countries ended up in prison camps. These extraordinary attempts to maintain an information blockade reflect a basic fact: the myth of prosperity has been absolutely essential to the regime's survival."[33]

It is no longer possible to deny access to information as completely as in the past, however, thanks mainly to the revolution in electronic communication. First, radios penetrated the information silence despite the fact that in North Korea shortwave radios were prohibited.

Next was the VCR. Smuggled in from China, with which North Korea shares a porous border, VCRs at first were scarce and expensive. As cheaper models and later DVD players became available in China, the older models found their way to North Korea and were affordable to many people. These are used mainly to view South Korean television dramas.

Through the China connection, North Koreans also have access to computers and the Internet, although on a very limited basis. Another electronic innovation with widespread impact is the cell phone. "One of the most striking developments in recent years has been the spread in the borderland areas of mobile phones, which are serviced by Chinese network operators."[34]

During the decade of the 1990s North Korea's economy diminished by nearly half, measured in GDP, and the country suffered widespread famine conditions from 1995 to 1997. Weather-induced food supply problems were exacerbated by the government's refusal to allow farmers small private plots, a reform that proved the salvation of China's agricultural economy. In an effort to end dependence on international food aid, the regime gradually relaxed restrictions on farmers' markets and petty trade, which began to supply a growing proportion of the population's needs. Hardline efforts to rein in even this slight liberalization are easy to explain, for as the economy develops along the lines of small-scale individual initiatives, the ability of the government to control the population weakens.

There are also changes under way in the social system. The notion of "origin" or family background as the determinant of social and political status is weakening. Descendents of military heroes and top officials have a "good" origin and get the best jobs, enter prestigious colleges, and have the best living arrangements. Those with a "bad" origin do manual labor in the provinces. Yet, some formerly disadvantaged groups have risen to the top of the socioeconomic hierarchy. Japanese-Koreans receive money from relatives in Japan who emigrated in the 1960s and invest it in the more relaxed climate of today. Likewise, Koreans with relatives in China receive help in business and trade dealings. Ethnic Chinese, the only minority in North Korea, have been able to travel outside the country and are key players in the "underground economy" and in smuggling.[35]

The official North Korean economy not only fails to provide for the livelihood of its people, it does not generate sufficient wealth to pay for foreign imports. There are other sources of revenue to pay the bills, all causing international concern. North Korea does a substantial business in arms sales. Of particular concern is the export of missiles and nuclear weapons technology to Middle Eastern countries such as Iran and Syria. Another source of revenue is drug trafficking. A third way of paying the bills is through counterfeiting. In one case, the United States accused Pyongyang of counterfeiting and blocked an account in a Macao bank.[36] Pyongyang refused to continue talks over its nuclear program until the money matter had been cleared up. After a period during which no bank could be found willing to accept the funds, North Korea finally received its money in June 2007.

Alexandre Mansuourov sees considerable cumulative evidence of the breaking down of North Korea's rigid authoritarianism.[37] The fear, isolation, elite unity, and *juche* ideology that have held the regime together are eroding away. As the traditional sources of control available to him have started to disappear, Kim Jong Il has turned to the military for support."[38] The creation of "military-first" politics in North Korea was expedient for Kim Jong Il so that he might effectively govern North Korea.

North Korea's Nuclear Program

North Korea has been at loggerheads with the international community since the end of World War II. The legacy of the Korean War and the broader security environment of the Cold War set relations into a mode of permanent hostility. North Korea's behavior has been erratic and unpredictable. The U.S. perception of North Korea is a function of hostility toward its Communist regime and the security threat it poses. However, the degree to which North Korea poses a security threat may be exaggerated. While it has a large army and the political role of the military is considerable, its forces are not up to modern standards.[39] Its nuclear weapons potential and delivery capability are worrisome, especially to Japan, but nuclear weapons have little strategic utility except as a deterrent. It is unlikely that Pyongyang would commit suicide by launching a first strike. North Korea has become increasingly isolated, and it has few cards to play. Since it refuses to play by the rules, it has little choice but to exploit the security challenge it presents to the world. The world community offers resources to North Korea in an effort to get it to change its ways. But if it changed its ways, it would have nothing to bargain with. Its ability to extract these resources "is intimately related to the threat it poses, and, in a sense, the status quo more closely resembles extortion than charity. The threat that North Korea possesses is its sole asset. It is unlikely to negotiate away this asset very easily."[40]

North Korea began its nuclear program in 1964, relying on a Soviet-supplied research facility at Yongban employing uranium mined in North Korea. It joined the International Atomic Energy Agency (IAEA) in 1974 and signed a safeguards agreement in 1977 covering its two nuclear research facilities. Under pressure from the Soviet Union, on December 12, 1985, Pyongyang joined the Non-Proliferation Treaty (NPT), which required complete inspection of nuclear facilities by the IAEA. The Soviets had promised four light-water reactors if North Korea joined the NPT, but they were never delivered. However, Pyongyang only agreed to these inspections in 1992. It announced its intention to withdraw from the NPT and the safeguards agreement on March 12, 1993, and from the IAEA in June the following year.

On October 21, 1994, the United States and North Korea signed the Geneva Accords of the Korean Peninsula. Had these accords been fully implemented, the peninsula would have been made nuclear free, and relations among the two Koreas and the United States would have been normalized. This was known as the Agreed Framework. North Korea was to have remained in the NPT and submitted its three graphite reactors and related facilities to International Atomic Energy Agency inspection. The United States agreed to supply North Korea with 150,000 tons of heavy heating oil in 1995 and 500,000 tons annually from 1996 to 2003. Even if all had gone according to plan, achieving the targets for heating oil delivery would have been difficult given North Korea's limited storage capacity. The Americans also agreed to lead a consortium to finance, build, and deliver two light-water reactors in 2003 and 2004.[41] North Korea would repay this investment with a twenty-year loan.

But none of this came to pass. A change in the political climate of the United States occurred as the Republicans took control of Congress in 1994 and set about creating new conditions limiting President Bill Clinton's freedom of action in Korea.

From the North Korean perspective, the death of Kim Il Sung in 1994 interrupted the negotiation process. After his death, there followed a three-year mourning period. During this time there was little movement in addressing international differences. Further complicating matters, in August 1998, North Korea fired a long-range ballistic missile that traveled through Japanese air space. The Japanese reacted to this event, understandably, as a serious security issue, and took measures to retaliate. Tokyo put its military forces on alert, suspended food aid, ended participation in the Korean Peninsula Energy Development Organization (KEDO)—including financial arrangements, refused to proceed with normalization talks, and threatened to condemn North Korea in the UN Security Council.[42] Meanwhile, the United States was frequently late in delivering the promised fuel oil and failed to move on the construction of the nuclear reactors.

Nevertheless, work on the different aspects of the agreement proceeded until the advent of the Bush administration. On June 6, 2001, the U.S. government outlined a new American posture toward North Korea. In effect, the new policy called for North Korea's disarmament. "The Bush administration's policy was to eliminate even the minutest elements of North Korea's military power and to secure absolute U.S. hegemony in Northeast Asia."[43] In his January 29, 2002, State of the Union speech, following the 9/11 attack, Bush included North Korea in the "axis of evil," along with Iran and Iraq. In October 2002, North Korea restarted its nuclear weapons program and, in response, the United States suspended its heavy oil program. North Korea denied entry to a KEDO delegation and resumed construction and operation of its nuclear facilities. IAEA inspectors were expelled on December 27, 2002. On January 10, 2003, North Korea announced its withdrawal from the NPT.

After the U.S. invasion of Iraq in March 2003, the North Korea matter shifted to a six-party format, in which China played a pivotal role. China's initiatives had less to do with concern over the potential use by North Korea of its nuclear weapons than with possible U.S. military intervention, an action that would put all of Northeast Asia in crisis. The United States demanded full compliance with the nonproliferation regime. North Korea demanded a legally binding nonaggression commitment from the United States. The talks began on August 27, 2003. North Korea wanted a less hostile posture on the part of the Americans, particularly as manifested by a nonaggression treaty. It would agree to dismantle its nuclear weapons program only if the United States abandoned its hostile posture. For its part, the United States was vague on what it was willing to do in the event North Korea gave up its nuclear weapons program. American conservatives criticized the idea of "rewarding" North Korea with concessions.

During the Clinton administration, the approach was to exchange the nuclear weapons program for a package including heavy oil and light-water reactors, which would not pose a weapons development problem. This approach ultimately went nowhere. The Bush administration took a hard line. In June 2004, the United States outlined a denuclearization program. "North Korea was required to make the initial concessions without any guarantee of reciprocation from the United States. Whereas the requirements for the DPRK were quite specific, those for the United States were vague and contingent— the United States, for instance, would not even participate in the new heavy fuel oil shipments."[44]

The other parties to the talks—China, Russia, Japan, and South Korea— have their own agendas. China seeks a greater role in Northeast Asia. In this the future of North Korea is pivotal. "North Korea has earned a reputation . . . for employing 'the power of the weak,' creating and using crises to extract concessions to compensate for its growing domestic failings. China, more than any other country, has been the target of these appeals."[45] For its part, Russia hopes to regain some of the initiative lost after the demise of the Soviet Union. But Moscow has cut back on its commitments to Pyongyang by, among other things, reducing its pledge to defend North Korea in the event of war to defending it only in the event of an unprovoked attack.

Until Pyongyang acquired a nuclear capability and presented a serious security challenge to Japan, Tokyo made little effort to establish normal official relations with North Korea. To do so would have aroused the suspicions of the United States, and the absence of such relations did not seem to interfere with economic opportunities. Pro–North Korean interests in Japan also provided a conduit through which Japan could maintain unofficial communication.[46] North Korean actions have moved Japan and South Korea closer together. Up to the 1990s these two countries entertained some degree of suspicion toward one another. Seoul, of course, harbored hostile feelings left over from the colonial era. Japanese politicians often complained that Korea had not been grateful enough for all Japan had done for it during the colonial period and felt the Koreans, and others, were being unreasonable in demanding apologies.[47]

Japan wants to resolve the issue of the kidnapping of Japanese citizens by North Korea during the late 1970s and early 1980s and is also concerned about North Korea's nuclear weapons and missile programs. In 2002, Prime Minister Koizumi visited Pyongyang to discuss, among other things, the status of the abductees.[48] Eight of the thirteen admitted abductees had reportedly died in North Korea, and there was little information regarding the circumstances of their deaths.[49] Five survivors and, eventually, their children were allowed to return to Japan. South Korea wants a peninsula free of nuclear weapons and better relations with the North. Under the KEDO agreement, Seoul would have had greater leverage vis-à-vis the North since it was to pay the greater share of the bill for the reactors and South Korean technical workers.

On October 9, 2006, North Korea tested a nuclear device. This action provoked international condemnation. In the UN Security Council, the United States sponsored a resolution to impose an arms embargo, a ban on all trade relating to weapons of mass destruction, a freeze on funds related to missile and nuclear programs, an end to counterfeiting U.S. currency, and a ban on trade in luxury goods. The proposal also called for international inspection of all cargo to and from North Korea. The resolution passed, but difficulties arose immediately over enforcement, especially the inspection of ships sailing to North Korean ports.

The test also cast a pall over the "sunshine policy" pursued by South Korea since 1998. President Lee Myung Bak, elected in December 2007, took a much harder line, proposing to link economic cooperation and aid to successful resolution of the nuclear issue. By the end of 2008, relations had worsened considerably. In January 2009, Pyongyang accused Seoul of "hostile intent"; in April it tested a long-range rocket and in May it conducted underground nuclear tests, drawing increasing international condemnation with each step. North Korean actions became more overtly hostile in 2010, with the torpedoing of a South Korean naval vessel in March and the shelling of a South Korean island in November.

While these escalating provocations followed a familiar pattern of extortion, it is now thought that they were also intended to keep the world off-balance as the regime prepared for another succession, from an obviously ailing Kim Jong Il to his youngest son, Kim Jong Un.

China, which provides 70 percent of North Korea's fuel and 40 percent of its food, has long been the Pyongyong regime's protector. Beijing has opposed tough sanctions that might result in the collapse of North Korea and a flood of refugees into China. Accordingly, China is disposed to continue and perhaps even increase the flow of aid. On the other hand, China is also concerned about a nuclear arms race in East Asia and the possibility of North Korea exporting nuclear technology, especially to terrorists. Japan might also go nuclear as a deterrent, a development that would unwelcome in China.

Reunification

Publicly, everyone favors reunification, if speaking softly about it. Young Whan Kihl observes that there are three ways reunification could occur. One is by force, an option that no longer seems viable. Another is by mutual consent, as occurred in Germany. This option also seems unlikely without substantial political change in North Korea. This leaves gradual reunification by negotiation and agreement, leaving both North and South with some kind of residual identity.[50]

Japan regards the North Korea problem to be the last remaining issue of the Cold War in Asia and as such needs to be resolved in that context. But at the same time, Tokyo worries that the situation has the potential of disrupting and jeopardizing the current security arrangement in the region, including especially Japan's own security. North Korea is the only country with which Japan has yet to negotiate normal diplomatic relations, leaving Japan's wartime legacy unsettled, at least at the official level.[51]

From China's point of view, the potential benefits of unification may be equally ambiguous. Without a North Korean security problem the United States might view its security role in Asia as diminished. Or without the security threat posed by North Korea, the United States might address itself full time to a containment strategy toward China. Security relations between the United States and China have worsened in recent years. The Bush doctrine, American interventionism, the tendency to bypass the Security Council altogether, along with references by Bush himself to the effect that China is a competitor not an ally, led China to the conclusion that the United States seeks world hegemony and the containment of China.[52] The financial crisis of 2007–2009, which originated in the United States, added another source of tension.

Russia is the only major power to openly advocate Korean reunification, which would be economically rewarding for Moscow. In addition to adding links to Russia's transportation networks, a unified Korea could open markets to Russian natural gas. Reunification could also facilitate repayment of North Korea's enormous debt to Russia.[53]

Predicting the trajectory of developments on the Korean peninsula is risky. For one thing, as Noland notes, very little is known about the workings of North Korea's government and economy.[54] The Bush administration's use of such provocative slogans as "axis of evil" and "regime change" may actually have accelerated North Korea's drive to become a nuclear power. Washington has resorted to the sanctions approach, an approach that has been used against Cuba for half a century, impoverishing the country but not achieving the goal of eliminating the Castro regime. Now the approach is being used in an effort to induce Iran to give up its nuclear program. The linkage between economic pressures and political change is tenuous at best.

Since the United States cannot seriously entertain the military option to achieve regime change in North Korea, the hope is that the regime will either change its own behavior or collapse. This may be one of those "be careful what you wish for" situations. The costs of reconstruction of North Korea would be enormous, and the international community is not likely to be willing to shoulder that burden any time soon.

12

Asian Tiger

The political history of South Korea has been both short and troubled. The area was part of the Japanese empire from 1910 to 1945. Following World War II, it was "temporarily" occupied by the United States, which intended to transfer authority to an independent, unified country. The emergence of new strategic realities in the form of the Cold War disrupted those plans. In occupying South Korea, the United States pursued two not necessarily complementary objectives. First, Korea was central to the containment of communism in Northeast Asia. Second, the United States wanted to promote South Korea as a model of democracy. Containing communism was the top priority, and it led eventually to the Korean War. Promoting democracy was, if anything, even more difficult than preventing the spread of communism. East Asia had little experience with democratic politics—Korea having even less than either China or Japan. Democracy was introduced by Americans and was not a product of internal South Korean political dynamics. As a result, the road to democracy has been a difficult one.

Postwar Governments

In 1948, Syngman Rhee was elected president of the Republic of Korea. Rhee had lobbied the U.S. government for years to become post-independence Korea's leader, and he had set up a government in exile as early as 1919. Rhee's strident anticommunism played well among American conservatives, and even though official Washington was less than enthusiastic, he was duly installed as South Korea's postwar leader. He continued in that capacity through three terms as president. He won a fourth term in March 1960, but by then Rhee's popularity had begun to wane and there was a widespread belief that the election had been rigged. Subsequent violent student demonstrations brought into question the legitimacy of his regime. Rhee's increasingly authoritarian rule and widespread government corruption generated growing public opposition. Student protests in April 1960 were met with police retaliation, and 125 students were killed. This action, clearly the wrong approach to take, in turn produced a wave of civil violence that forced Rhee from office. The successor government was headed by Prime Minister Chung Myun.

In 1961, a pattern of military intervention in the political process began to emerge. In May of that year, the army seized power in a bloodless coup when Prime Minister Chung's government proved unable to deal effectively with economic problems or maintain order. A military government under General Park Chung Hee established tight control over society, the economy, and the press. Park attempted to "civilize" his rule, and he was elected president in 1963, reelected in 1967, and, after amending the constitution to allow for a third term, was reelected again in 1971. Park's government was successful in bringing government corruption under control, stimulating the economy, and introducing the first of many five-year development plans. From 1962 to 1972, the economy grew rapidly under the impetus of industrial expansion and a successful export campaign.

Economic growth was not an unmixed blessing, however. While a few families amassed large fortunes through industrial activities, material conditions improved only marginally for the economically less fortunate. Overall, there were serious problems in many areas. Employment opportunities in industry drew large numbers of people from rural agricultural areas into the cities, where housing and services lagged behind. Labor unions were outlawed, so wages did not keep pace with inflation. Working conditions in textile and small-scale consumer industries where women were the main employees were unhealthy.[1]

Meanwhile, North Korea took advantage of South Korea's political turmoil by adopting an increasingly aggressive posture. Pyongyang had been far from cooperative for some time. On January 21, 1969, armed North Korean agents attacked a government building in Seoul. On January 23, the U.S. intelligence ship *Pueblo* was captured by the North Korean military. At the resulting trial the ship's captain, Lloyd Bucher, was put on public display, which proved to be a major embarrassment to the United States. Later the same year, North Korea shot down an American reconnaissance plane, and North Korean armed agents continued to infiltrate the South. Tunnels were built under the DMZ (Demilitarized Zone), some large enough to accommodate an army on the march.

In October 1972, Park dissolved the National Assembly and declared martial law, claiming authoritarian rule was necessary to improve South Korea's position in reunification talks with the North.[2] Then in December of the same year he revised the constitution of 1969, giving himself almost unlimited power. In 1974, a Korean resident of Japan made an unsuccessful attempt to assassinate Park in Seoul, killing Park's wife in the process. A second assassination attempt in 1979 by Kim Jae Kyu, the head of the Korean Central Intelligence Agency and Park's right-hand man, was successful.

General Chun Doo Hwan, the head of the Defense Security Command, headed the investigation into Park's assassination. His investigation led to a violent confrontation with other military leaders from which Chun emerged, together with his supporters, at the head of the Korean military. In May 1980, Chun extended martial law, resulting in violent protests around the country. In August he declared himself president and was formally elected to that office in February 1981. Political problems remained, and opposition to Chun's authoritarian rule intensified.

In 1987, labor unrest and general dissatisfaction with the government led South Koreans leaders to draw up yet another constitution, which mandated the popular election of the president to a single five-year term of office. Other provisions included the establishment of judicial independence. The importance of the National Assembly was enhanced. Civil liberties and the right of labor to organize, bargain, and strike were guaranteed.[3]

Chun's tenure as president was marked by three patterns of development. First, the economy grew significantly, bolstered by expanding foreign trade. Living standards improved for the masses of the people. Second, civil liberties suffered as a result of Chun's rigorous authoritarianism. Finally, to his ultimate undoing, Chun and members of his family engaged in unbridled corruption.[4]

Elected president in 1988, Roh Tae Woo was confronted with inflationary pressures brought on by Korea's overheated economy. Roh's term was marked by efforts to improve relations with opposition politicians and with the North. Diplomatic relations were established with the Soviet Union in 1990 and with China in 1992. While the prospects for better relations between the two Koreas improved from time to time, the likelihood of reunification dimmed. In 1991, North Korea agreed to the establishment of a two Koreas policy by accepting separate membership in the UN for both North and South Korea.

Roh Tae Woo and his predecessor, Chun Doo Hwan, were arrested and convicted in August 1996 of treason, mutiny, and corruption. They, together with fourteen former generals, were also tried for complicity in the 1979 coup following Park's assassination and for their connection with the 1980 massacre of demonstrators in Kwangju. Chun's death sentence was later commuted to life in prison, and Roh's twenty-two-and-a-half-year prison sentence was reduced to seventeen years after appeal. Both were pardoned by President Kim Dae Jung in 1998. Chun, stripped of his fortune, returned to Seoul, to a life of obscurity.

Kim Young Sam, a former opposition leader who merged his party with Roh's, was elected president in 1992. He was the first person without a military background to be elected president since 1960. He launched a campaign to eliminate corruption and administrative abuse and encouraged economic cooperation with the North. While he was concerned with promoting the integrity and legitimacy of the regime, he was insufficiently attentive to policy issues. His efforts to promote clean and moral politics were damaged when an aide was charged with influence peddling, but most damaging was the conviction of his second son on corruption charges. "In the context of Korea's Confucian culture, the father is the source of moral authority of the family and his son's illicit acts caused Kim Young Sam to lose face and moral authority as a political leader."[5] Whereas he started his tenure as president with great momentum, he ended it a failure with a popular approval rating between 5 and 10 percent.[6]

In 1997, several of region's most rapidly developing economies, known as the "Asian Tigers" (Singapore, Hong Kong, Taiwan, South Korea, Thailand), experienced severe financial crises. The problem began with the bursting of the Japanese economic "bubble" and first manifested itself as a financial crisis brought on by the collapse of the Thai currency, the *baht*. It quickly spread to South Korea and Indonesia. Increasing financial risk led foreign investors to remove their money from Indonesia, causing a financial collapse. The South Korean economy, suffered a similar fate. The financial crisis was so severe that South Korea was forced to seek loans from the International Monetary Fund (IMF). In short order, South Korea ran through its financial reserves and found itself on the verge of default. On December 3, 1997, the IMF came to the rescue with a substantial loan to bail out the South Korean economy. But this loan came with strings attached. Seoul had to agree to the usual IMF conditions: currency stabilization, budget cuts, tax increases, and a commitment to meet its foreign debts. The amount of the loan was at the time the largest international rescue effort in history: $58.35 billion.

Kim Dae Jung, a pro-democracy dissident who had been active during the periods of military dictatorship, was elected president in 1998 and undertook an initiative to improve relations with Japan as well as the United States. The economy began to recover from the financial crisis in 1999, and Kim undertook a "sunshine policy," which was intended to put relations with the North on a more open and productive footing and, it was hoped, induce Pyongyang to undertake its own political reforms. In 2000 Kim made a historic visit to Pyongyang and held discussions with Kim Jong Il. The Clinton administration was receptive to a summit meeting but failed to achieve this goal before the end of Clinton's term. The Bush administration postponed the prospective talks until after a comprehensive review of foreign and defense policy.[7] Kim's effort toward a stable relationship and eventual reunification was further undercut by Pyongyang's belligerence and its weapons development program. Its testing of long-range missiles, that made Japan a potential target had already provoked the Japanese to seriously entertain reviewing their security policy. In addition to its foreign relations problems, Kim's government was further weakened when it was hit with corruption charges in 2002, charges that came to include his own family. Further embarrassment came when the National Assembly rejected his nominee for prime minister. Despite these difficulties, his chosen successor, Roh Moo Hyun, was elected president in December 2002. In 2003, the main political parties were implicated in a fund-raising scandal that also included many prominent people in the business community. In 2004 the president was impeached and removed from office over a relatively minor election law violation. Roh had publicly supported the new Uri Party (formally Yeollin Uri, or "Our Open Party"), an action that was illegal since the president is supposed to be neutral. During the impeachment proceedings, Roh was also accused of incompetence. But the Constitutional Court reversed the action of the legislature and restored Roh to office in May 2004. During the brief period when there was no president, Prime Minister Goh Kun was acting president and the Uri Party gained a majority in the April National Assembly elections. This was the first time a left-of-center party had gained control of parliament. Roh officially joined the Uri Party in May. In April 2006, Han Myung-Sook, a member of the Uri Party, became the first woman to be selected to be prime minister in South Korea.

In December 2007, Lee Myung Bak, a former Hyundai executive and mayor of Seoul, won the presidency as the candidate of the Grand National Party, formed in 1997 in a merger of conservative groupings. This marked a shift to the right in South Korean politics and signaled a loss of patience with efforts to mollify the North, but Lee's strongly pro-U.S. posture has also cost him politically at home.

The Political System

South Korea currently has an estimated population of 50 million, most of whom share the same ethnicity. Korean is the official language, with the country claiming a literacy rate of 97.9 percent. English is widely used owing to the American presence and the utility of English in world commerce. In recent years, South Korea has been progressing along a democratic development trajectory. Relations with the United States remain strong, although public enthusiasm for the American military presence is weakening. Post–Korean War generations are less concerned about the threat from the North and often pressure the government to improve relations.

Despite its ups and downs, "Korea has made significant progress toward establishing pluralistic governing institutions and protecting the political and civil liberties of its citizens."[8] Nonetheless, the country faces serious obstacles to becoming a consolidated democracy. Among the contentious problems are regional factionalism, conflicts between labor and management, and severe ideological divisions. "Korea has yet to be geographically, socially, culturally, and politically unified within its own borders."[9]

Korea has, in all, amended its constitution or wholly rewritten it nine times since 1948 within the context of six republics. The first constitution established a presidential system with the president appointed by the legislature. Under a 1952 amendment, the president became popularly elected. A bicameral legislature with a prime minister was also established. A 1954 amendment removed term limits for the president and emphasized a capitalist economy. But these actions undertaken by Syngman Rhee to perpetuate his own rule provoked popular opposition, and a more democratic constitution emerged in 1960 under the Second Republic. This constitution created a cabinet, a bicameral legislature, electoral and constitutional commissions, popular elections for Supreme Court justices and provincial governors as well as a natural law–based system of constitutional rights. Following the 1961 coup, the Third Republic added judicial review to the constitution in 1962.

The constitution of 1972 during the Fourth Republic reflected the authoritarian rule of Park Chung Hee. The presidential term limits were removed and governing power was centralized. After Park's assassination in 1979, the Fifth Republic was established under the 1980 constitution. The powers of the presidency were reduced, and the president was to be indirectly elected. The legislature was made unicameral with a cabinet system.

In the late 1980s prodemocracy protests led to further political changes and another constitution. The constitution of 1988 established the Sixth Republic and a more democratic regime. Civil liberties received greater emphasis but there were restrictions such as those imposed by the National Security Act.

Today the government of South Korea is divided into three distinct branches, reflecting the American preference for the separation of powers. The executive branch consists of the head of state, or president, who is popularly elected for one five-year term and who possesses considerable authority. There is also a separate head of government, the prime minister, plus three deputy prime ministers. The cabinet, called the State Council, is appointed by the president on recommendation by the prime minister. The prime minister is appointed by the president with the approval of the National Assembly. Recommendations for the deputy prime ministers and cabinet members are made by the prime minister prior to approval by the president.

The legislative branch is a unicameral assembly with 299 members serving four-year terms. Of these seats, fifty-six are elected by proportional representation and 243 come from single-member districts. Typically, the prime minister is the leader of the largest party in the legislature; if there is no majority party, the prime minister is the head of a coalition. As in other parliamentary systems, the legislature, or *kukhoe*, can be dissolved by the prime minister and new elections held. If a vote of no confidence causes the government to "fall," new elections must be held.

As in the U.S. Congress, the organization of the legislative branch relies heavily on a committee system. These committees have the authority to amend bills, hold hearings, request information from the executive branch, and question high-level executives. However, this arrangement does not yet work well. In the first place, the committees typically do not meet very often. Committees are also venues for partisan competition. "A sense of identity is missing in the committees. Expertise is not appreciated, and reviews of legislation are on the whole hastily conducted."[10]

Despite reforms, the president still exercises considerable influence over the legislative process. Even when there is substantial opposition to a bill favored by the president, the likelihood is that it will be rammed through without compromise.

The judicial branch consists of a Supreme Court, a Constitutional Court, and lesser courts. The membership of the Supreme Court consists of a chief justice and as many as thirteen additional justices serving six-year terms. Justices are appointed by the president with National Assembly approval. The nine members of the Constitutional Court, six of whom must concur before a law can be declared unconstitutional, are nominated three each by the president, the National Assembly, and the chief justice. The latter is also nominated by the president, in effect giving him the ability to choose six members of the court.

There are two main parties—the Uri and the Grand National Party (GNP). There are also several minor parties. But these parties do not function in the conventional democratic sense of focusing attention on issues and public policy options, mobilizing public opinion, and facilitating the electoral process. They also lack the conventional sources of support found in other countries with competitive party systems. Neither class identity, ideology, nor social values, including religion, serve to define the "core" of the political parties. Instead, they reflect regional loyalties and are burdened by personal ties to political bosses. There is also an emphasis on "anachronistic Confucian ideals"[11] such as paternalistic authority.

During most of its history, Korea has been governed by authoritarian regimes. Typically, there was a ruling party organized and led by the government. The opposition frequently encountered repression by the government and it favored reform and democracy. As a result, between the two there was deep division and hostility. This hostility continues to describe interparty relations today. Part of this is due to the enduring impact of Confucianism, in which "such values as compromise, negotiation, bargaining, and accommodation are all alien, if not antithetical."[12]

The deficiencies of the political parties make the South Korean electoral system less than an expression of public opinion.[13] The political system has also been weak in terms of its ability to govern and its stability. Nevertheless, there appears to be discernible progress in stabilizing the South Korean political system in the early twenty-first century. The successful transitions of power in the Sixth Republic have built a good foundation that has endured since the late 1980s.

The South Korean Economy

With a population of 50 million and a population growth rate of .49 percent, South Korea faces the prospect of an aging population. Currently 28 percent of the workforce is sixty-five or over. Still, the economy has continued to grow since the financial shock during the 1990s. Growth rate in the GDP has been in excess of 4 percent. In 2003, China became Seoul's largest export market, and the following year the bilateral trade between the two countries exceeded that between South Korea and the United States.

The *chaebols*—Korea's huge family-owned and family-managed business conglomerates—"grew enormously in economic and political power under the careful guidance and protection of successive military regimes."[14] The reformist government of Kim Young Sam attempted to correct the abuses of the *chaebols*, but without success. This failure contributed to the financial crisis that swept Korea, and other Asian economies, in late 1997. An IMF loan rescued the Korean economy, but despite the reforms called for by the IMF, the *chaebols* continue their dominance. In fact the economy is now more concentrated than it was before the crisis. "Where thirty *chaebols* once reigned, now just five dominate, thus increasing the leverage of each one over the government."[15] On the other hand, the fact that Korea was forced to close or restructure its largest banks gave Korea an advantage in weathering the global financial crisis that began in 2008.

U.S.–South Korea Security Relations

Following the end of World War II, the United States ran South Korea for three years through the United States Military Government in Korea. According to the Cairo Accord, this military government was to facilitate the transition from colonial status to independence. The military government, unpopular with Koreans, confronted political instability, much of it stirred up by Communists, and was completely unprepared to meet the challenges it faced.

This arrangement ended on August 15, 1948, when an independent Republic of Korea came into existence. The military connection remained, however, as the threat from the North intensified. Korean forces were under U.S. command, which was nominally acting under the authority of the UN. Today the commander of U.S. forces in Korea heads the UN authority with a mandate to maintain the terms of the 1953 armistice and to protect South Korea from attack.

In 1954, the United States and South Korea signed a mutual defense treaty, one of the multilateral and bilateral alliances the United States created within the containment doctrine. Under this agreement, the United States continues to defend South Korea. For its part, South Korea provided assistance during the Vietnam War and more recently in Iraq. In 1978, the United States and South Korea created the Combined Forces Command, allowing the ROK forces a greater degree of independence. Military decisions are supposed to be made by this joint command structure, which is still headed by an American general with a South Korean deputy.

In the late 1960s, South Korea committed itself to a goal of military self-sufficiency, which the United States supported with substantial assistance for the modernization of the South Korean military. In 1974, the arrangement was formalized into South Korea's Eight Year National Defense Plan. In 1977, the Carter administration suggested that all U.S. forces should be withdrawn within five years. The proposal drew sharp criticism from South Korea, Japan, and from both Congress and the military in the United States. The plan was quietly dropped.

While the goal of military independence served to strengthen South Korea's resolve and potentially relieve the United States of responsibility, problems sometimes arose. There were frequent military interventions in the political process, something looked upon with disfavor by the United States, which wanted to showcase South Korea's democracy. In 1980, the Korean military suppressed and anti-government demonstration in Kwangju, resulting in many casualties. Many Koreans claim that since Korea's military was under the authority of an American general the United States must have been complicit in the action. The American military presence has become increasingly unpopular, particularly among younger Koreans, who have no memory of the Korean War, much less of the Japanese occupation.

In response, the United States has tried to lower its profile in South Korea. One proposal is to move the large American base in Seoul to a less conspicuous location. The conflicts in Iraq and Afghanistan drew down American force levels in Korea by as much as a third. At the end of the Korean War, there were 328,000 American military personnel in South Korea. This number had dropped to 55,000 by 1960 and then to 52,000 by 1964. There were 32,000 U.S. Army personnel and 12,000 U.S. Air Force personnel in 1990. In 2010 the total stood at around 28,500.

III

Japan

13

Japan in Isolation

Compared to other Asian countries, such as India and China, the recorded history of Japan is not only short but has neither the substantial political tradition nor the record of wide-ranging intellectual achievement that is characteristic of other parts of Asia. There is nothing like the intellectual and cultural legacy of the subcontinent of India, for example, which was the birthplace and home of both Hinduism and Buddhism. Japan existed for centuries in the shadow of China's unrivaled achievements. In fact, very little is known about Japan before the seventh century C.E. A written language did not exist until the fifth or sixth century C.E. Before then, the only records available were based on oral traditions, some of which were later recorded in written form.[1]

The Influence of China

The dynamics of Japan's internal historical evolution often reflected developments originating elsewhere. For instance, language, literature, politics, and philosophy reflected Chinese influence, which came to Japan by way of Korea. In their long-term relationship, Korea claims some credit for Japan's intellectual development. The Japanese civilization that developed over time was an amalgam of foreign influences mixed in with native traditions. Historically, the Japanese have sought to preserve their cultural identity within a larger, universally valid social philosophy that was developed in China—Confucianism.[2] Political institutions were shaped between the sixth and eighth centuries based on the model of Tang China. The Japanese imperial institution was predicated on the Chinese doctrinal definition of the central role of the emperor in the political system.[3] The idea of the sovereignty of the emperor was the bedrock of the Japanese political system until the twentieth century.

For the first 600 years of its recorded history, Japan was composed of a loose collection of local political units nominally held together by a Chinese-style monarchy. During that period, Japan's political institutions, economic growth, and cultural achievements were modest by the standards of the time. In fact, during much of this period, the country suffered from chronic instability and conflict.

It was not until the twelfth century that some semblance of political integration occurred. In 1192, after a prolonged period of civil war, unification was achieved in the form of a military dictatorship. The monarchical form of government in and of itself did not prove vigorous enough to unite all the warring factions. The institution of the monarchy was weak and basically an abstraction, lacking the institutional or conceptual standing of its Chinese counterpart.

Following a prolonged period of civil war, a military dictatorship called the shogunate, or *bakufu*, emerged. In theory, the *shogun*'s official capacity was that of commander in chief of the imperial army. In a constitutional sense, sovereign political authority remained with the emperor, to whom the shogun paid allegiance. The actual power of the government to rule, however, was in the hands of the shogun but only so long as he was able to retain military supremacy, something that was always subject to challenge. "Legitimacy lay with the Court, where the sovereign linked the present with the semi-historical past. . . . Matters of governance, however, were the province of the *shogun*, who, as supreme hegemon and head of the military houses, delegated responsibility to his vassals."[4] For nearly seven centuries this arrangement prevailed, with the emperor having little more than ceremonial significance and sometimes living under conditions approaching house arrest. While this isolation prevented the emperor "from having the slightest influence over public affairs," it also "increased the mystery and awe with which the contemporary society invested the persons of the Court and their works."[5] For the most part, the arrangement produced stability and facilitated national integration.

Although the emperors did not rule, they did reign, which is a matter of considerable constitutional significance. The imperial institution legitimized the state and the authoritative relationships contained within it. This made the philosophy of government, the obligations of rulers, and the duties of citizens clear and understandable, if not always agreeable, to all. There were, of course, frequent struggles for power and military encounters over how political power would be exercised and by whom; but at least the rules of the game were reasonably well defined. The sovereignty of the emperor remained a vital part of Japanese political philosophy and became even more significant during the authoritarian period of the 1920s and 1930s. After World War II the sovereignty of the emperor was replaced with the doctrine of popular sovereignty.

The Three Shogunates

The system that prevailed beginning in 1192 consisted of three great shogunates, each based on the political dominance of a particular clan. In all three cases, political power was seized, after intense warfare, on the strength of the military ability of the successful leader. The first of these three military houses—the Minamoto—lasted for 200 years, during which the processes and procedures of the state were put in place. After a successful challenge from another clan—the Ashikaga—the second shogunate came into existence, lasting from 1392 to 1573. But from 1467 to 1568 the country was plagued by almost continual warfare. During this time, devastation extended from the emperor and his courtiers, who "barely survived by begging alms from individual lords," to the commoners, who perished by the thousands from famine and disease.[6] Central control of political affairs dissolved, and governing power was in the hands of local petty rulers. At the time, the country was divided into small feudal enclaves, each dominated by the local lord, whose ability to rule was predicated on his band of warriors. The lord's power was based on his military strength, which in turn derived from a system of personal loyalties. Society was held together, to the extent it possessed cohesion, by the Confucian system of ethical loyalties. There was little if any formal development of political institutions. The high social status of military men, interestingly, is the reverse of the Chinese experience, in which the soldier was placed near the bottom of the social hierarchy.

The long period of warfare finally came to an end and political unity was restored through the efforts of three *daimyo*, or feudal barons. They were able to persuade other lords to join together and form a coalition that ultimately defeated the opposition and unified the country. These *daimyo* were Oda Nobunaga (1534–1582), his chief vassal (feudal retainer) Toyotomi Hideyoshi (1536–1598), and his vassal Tokugawa Ieyasu (1542–1616), who received the title of shogun in 1603. Following on the period of consolidation under Oda Nobunaga, Hideyoshi undertook measures leading to the emergence of the modern Japanese state. He employed two very effective strategies to consolidate his political position. First, he was able to gain greater administrative control over the land than had existed prior to that time and thereby was able to control the peasants who worked on it. In the 1580s, he ordered a resurvey of the land in order to determine its productivity and to identify who was responsible for the payment of taxes. By clarifying this responsibility, the government was able to be more successful in raising revenue. Even more importantly the government could now keep track of the rural elite and especially the politically ambitious local lords.[7] The Tokugawa also placed additional restrictions on the emperor, and by 1615 they had established "systematic control of the imperial institution."[8]

Hideyoshi's second measure was to prohibit the possession of swords by anyone other than his own soldiers. To achieve this end, he confiscated all weapons in the hands of civilians. These were then melted down and used in the construction of a Great Buddha monument.[9] This absence of weaponry in private hands made it nearly impossible to raise popular rebellion against the government. Hideyoshi's efforts led to the emergence of a professional warrior class called *samurai*.[10] These warriors were the personal retainers of feudal lords.

The Tokugawa would be Japan's third and most famous shogunate, lasting from 1603, when Ieyasu assumed the title of shogun, until 1868 when the status of the emperor was restored and the shogunate abolished. In order to maintain control over the unwieldy feudal coalition that was the Japanese political system, the Tokugawa established a complicated system of governance. One of the most important devices was the reassignment of control over land to different feudal lords, depending on their reliability. In this way, those suspected of disloyalty or of harboring troublesome political ambitions could be kept in close check. They might be given lands on the fringes of the empire, where they could do little mischief, or close to the seat of government, where they could be kept under surveillance.

A second technique used to discourage political opposition was the alternate residence system whereby the *daimyo* were required to maintain a residence in the capital as well as the one on their lands. When back at their fiefs, they were required to leave their heirs behind in the capital as security for their loyalty. The practice of holding the relatives of their followers hostage in order to guarantee loyalty had been used by Japanese rulers for some time. The alternate residence system was a financial drain on the feudal barons that diminished their military potential.[11]

A third device was seclusion. Both China and Japan feared Western influences would prove socially and politically disruptive. Westerners, and especially Catholic missionaries, were perceived as constituting a corrupting influence. Europeans were suspected of seeking to extend colonial control over Japan. To prevent this, the *bakufu* prohibited trade and cultural contacts. Actually, Christianity had been banned by Hideyoshi in 1597, but the ban was not vigorously enforced. Another ban in 1612 issued by the Tokugawa led to the expulsion of missionaries and the persecution of Christian converts.[12]

Japan's insularity, the product of 250 years of isolation from the rest of the world, promoted a semi-mystical nationalism. This nationalism was reinforced by state-supported indoctrination, which resulted in "a religious or semi-religious belief that the country is the centre of the world." The policy of seclusion required isolation not only from the West but from Asia as well, which, ironically was the source of Japan's culture. The Chinese concept of the Middle Kingdom was adopted to make Japan the center of the world, and "the stress was laid on 'Japanism' and the natural purity which existed before it was corrupted by a heavy coating of Chinese culture." The doctrine of cultural purity led, inevitably, to racism, "with the Indians in particular being regarded as an inferior species. It should be stressed that the main targets of these racist teachings were not Europeans but other Asians."[13]

The policy intended to exclude other cultures and promote "Japanism" was effective until the middle of the nineteenth century, when a more determined effort to open Japan to commercial and diplomatic contact was undertaken. Despite efforts to avoid the effects of corrosive cultural influences, Japan had participated in political and economic relations with other Asian countries, on a limited basis and on its own terms, for some time.[14] For one thing it sent tribute missions to China.

In many places, the trajectory of national development is significantly influenced by wars. Countries that fall victim to invasion and defeat reflect these experiences in their cultures and institutions. The more frequent the event, the greater the influence. Contrariwise, countries that have been spared such experiences have national development patterns reflecting their internal dynamics. China is a prominent example of the first type. Apart from its defeat in World War II, Japan has never been successfully invaded by a foreign power. The only serious threat occurred in the thirteenth century, when the Mongol invasions of 1274 and 1281 were foiled, the second due largely to the timely intervention of a typhoon. Japan reflects many aspects of the Chinese experience, but it was spared the philosophical, demographic, and institutional influences of foreign invaders.

As in China and Korea, the absence of foreign contacts slowed the evolution of Japanese social and political institutions. The three countries are an interesting contrast in how each dealt with foreign challenges once they were encountered. It is likely that since the Japanese were not forced by invasion and occupation to deal with such influences, they could ultimately do so at a more leisurely pace and on their own terms. The Chinese, Indians, and a host of other peoples had Westernization forced upon them. Moreover, the Japan of the mid-nineteenth century was in a good position to respond creatively to new challenges. Indeed, in many respects, Japan was in a better position to meet the challenges of "Westernization" than the West itself had been at a similar stage of development.

The character of Japanese feudalism was sufficiently resilient to permit a successful response to the challenges of modernization. Compared to the West, which had a legalistic type of feudalism, the Japanese system was ethical. Political arrangements based on law can be formally changed only by competent authority, and disputes as to what constitutes "competent authority" can lead to the complete breakdown of political order. Ethical structures, on the other hand, are more adaptable, and loyalties can be transferred without undermining the integrity of the system. Ethically defined political order is more adaptable in a structural sense than order that is defined in objective legal terms.

The Rise of the Imperial System

Apart from its philosophical foundations, there were similarities between Japanese and Western feudalism. Both involved bodies of armed men obligated to render aid and service. For European knights, the relation was contractual; for Japanese samurai it was ethical. In Europe, the peasants were bound to the land and committed to support the lord with work and military service. But in Japan, the office of the emperor was more developed as a political institution than was its Western counterpart, and the role of an institutionalized religion similar to that of the Roman Catholic Church was missing. This would prove an advantage in easing the process of building secular political institutions. The burdens upon the Japanese peasants were less, as they were not expected to perform as many tasks (for example, participation in foreign wars), nor were they expected to provide as much corveé or unpaid labor as were the common people in Europe. A potential source of internal political opposition derived from disaffection among the common people was missing in Japan.[15]

Three characteristics described Japan in the first half of the nineteenth century. First was the policy of exclusion or national isolation. Called *sakoku*, this policy was widely supported and was assumed to be based on long-standing tradition. In 1825, the Tokugawa *bakufu* declared that Western ships approaching the coast of Japan should be fired upon and driven away. The Tokugawa regime based its legitimacy on this policy. Following the Chinese example, trade was permitted only with China and the Dutch at Nagasaki. Second, given its isolation, Japan's knowledge of the world outside was sparse and frequently incorrect. Third, the political system was based on a dual arrangement consisting of the divine emperor who did not rule and a military dictatorship that did. While authority theoretically was vested in the emperor, the shogun exercised it in his name. The Japanese "rationalized the court-*bakufu* relationship by theorizing—again with no basis in historical fact—the emperor and court in Kyoto invested the shogun and *bakufu* in Edo with all authority to rule Japan."[16]

The period from the mid-nineteenth century until the 1920s was a time of rapid transformation in Japan. This period corresponded to the last decades of the Qing dynasty in China and the emergence of the fledgling Chinese republic. It was a time of intense Sino-Japanese interaction. "Actual contacts between Chinese and Japanese were renewed on a regular basis for the first time in centuries. Japanese began traveling all over the Chinese map. Thousands of young Chinese, both male and female, flocked to Japanese institutions of higher learning, and hundreds of Japanese instructors were invited to teach at Chinese educational institutions. There was cultural contact on a broader level than had ever before been achieved."[17]

14

Japan and the World

For 200 years prior to the visit of an American naval force under Commodore Matthew C. Perry in 1853, Japan had been largely successful in keeping itself sealed off from the outside world and especially the West. Part of this success can be attributed to the fact that Japan was on the margins of the area of most intense Western imperial interest. Isolation was abetted by the Dutch who, as the first Europeans to deal with Japan, successfully kept other Europeans away from the few trade or other commercial opportunities made available by the Japanese. Russia was the first to challenge the Dutch monopoly of foreign trade when in 1792 it received permission to trade on a temporary basis. England and finally the United States followed with attempts to open Japan to trade and diplomacy. Up until the middle of the nineteenth century, most Western nations were interested mainly in South and Southeast Asia and China, where there was greater commercial opportunity. Sooner or later, however, Japan would have to come to terms with the expanding network of international activities.

The End of Seclusion

The Japanese had known for some time of the Western presence in Asia. They also knew they were dealing with a force of some consequence. In 1808, a British warship visited Japan and threatened to use force if it were not provided with supplies. The Japanese were also aware of the Opium Wars in China beginning in 1839 and the consequences of these wars for China. Thus when Perry visited Japan in 1853, many among the Tokugawa elite realized their country faced the very real possibility of war with the West, a war they would probably lose.

Nonetheless, their initial reaction to the American proposals to establish formal relations was to reject them. Perry returned the following year and gave the Japanese an ultimatum that if they rejected his proposals, he would make war. Fearing they were confronted with imminent attack, the Japanese capitulated and received Perry, with whom they negotiated the Treaty of Kanagawa, which was signed on March 31, 1854. Perry was successful not just because he threatened military force. He came prepared with an unambiguous set of proposals. Perry also made good use of gifts and ceremonies, which favorably impressed the Japanese.[1]

By then, the Russians were entering the picture, creating even greater uncertainty in Japan's international position. In another treaty signed in

1854, the Japanese opened two minor ports to the Russians. Another treaty, negotiated in 1855, included the practice of extraterritoriality, or extrality, which is a concession by the host country exempting a foreign power from some aspects of domestic law. In the contemporary world, the practice of diplomatic privilege, in which accredited diplomats and their families are not subject to prosecution for criminal offenses in the country where they serve, is an example.

The concessions that the Japanese had made to Perry were insignificant compared to those extracted by the American consul, Townsend Harris. The Treaty of Amity and Commerce, or the Harris Treaty, signed in July 1858, granted the United States access to major ports, the stationing of Western diplomats in the capital Edo, extraterritoriality, and a structure of fixed Japanese tariffs to allow for the easy importation of Western goods.[2] Harris was able to persuade the Japanese to open trade with the United States by arguing that if they failed to do so Europeans would use force to extract even more onerous concessions. The provisions of the agreement included many of the concessions to Western demands that China had already made. Even though the treaty was opposed by many conservative *daimyo*, it was accepted by the emperor, thus making criticism of it impolitic.[3]

Most Japanese regarded the West as barbarian and corrupt, but a few saw the need to promote the study of Western ways, and especially Western learning in science and technology. It was fortunate for the Japanese that the political integrity of the shogunate was declining at the same time that pressure from the outside world was increasing. Had the integrity of the political system under its military rulers been stronger, it might have been able to resist modernization more effectively, perhaps with the same kind of dire consequences that were occurring elsewhere. The weakness of the government made the exclusion policy, which had become sacrosanct by the eighteenth century, politically easier to overcome. The growing number of Japanese who saw the twin needs for accommodation with the outside world and modernization within confronted a political leadership that was becoming weak and irresolute and increasingly unable to maintain a united front against outsiders.

The advocates of the policy of exclusion were, of course, right to argue that contact with the West would prove disruptive. They were especially concerned about the ability of Christianity "to lead the people's minds astray."[4] Opposition to Christianity was encouraged by leading Buddhists who, quite naturally, found the foreign religion a threat to their influence.[5] In the final analysis, however, the Japanese really had little choice; they could either accommodate themselves to outside influences or, like the Chinese, be overcome by them.

Trouble first appeared in the economy. The sudden intrusion of Western commerce undermined traditional Japanese economic practices, resulting in severe inflation. The political discontent that followed created added problems for the government and hastened the process of political restructuring.

The physical presence of many Westerners was a source of strain in a society unaccustomed to linguistic and ethnic differences. The arrogance and peculiar behavior of the foreigners encouraged self-examination among the Japanese that contributed to the reinforcement of an already strong sense of national identity and a desire to compete with foreign nations on their own terms. The Japanese did not suffer from the cultural superiority complex that inhibited Chinese development and were thus in a better position to accept the necessity of change.

Given the politically unsettled conditions during the 1850s and 1860s, the government had to meet the mounting challenges to its authority by either accommodating the demands for change or suppressing them. It tried suppression first, which simply made matters worse. Reform factions came to realize that little could be accomplished within the existing political structure. Rather than call for revolution, the ideology for which did not exist anyway, the advocates of modernization favored restoration. The emperor served as the rallying point for the progressive movement, which advocated the return of governing authority to the throne. In so doing, of course, they intended to create new and more effective political institutions, not simply substitute an absolute monarchy for the military dictatorship of the shogun.

In 1863 the government attempted to expel the Western "barbarians," but the effort failed; it was altogether too late for that. Many Japanese recognized the superiority of Western militaries. The *bakufu* initiated a program of modernization and reform of the military in 1866, but many of its troops still employed swords and pikes, while others lacked motivation. The shogun's armies were deficient in modern organization and technology, and they were often poorly led and suffered from morale problems. The imperial forces prevailed, the shogunate was liquidated, and the imperial structure was formally "restored."[6]

The Meiji Restoration

The restoration leaders were young and talented men who did not have a vested interest in the status quo. They were relatively free of the constraints of cultural tradition and personal loyalties. Since innovations did not threaten their prestige or status, they were in a good position to make changes, something the traditional elite could not bring itself to do. Accordingly, Japan was in a better position to meet the challenge of Western imperialism than were other

Asian countries. While at the time it came into contact with the West it was economically backward, it possessed the resilience to respond constructively. Its technology and the skill of its workers were no greater than those of China, for example, but its system of production was more effectively dispersed throughout society, allowing for "a particular dynamism and flexibility" in its approach to national development.[7]

Japan's encounter with the West brought it into contact with two totally different national histories. Before its first war with China in 1894–1895, Japan had little experience of extensive contacts with its neighbors, much less wars with them. This contrasts sharply with Europe, where for centuries the emerging states were increasingly interactive and where all the time a war was likely going on in one place or another. European history had been competitive and often hostile. Japan had not been competitive with its neighbors and for the most part had not developed a sense of antagonism toward other nations. As a result of its tradition of isolation, "Japan lacked a clear image of a national enemy throughout most of its history. Japan was thus one of the few countries in the world which did not regard its neighbors as enemies."[8] The West introduced into Japan both "modern" concepts of international competition and antagonism.

As White, Umegaki, and Havens discuss in *The Ambivalence of Nationalism*, Japan's brief relationship with the outside world included "an internationally active nation-state, the growth of modern nationalism" and a short stint as a major power in East Asia. However, they go on to note the Japanese have never enjoyed a true sense of certainty as to the character of their international role and the direction it should take. This ambiguous sense of purpose and orientation is attributable to Japan's rapid transition through many stages as a state: from blissful ignorance of Western norms of international relations through periods of apprehension and fear that Japan would fall victim to these norms.

Throughout its modern history, Japan emulated the rules and norms of international behavior designed by the West while resisting them at the same time. For the first few decades of the twentieth century, the foreign policies of imperial Japan were maintained through cooperation with the Anglo-American maritime powers. Given the overlapping of national ambitions, however, this course of action could not be sustained for long, and eventually Japan found itself heading toward a collision with these same powers.

The Advent of Imperial Japan

The term "imperial Japan" was employed before a policy of foreign conquest was adopted by the government. Its use began in the Meiji period and refers to a system of governance in which the emperor is supreme.[9] As Japan's international horizons expanded, the designation "imperial" was adapted to a definition more conventionally employed in the West.

In acquiring an overseas empire, Japan's attention was first drawn toward Korea. Historically, Korea had played an important role in determining the cultural makeup of Japan. Direct and continuous official relations between the two countries were limited, however, and they were never fond of each other. One of the few significant events in Japan's relations with Korea occurred in the sixteenth century, when a Japanese military expedition was launched against that country. The campaign did not last long, but the long-term consequences served to harden Koreans' dislike for Japan.

In the 1870s and 1880s, Japan began pursuing a more assertive policy toward Korea, resulting in an inevitable confrontation with China, which had a historical claim of suzerainty over Korea as a tributary state. This confrontation eventually resulted in the Sino-Japanese War of 1894–1895. Their defeat at the hands of the Japanese encouraged the Chinese to contemplate reforms. But those advocating change in the ossified and effete Chinese system were few, and they lacked a clear vision. Proposed reforms were sidetracked and monies intended to update the pathetically backward Chinese military were squandered.

The modernizers in China needed a model and, despite their differences, it was to Japan that they looked for guidance. Their common experience with Western imperialism led to a shared feeling of Asian community but, as would be revealed in the next century, Japan had an entirely different idea of what that meant. Far from being the natural allies against common threats as some in China thought, the Japanese came to regard China as a target of opportunity, not an equal but an inferior to be made to follow Japan's lead. Nonetheless, many Japanese had established personal relations and cultivated mutual trust and cooperation with their Chinese counterparts.[10]

Japan annexed Korea in 1910. For the next thirty-five years, the Koreans suffered exploitation and abuse, with 700,000 of them forced to work as little more than slave laborers in Japanese-controlled mines and factories. Many Koreans were eventually transported to Japan itself, where they were forced to help meet the demand for industrial labor. The Japanese called this "the implementation of the national mobilization order to Koreans."[11]

Like China, Japan viewed Korea as "an area of strategic importance."[12] Another area of importance was southern Manchuria, where Japanese successes not only "sanctified Japanese rights and interests in Korea and Manchuria," but also "created a new pantheon of national heroes and a pervasive sense of nationalism."[13]

Japan's influence grew rapidly after the first Sino-Japanese War. Participation along with the Western powers in the suppression of the Boxer Rebellion in China in 1900 further enhanced Japan's international stature. Concern about Russian intentions in Asia led Britain to make a naval alliance with Japan in 1902. The Russo-Japanese War of 1904–1905 resulted from the clash of Russian and Japanese interests in Manchuria and Korea. The humiliating Russian defeat had enormous implications. Among other things, it contributed to the disintegration of the tsar's regime in Russia. It showed that European nations were not militarily invincible vis-à-vis non-Europeans, a lesson not lost on other colonial peoples. Victory catapulted Japan into the status of a major military power. Following the annexation of Korea in 1910, Japan was able to bring to an end, in 1911, the extraterritorial concessions made earlier in treaties with Europeans. From Japan's point of view, equality with the West was achieved by the end of World War I, when it sat with the victors at Versailles, although it had played only a minor role in the war. Despite its growing might, however, Japan was regarded by the West as essentially a regional power, not to be taken too seriously in global matters. China, on the other hand, continued to be treated very differently.

The increased power that Japan so desired was dependent on modernization, which was itself a mixed blessing. The price of industrialization was a certain degree of social dislocation. Population growth, adding to the pressure for economic development, resulted in growing dependence on foreign imports and markets. The unity of thought that had existed for centuries gave way to diversity and complexity. Urbanization brought with it rural anxiety and proletarian unrest. Leadership tension between military elites and political/economic elites eventually resulted in a military dictatorship. Demands for greater popular participation were politically destabilizing and difficult to satisfy, especially given the tendency to regard political opposition as subversive. The pursuit of an ambitious foreign policy agenda, and especially the emphasis on the military options, led to international rivalries.[14]

Sensitive to these and other divisive consequences of modernization, the governing elite stressed the importance of an ideological bond to hold society together. The development of such an ideology became one of the highest priorities of the state. "It was not enough that the polity be centralized, the economy developed, social classes rearranged, international recognition striven for—the people must also be 'influenced,' their minds and hearts made one."[15] To guard against political deviation, the police "came to see themselves as responsible for surveillance of all thought that might disturb the national polity."[16] An important milestone in this process was the issuance of the Peace Preservation Ordinance of 1887, which not only prohibited secret organizations and meetings, but also gave the police considerable authority to interfere in political activities.[17]

The Rise of Totalitarianism

From the 1890s, when the emperor-centered system crystallized,[18] until 1945, Japan's formal constitutional system was representative in character. In the early part of the twentieth century, there was perceptible movement in the direction of further democratization of politics. Political parties sought to gain a greater share of political power, efforts which initially met with a measure of success. In the aftermath of World War I, a social movement emerged advocating a variety of democratic reforms. This broad-based movement consisted of political groups ranging from labor unions to student organizations. But the liberalization of the regime began to lose its momentum by the end of the 1920s as the conservative elite successfully extended its control over the apparatus of government.

Japan lacked a commitment to the spirit of democracy, and eventually it failed to function in a democratic fashion. Instead, politics were dominated by powerful elites: army and navy service chiefs whose direct responsibility to the emperor gave them much independence; the leadership of the civil bureaucracy, a group of people, especially former prime ministers, who had access to and the confidence of the emperor; and the heads of the *zaibatsu* combines—large, family-controlled financial and business conglomerates. The lower house of the Diet, given its control over permanent laws and the budget, was also a center of power, but this power diminished with the drift toward authoritarianism.[19]

Among the more significant restrictions on democratic politics were the Public Peace Police Law, enacted in 1900, and the Special Higher Police, established in 1911. The former was aimed at any group deemed antigovernment. Such groups were required to register with the government, and their meetings were frequently disrupted by police. Labor organizations were regarded as disrupters of the peace, and strikes were illegal—provisions that seriously weakened the labor movement.[20] The Special Higher Police came to be known as the "thought police" and were charged with controlling social movements and with suppressing the spread of dangerous foreign ideologies.[21] The provision making strikes illegal was soon repealed, however.[22] These measures were followed by the enactment of the 1925 Peace Preservation Law, which defined permissible ideological limits for individuals and groups. It prohibited advocating change in the basic political structure of Japan and the philosophy upon which it was based.[23]

Japan's eager entry into world politics as an imperial power and its embrace of totalitarian-fascist politics were due mainly to internal political and social dynamics. Another factor was the outside world and the opportunities and challenges it presented. "Ever since Commodore Perry's visit to Japan in 1853, international politics have been decisive in the development of Japan's legal and political institutions."[24] Some scholars have argued that had there been no external influence, Japan might have continued its slow evolution toward full parliamentary government.[25] In the event, however, these influences upset the elite balance in favor of the military and an emperor-based political cult.[26]

From the time of the Meiji Restoration to the 1930s, Japan's political development reflected an enduring sense of insecurity, both physical and cultural. This insecurity led to an exaggerated ambition for national power, respect, and equality. These motives, intertwined and often inseparable, made up the chemistry of a distinctive nationalism, a force which impelled Japan along its particular historical path. Japanese nationalism, unlike that in Europe, lacked strong mass support but nevertheless possessed a dynamism provided by the bureaucracy, the military, and powerful economic interests.[27] This nationalism, moreover, was fed by international developments. World War I upset the balance of power among European nations in East Asia, allowing Japan, under the guise of the Anglo-Japanese alliance, to seize German holdings in China's Shandong Province and German-held islands in the South Pacific: the Carolines, Marianas, Marshalls, and Palau and Yap, names that would become familiar to Americans during World War II.

Japan's nationalism further intensified as relations with the United States worsened. In January 1915, Japan made twenty-one demands of China, furthering a process of encroachment on the sovereignty of China that began with the 1894–1895 Sino-Japanese War. This move was particularly significant for two reasons. It was a departure from the understanding developed among world powers over the preceding decades not to act unilaterally with respect to China. It also marked the growing estrangement between Japan and the United States, which had become the main protector of the new Chinese Republic founded in 1912.[28] Estrangement between the United States and Japan was exacerbated by the issue of race. In 1905 the California legislature passed a resolution calling for a ban on immigration. Congress passed the Japanese Exclusion Act in 1924, which understandably rankled the Japanese and made them even more sensitive about their national identity.[29]

In the late 1920s, while relations with China worsened, conservatives adhered to the view that Japan's overall security situation was being compromised by the activities of political radicals operating within the country. This argument was used to justify the massive arrests of leftists in 1928–1929. Conservative anxiety was further stimulated by economic problems that made left-wing politics and ideologies more attractive among the lower classes. The preferred conservative approach to dealing with matters of this kind was not to address the economic problems but to repress the politics and ideologies that were produced by them.

In the decade prior to World War II, political instability brought on by the economic distress of the Great Depression affected many countries. Authoritarian political measures were frequently employed to cope with this instability, promoting, in some cases, the rise of fascism. Japan did not escape the crushing social and political effects of the worldwide economic crisis. Its economy, already severely weakened in the 1920s, declined even further during the 1930s. Industrial and agricultural workers, both hard hit, were desperate to find relief from their plight. Moreover, a political climate came to prevail in which the public was eager to assign blame for the worsening situation. A scapegoat was found in political parties. The question became who should rule—the civilian elite, who many felt were responsible for the country's problems, or the military, whose record, thus far, contained only successes.

Foreign relations contributed to the rightward drift of politics in another way. Ultranationalistic groups exploited patriotic enthusiasm when the Japanese position in Manchuria appeared to be at risk. After the first war with China, among the concessions extracted by Japan was the right to engage in commercial activities in Manchuria.[30] While legally Manchuria remained under Chinese sovereignty, the Japanese acted as though it belonged to them. The success of Chiang Kaishek and the Guomindang in their efforts to overcome the problems of disunity in China during the period 1926–1928 and the ensuing rise of Chinese nationalism were viewed with suspicion in Tokyo.[31] The prospect of China putting its political house in order was seen as threatening Japanese interests in Manchuria.

Many Japanese saw Manchuria as a vital economic asset which they could ill afford to surrender. In the face of Chinese efforts to restrict Japan's freedom of action, the army contrived a bomb incident in Manchuria in September 1931. The Chinese, of course, were blamed for taking hostile action, which was used as justification for a full-scale retaliation against Chinese troops. Not everyone in Japan was enthusiastic about these developments, however. The civilian government in Tokyo wanted an end to hostilities and ordered the army to stop, but the advance continued anyway. This became known as the Manchurian Incident, and it was one of the factors spurring rightist revolutionary activity in Japan during 1931–1936. The most significant of such developments were the assassination of Premier Inukai Tsuyoshi in 1932 by a group of young military officers committed to a doctrine of patriotic zealotry, and the Young Officers' Rebellion of February 26, 1936. The Young Officers' Movement had developed among the cadets at the Military Academy in Tokyo during the 1920s. The followers of the movement were ultrapatriots who considered Japan's leaders to be traitors.[32] The core idea of this ideology was the unique character of Japan. Its racial purity and racial consciousness were contained in "an imperishable national principle. Japan was not only unique but superior to any other nation."[33] The Young Officers' Rebellion led to a purging of the military, the suppression of leftist and liberal political factions, and assassinations of leading generals and politicians, all in the name of patriotism. In subsequent trials, the movement's leaders were sentenced to death. Later, they would be considered heroes. Most of those who were tried, and most were not, received light sentences and were free after a few years.[34]

The success of European fascism attracted the attention of the Japanese Right and served as an attractive political model. Indeed, Japan's increasing restlessness and international ambitions made it a likely candidate for a pattern of development similar to that occurring in Germany and Italy. The government had used education, the media, and various grass-roots organizations to encourage chauvinistic nationalist sentiment in support of the hard struggles for industrialization and international stature. Now the government was caught in a trap of its own making and reaped the whirlwind: "Such was the success of Japanese society in marrying an ancient, premodern, undemocratic structure with modern machine civilization."[35]

The growing military confrontation with China over Japan's continental empire strengthened the hands of the militarists and jingoist bureaucrats. From 1932 to 1936, the country was governed by cabinets that were on two occasions headed by admirals. While there was considerable sentiment for a more pacific approach to international issues, these voices were drowned in the cheers that accompanied military success. The Japanese also found little to discourage them in the broader international context. Their imperial inclinations were encouraged by the West's weak response to Japanese aggression in China.[36]

Japan's second war with China began in 1937, although sporadic fighting between the two had been occurring since the beginning of the decade. Japanese of nearly all political persuasions looked at their country's involvement in China as sanctioned by economic need. Apart from narrow self-interest, many also considered it their destiny to create a new order in Asia that would expel Western influences and establish a new structure based on Asian concepts of justice and humanity.[37] And it fell to Japan, of course, as the strongest nation in Asia, to assume the leadership role in defining and implementing these concepts.

Japan's defeat in World War II should not be construed to mean that the intellectual and political legacies of the prewar years have been totally discredited and forgotten. Authoritarianism may not travel well in the contemporary world of Japanese prosperity and growing world influence. Old-style imperialism has been discredited, and the acquisition of overseas possessions by military force appears to be a thing of the past. But international influence is not limited to those countries with the best armies. Now technology and money are, if anything, more important. Like all countries that have had the opportunity to exercise international "leadership," the Japanese are enjoying the heady pleasures of success. This success was fairly easy to come by following World War II, but it may be harder to sustain in the future as other Asian countries, most notably China, continue their ascent. There is the possibility that, under pressure, Japan may revert to its old ways. Liberal-democratic values are continually under assault, even in those countries where they have been long established. In Japan, the roots of these values do not go very deep.

15

Japan at War

Japan joined the race for economic and political modernity in the mid-nineteenth century. The foreign policy it embraced to achieve these goals reflected both the Western-inspired approach to national development and Japan's own particular circumstances. Lacking natural resources of their own, the Japanese sought to fill the void by acquiring an empire, which inevitably brought them into direct conflict with their neighbors, China and Korea. In this they convinced themselves that they were doing only what they were entitled to do, that is, applying the same imperial model that Western nations were then using. "In exercising its right to survive as an independent nation in the modern world, it was right and proper for Japan to seek an exclusive sphere of influence in adjacent territories so as to secure her sources of raw materials."[1]

The Japanese sought economic development not only for its own sake; they also realized that modern war required resources and a strong industrial base. When war did come, Japan was not adequately supplied with either. A modern military requires, more than anything else, fuel for the machines of war. Japan had no petroleum resources of its own and imported almost 80 percent of its needs from a single source—the United States. Synthetic fuel was a possibility but Japan also depended upon the United States for the technology for a synthetic fuel industry.[2]

Collision Course

The Japanese achieved their first major strategic success when they defeated China in the mid-1890s. But with this very success, the Japanese had planted dragon's teeth that would lead them to ultimate disaster. Japan's ambitions were in direct conflict with those of the European countries and especially with the emerging interests of the United States. "The road to Pearl Harbor was paved with the unwillingness of the Western powers to accept a New Order in East Asia that discriminated against their hundred-year-old rights and privileges, a New Order indeed that was based on Japanese monopolies."[3]

Japan confronted a dilemma. Plans to achieve economic development depended on access to and exploitation of resources in China. While the resources were taken by force, exploiting them required a peaceful environment, which was not forthcoming because of resistance by the Chinese. Eliminating this resistance required the application of military effort that delayed economic progress. By 1933, half of the government's budget was going to the military.[4] Moreover, military operations eventually galvanized international opposition and led to World War II in the Pacific.[5]

The United States and Japan were clearly on a collision course and they began drawing up war plans directed at each other long before the event. The American plan, dubbed Plan Orange, anticipated a Japanese attack on Guam and the Philippines. Under this plan U.S. forces would hold out until rescued by the Pacific Fleet. In the Japanese plan, too, Guam and the Philippines were the targets. The difference in the two plans was that in the Japanese version, U.S. ships would be met by submarine and carrier-based air strikes. Surviving elements would be destroyed in a grand, conclusive battle by the Japanese fleet.[6] This idea of a decisive naval engagement would remain a fixture of Japanese strategic thinking throughout World War II, although when war finally came, Japan's strategy was modified. Admiral Yamamoto Isoroku argued that Japan should not wait to ambush the American fleet as it steamed to the rescue but should instead launch a preemptive strike. One reason for the decision to attack the United States was the fear that U.S. naval construction would lead to American superiority. Should the United States decide to take action, Japan would be vulnerable to seeing its navy crushed by superior forces—forces that would likely be in existence by 1942.[7] Yamamoto convinced the government to attack the U.S. fleet as it lay at anchor in Pearl Harbor. By the time the ships had been replaced, Japan would be secure in its Asian stronghold.[8] At least that was the plan.

American suspicion of Japanese intentions and Japanese concern that the United States might interfere with their international plans led to an expectation of eventual war. In fact, war scares were common in the 1920s and 1930s. American restrictions on Japanese immigration exacerbated the situation. Thus the struggle for naval supremacy and latent racism were volatile issues that were brought to a head by Japan's invasion of China.[9]

Confrontation in China

Japan began its imperial activities in the late nineteenth century. But little serious effort was devoted to the development of a philosophy that would justify these activities in terms other than narrow self-interest. Despite the scope of its foreign ambitions, Japan's policies designed to achieve them were not governed by any comprehensive strategic doctrine. "Japan had no unified, or even consistent, foreign policy from the end of the first World War to the end of the second. The results would prove disastrous."[10]

Prime Minister Konoe Fumimaro announced on November 3, 1938:

"What our Empire ultimately seeks is to establish a New Order in East Asia by which the Empire is to secure an eternal stability in that region. Here lies the ultimate goal of the present expeditionary force. . . . Our Empire wholly trusts the powers to adapt themselves to this new situation in East Asia by accurately recognizing the real intention of Our Empire."[11] In 1940 the fundamental national plan stated:

> Now the world has come to a great turning point in history. New formations of politics, economics and culture have begun to emerge, based upon the development of several groups of nations. The Imperial Nation (*kokoku*), facing the unprecedented ordeal, is determined to accomplish this national principle. It is of the most urgent importance that the Imperial Nation strive for the establishment of a national defense system by conquering every difficulty and by making fundamental renovations in all aspects of our government.[12]

The Japanese were unsophisticated in the business of foreign relations and, uninformed by experience, had little appreciation for what they were getting into. "One of the notable characteristics of the Japanese political evolution of the early thirties was the substitution of violence and emotion for reason as the effective force behind government policies in the interest of an expansive and aggressive foreign policy."[13] Carried forward for a period of time by the success of these violent measures and sustained by the inflated emotion of emperor worship, sooner or later the lack of foreign affairs planning grounded in an understanding of those with whom they were dealing would become tragically evident.

The jingoistic trend in the 1930s was aided and abetted by the press and popular culture. Through selective press coverage, "the complex realities of the military occupation were reduced to the simple and sanctifying patterns of myth."[14] The myth of Japan's imperial mission was contained in all manner of media, from books and magazines to movies and music. The most enthusiastic advocates of this mythology were to be found in the military itself, especially among junior officers. These young men embraced with religious zeal a combination of samurai heroism and self-sacrifice with modern national grandeur. No one but the military itself could be trusted with this patriotic mission. "The junior officers insisted upon the wholesale removal of the old ruling elites. Only the army was pure enough to be entrusted with the Emperor's country."[15]

The new Japanese empire had three dimensions: military conquest, economic development, and mass migration (colonization). The first involved a force known as the Guandong Army, which engaged in a series of campaigns from 1931 to 1933. Following military success, Japan brought an area extending from the Amur River and the Soviet border in the north to the Great Wall of China in the south—in other words all of Manchuria—under military occupation.

The Japanese army did not limit itself to fighting battles and occupying territory. Some elements of the army schemed to influence Chinese political developments.[16] "The notion that warlords in North China could be induced to oppose Chiang and support Manchukuo had blossomed among local Japanese Army commanders soon after the Manchurian Incident."[17] By the summer of 1938, those hardliners dreamed of nothing less than all of China under Japanese control.[18] Not only was the army interested in politically separating Manchuria from the rest of China, but the existence of an independent Manchukuo, as they called it, gave the army a considerable degree of independence from Tokyo.[19]

Second, under a new regime of colonial management known as the "controlled experiment," the Japanese undertook a program of planned economic development and state capitalism. The project involved the integration of the two economies, tying Manchurian development to domestic production goals through the creation of the Japan-Manchuria bloc economy.

A third important aspect of Japanese imperialism in China was colonization. Japan sought to relieve the social ills of its rural areas by sending the rural poor to colonize lands in Manchuria. This effort was aided by the need to relieve unemployment pressures brought on by the Depression.[20] This entailed an ambitious plan to send five million Japanese farmers to settle in the Manchurian hinterland, a project designed "to create a new generation of 'continental Japanese' who would secure a more thorough domination of colonial society."[21] These Japanese emigrants received incomes higher than those of the colonial peoples among whom they were living and higher than they could have expected had they remained in Japan. There was little in the way of assimilation as most Japanese intended to return home. They tended "to lead lives that were separate, as well as privileged."[22]

The civilian government in Tokyo was concerned about the military's endeavor in Manchuria. Even the emperor was concerned about the army's activities. It was suggested that the army could be reined in by a formal command from the emperor—a rescript—but it was feared that should the army ignore it, it would be a serious blow to the emperor's prestige.[23] To get around this problem, the occupiers created a puppet regime with Chinese officials nominally in charge but with real power in the hands of Japanese. Thus, in March 1932, the "independent" state of Manchukuo was created. Tokyo recognized this new state and gave the Guandong Army responsibility for its security.[24]

In the early 1930s the Japanese army in China began to operate independently of the government in Tokyo. Commanders seemed unable to control their more radical subordinates yet used this situation effectively as leverage against the government. "Internally, the army authorities placed themselves in a position subject to radical pressure by appeasement. Externally, they were to use radicalism as an instrument to gain power."[25] Civilian political leaders were unsuccessful in reining in the army, and to make matters worse, radical militarists began a campaign of assassination of officials unsympathetic to their cause. This led to an unsuccessful coup in 1933. Top military commanders met government demands that they rein in the radical officers with the response that they were essentially helpless to do so.[26] Firebrand elements in the military recruited civilians into "national-defense societies," an undertaking greeted with enthusiasm by the public. "Such groups became a powerful political tool for the army, mediating a new relationship between policy makers at the center and a politicized public at the peripheries of power."[27] The government met the growing threat by embracing the very ideas advocated by the radicals. Thereafter there was little difference between government policy and the ambitions of the military.[28]

The Greater East Asia Co-Prosperity Sphere

One element of Japanese ideology was a deep suspicion of communism and fear of revolution. Anti-Japanese demonstrations in Manchuria were seen as Communist-inspired.[29] What came to be called by the Japanese the Greater East Asia Co-Prosperity Sphere meant not only liberation from Western imperialism, but also protection from international communism.

The more Japan succeeded in its foreign undertakings, the more authoritarian its domestic politics became. In the 1930s, the Japanese people were intensely patriotic and loyal to the imperial system, reinforced by a rigid orthodoxy. A time was eventually reached when even the slightest manifestation of disloyalty became the worst sort of crime. On one occasion, an individual convicted of a 2.75 million-yen swindle was given a light sentence that was immediately stayed. Another person, convicted of membership in an illegal political party, served a long jail sentence.[30]

In China, the Guandong Army experienced "mission creep," to use today's terminology. Instead of confining its efforts to securing Manchukuo, it was determined that additional territories were needed to achieve full security. Five provinces in North China had to be added to the core security zone as protection against China. Control of Mongolian borderlands was necessary as security against the Soviet Union. Islands in the South China Sea were needed to guard against British attacks on shipping.[31]

The main vehicle employed by the Japanese to exploit Manchuria economically was the South Manchurian Railway. Mantetsu, as it was known in Japanese, was a semi-public entity created in 1906 to manage the railway system that Japan had taken from Russia as a result of the 1904–1905 war. Mantetsu was soon expanded "into an enterprise of staggering proportions."[32] In addition to approximately 700 miles of railway track and associated bridges and tunnels, Mantetsu also owned and managed a diverse array of other enterprises, including coal mines, port facilities, warehouses, hotels, schools, hospitals, tax collection, and public utilities.[33]

Japan's grand strategy was well beyond its capabilities. "The Japanese government was by December 1933 committed to a policy which proposed to neutralize the influence of the Soviet Union, the Nationalist government of China, and the Anglo-American nations by a diplomacy rooted in the efficacy of Japan's military forces."[34] Japan focused on North China as it was closest to its puppet regime in Manchukuo, it was most vulnerable to communist activity, and it was also of considerable economic significance.[35] The Japanese exploitation of the resources of North China was not lost on the Chinese Communists, who took propaganda advantage from the situation.[36] Nor did Japan benefit from its imperial efforts, taking less from Manchukuo than it gave in return. The Pacific War deprived Japan of any gain from the investment it had made in Manchukuo.[37]

Whatever the Japanese had in mind with the slogan "Greater East Asia Co-Prosperity Sphere," they seem to have convinced themselves that their efforts would be welcomed by the conquered nations.[38] Japan's foreign policy doctrine was anachronistic and was based on intellectual foundations that were the product of a romanticized, heroic past. In the military mind of the Japanese, war involved grand battles with victory going to the side with the most enthusiastic warriors. The Japanese made the same strategic and tactical errors that the French had made in World War I. The French had placed their confidence in élan, or fighting spirit. The result was the decimation of a whole generation of French manhood.[39] Likewise, the Japanese "wasted precious patriotic lives in the Pacific War. . . . Japan counted so much on individual fighting skill, patriotism and the spirit of sacrifice, and then squandered them. Thus when the war ended, it had almost drained the sources of patriotism which Japan had cultivated for centuries."[40]

In another ironic twist, Japan was outclassed in both science and technology, and the war proved to be a learning experience. "The unsuccessful attempt to win the 'war of science and technology' left Japanese institutions, human skills and public attitudes remarkably well prepared for the massive import of western technology in the years which followed the surrender to the Allied powers in 1945."[41]

The Tripartite Pact

On September 27, 1940, Japan joined with Germany and Italy to form the Tripartite Pact, which was intended to create a new world order based on an authoritarian-fascist model of the ideal state. The alliance itself was based on few if any genuinely shared interests. The three had little in common apart from the same enemies and a similar desire to expand political control. The only thing that kept them from being enemies themselves was the fact that they did not covet the same territory. The adage "the enemy of my enemy is my friend" was sufficient reason for a union of convenience, even if the partners in this alliance were culturally and racially alien.

There was some common ideological ground among the Axis allies (the Japanese found German and Italian fascist ideas attractive), but these were superficial and disguised fundamental differences. The emperor-centered ideology of Japan had a strong mystical quality, while Nazism was predicated on the cold calculus of a master race headed by a master leader. The Japanese defined their purpose in terms of a spiritual devotion to the emperor while the *Führer* principle employed by Hitler demanded a more practical loyalty. The Japanese lacked a clear mission other than to assert power and establish control in service to a vague idea of a "greater" Asia for Asians. This notion was born of a fundamental feeling of inferiority that needed to be overcome by defeating the superior forces of the West using the West's own methods. Only in this way could Japan "prove" itself.

At first, Japan's supernationalist ideology, "Asia for Asians," resonated with emerging movements in various parts of Asia seeking to end European colonialism. Some of these resistance movements attempted to establish links with the Japanese on the theory that getting rid of the British or French, for example, was the first and most important priority. Even the prospect of colonial rule by the Japanese was not viewed as an unthinkable option since, being Asian, the Japanese would be preferable to white-European-Christian domination. Despite attempting to articulate a philosophy of common race and culture, however, the Japanese were inept in its practical implementation, being more often than not more abusive of their Asian brothers than the Europeans had been.

Probably the best known of these groups was the Indian National Army (INA) which, under Subhas Chandra Bose, actually fought with Japanese forces against their own people in the British army. This was enormously embarrassing to the British, who put great stock in the loyalty of their Indian troops. Still, the Japanese were not sure what to do with the INA; some Japanese commanders wanted to limit its role to propaganda.[42] Another example is Ne Win of Burma, who worked closely with Japanese forces during the war and received training from them. After the war, when Ne Win became the shadowy political leader of Burma, he continued good relations with Japan.

Japan's failure to exploit anticolonial sentiment was due in large measure to its own arrogance. "Japanese plans to mobilize the energies of anticolonial nationalism in service of their vision of a Japanese-ruled Greater East Asia was merely a more elaborate expression of an overweening faith in the assimilating ability of their institutions."[43] If colonial people were to be drawn to Japanese institutions because of their superiority, however, the Japanese did little to promote that result. In education for example, a dual system was maintained. Superior schools were reserved for Japanese residents. Another system for local people was "designed chiefly to provide vocational training and inculcate loyalty."[44]

The condescension of the Japanese limited their ability to exploit anticolonial sentiment. For the Japanese imperialists, national self-determination in the traditional sense was outmoded since small countries could not hope to compete with the larger, more powerful ones. Hence, this meant that "the only truly independent countries were those which possessed all the elements of national power, and that the weak nations of the world could exist only under the protection of one of the giants."[45] Accordingly, the Asian nationalists should seek inspiration and guidance from Tokyo, and the "liberated" countries of Asia should come under the tutelage and control of Japan.

In a Diet speech given on January 22, 1942, Prime Minster Tojo Hideki offered the Philippines and Burma the promise of independence in return for their cooperation.[46] But the Japanese army was incapable of cultivating support among the people of these countries. Despite the unpopularity of Western colonialism throughout most of Asia, the Japanese had managed to make themselves even more unpopular. "Even if there was a noticeable lack of enthusiasm for the white man's return, scarcely a hand was lifted in support of the Japanese. They clearly had failed to identify the interests of Southeast Asians with their own."[47]

Japan's early successes in the war were due less to its own military prowess, which was nonetheless considerable, than to the decrepit state of European colonial rule, weak defensive preparations, and naiveté, especially on the part of the United States, which could not imagine itself being attacked. British, Dutch, and French forces were woefully unprepared, being really only colonial armies of occupation, and were, for the most part, quickly overwhelmed. The pace of the Japanese advance produced considerable anxiety that Australia, New Zealand, and India might be overrun. In great mortal danger from the Germans, Britain was hard pressed to sustain even a minimal effort in Asia. Thus, Japan was in a good position to succeed in ending European hegemony had it not become overextended and made the mistake of attacking Pearl Harbor, forcing the early entry of the United States into the war.

Japan's war plan was based on obsolete strategic concepts.[48] Land warfare, in an island nation as Japan was, had little place in the thinking of Japanese military planners, who concluded that the way to win a war was to smash the enemy's naval capability. This indeed was how Japan had defeated Russia in the Battle of Tsushima in 1905. Japan thus prepared itself for the "great naval battles" that it assumed would in the end be decisive. Such a strategy led to the attack on Pearl Harbor, but this was at best a pyrrhic victory as U.S. losses were mainly battleships, much loved by admirals but by World War II of diminished practical value. In fact, their effectiveness had been substantially reduced as early as World War I by the advent of airplanes and submarines. Aircraft carriers, the really important tools of war in the Pacific, escaped the attack on Pearl Harbor.

Japanese military doctrine placed too much emphasis on samurai romanticism and not enough on practical realities. Although Japan had qualitative superiority in some weapon systems, carrier planes for example, it had major deficiencies elsewhere. It did not use submarines effectively, and its ground forces were poorly equipped. In the final analysis, however, Japan did not have the resources and staying power to sustain a prolonged war with the United States given the latter's industrial and manpower advantages. It was only a matter of time before Japan was ground down and forced to surrender.

Aftermath of the War

Japan was not held accountable for its wartime depredations to the same extent as Germany. There were war crimes trials but they did not have the moral significance, nor did they attract the same degree of attention, as did the trials of leading Nazis at Nuremburg. Japanese troops often behaved viciously toward their victims, and there are many stories of brutality, from the Bataan Death March to the Nanjing Massacre. But these have not tarnished Japanese moral integrity, at least in the West, to the same degree as did the Nazi "Final Solution" campaigns against Jews, Gypsies, and others. The key difference is that German actions were consciously and willfully sanctioned by ideology, and were official policy of the government. Japan continues to blame the atrocities for which it was responsible on "excesses of local commanders."

For Japan, these were just the "unfortunate" and "regrettable" horrors of war. For their part, the Germans own up to their past and regularly make gestures of atonement. The Japanese still refuse to apologize unequivocally for the war, hedging with such language as "having deep regrets over unfortunate incidents," and denying that some atrocities even happened.

Several issues were left unresolved in the wake of World War II, issues that would later provide the focal points of Cold War confrontation. The most important of these issues were the question of divided Germany, the partition of Korea, and the political future of French Indochina. The latter two resulted in wars, while the German question on several occasions very nearly brought about hostilities between the NATO allies and the Soviet Union. For Japan, European issues were of little concern, and Europe played no role in Japan's postwar development. But the two controversies in Asia were of great and immediate interest.

For Germany, Indochina, and Korea, World War II resulted in partition. Apart from the containment of communism on the international level, an effort in which Japan was an important although junior partner, the postwar Western strategy also affected Japan's internal politics. After a brief period of liberalization in which labor organizations, left-wing political groups, and even the Communist Party were allowed to operate openly, and indeed were encouraged for a time, the Japanese government and the American Occupation moved to restrict further radicalization of Japanese politics. Fearing communism would gain a foothold in economically depressed Japan, a more conservative approach to political development was put in place, an approach that set the tone of politics and public policy for the next several decades.

In the developing Cold War context of the late 1940s, and under policy guidance from the United States, Japan was drawn into a posture of confrontation with the Soviet Union. Despite their dislike for the Soviet Union and what it stood for, Japanese hostility toward communism did not match the kind of ideological zealotry that possessed the United States. While the brand of communism practiced in the Soviet Union or Eastern Europe was always unattractive to most Japanese, they did not feel compelled to crusade against it. But necessity dictated that Japan follow the strategy set down by the United States. Cold War politics aside, there remains the Northern Territories question, whereby the Soviet Union continues to occupy islands taken from Japan following World War II. The failure to develop a more constructive relationship between the two countries was largely a consequence of Soviet intransigence on territorial issues. Japan's basically unfriendly relationship with the Soviet Union endured throughout the Cold War and has been inherited by the Russian Republic.

The war in the Pacific produced several enduring consequences that would shape the patterns of international relations for decades to come. One was the demise of the ancient Confucian political system in China and its eventual replacement with a Chinese hybrid form of communism. Another was the geopolitical division of both Korea and Indochina. A third was the rapid decline of Europe as a strategic presence in Asia. A fourth was the growth of U.S. involvement, partly because of its own expanding interests and partly as a function of Europe's withdrawal. The last important development was the advent of nuclear weapons. Each of these carried great implications for Japan.

China and Japan had never developed close ties. Its two wars with China made Japan almost universally disliked among Chinese. The Communist Revolution in China made the estrangement between the two countries even more complete. For practical and ideological reasons, China aligned itself with the Soviet Union, whose own relationship with Japan was adversarial. China soon tired of taking directions from Moscow and found that Soviet help was not all that useful. After the Sino-Soviet split in 1962, China chose to isolate itself from nearly all contacts with the outside world and attempted to achieve the goals of a communist society mainly through the intense application of ideology or "correct thought." China's tortured revolutionary antics were viewed with dismay in Japan. It was only following the withdrawal of U.S. forces from Vietnam in 1973 and the demise of Maoism a few years later that China sought a different approach, including constructive relations with Japan and other countries.

The partition of Korea and Indochina resulted in two bitter and inconclusive wars, neither of which involved Japan directly, but both proved to be significant and, more importantly, of enormous economic benefit to Japan. Europe's general disengagement from Asia left not only a power vacuum, which was filled by the United States, but also an economic vacuum, which presented Japan with considerable commercial opportunity. The expanding security role of the United States in Asia and the global Cold War environment put Japan in a good position to take advantage of the situation by exploiting its alliance with and importance for the United States.

In the case of the development of nuclear weapons and their role in determining the character of international relations, Japan has a special role to play. As the only country against which nuclear weapons have ever been used, Japan's position on the issue carries a moral authority that only it possesses. As might be expected, the Japanese experience produced in them a strong antagonism toward the existence of nuclear weapons. This attitude led to the three non-nuclear principles that have been the basis of government policy since the war. The principles are: no manufacture, no possession, and no positioning of nuclear weapons in Japan. While the first two have been observed by the Japanese government, the government has been less than adamant in adhering to the third. The U.S. military routinely positions nuclear weapons in Japan, a phenomenon that is widely known and often condemned.

16

The Japanese Miracle

Japan's postwar economic recovery was its second period of rapid industrial expansion and growing technological sophistication; the first was the period of economic modernization following the restoration in 1868. Japan was considered of such minor importance as to pose no significant threat to the economic interests of the European imperialists.[1] Even Japan's military activities in China during the 1890s and its defeat of Russia in 1905 did little to alter the prevailing view that Japan was only a regional power. After World War II, Japan returned to the status of insignificance as far as the major powers were concerned. American patronage of Japan after the war provided a welcome cloak of obscurity and time to rearrange national priorities. "Washington's tutelary shadow was a convenient screen behind which they could reach the center of the stage without upsetting anyone."[2] But this convenient arrangement could not last forever. Economic achievements in the 1970s and 1980s brought the Japanese once again the full and occasionally hostile attention of the international community.[3]

When Japan embarked on its national development program in the late nineteenth century, it was well positioned to achieve economic growth. After the Meiji Restoration, the role of the professional warrior class, or samurai, disappeared along with the feudal system of which it was a part. With the coming of the modern state, financing used to support the samurai could be redirected into economically productive investment. Moreover, the samurai themselves constituted a pool of manpower, much of it educated and literate, now available for economic and political modernization. "And it may be, then, that the rapid transformation of Japanese society in the Meiji era was in large measure achieved because of the tools, training, education, leadership and experience brought to it by members of the former feudal class."[4]

Japan managed to make the transition from an agricultural to an industrial economy without experiencing the massive social dislocation that frequently attends this process. Rural poverty and urban unemployment were problems of much smaller magnitude than the experiences of other countries in the early stages of industrialization. The combination of private entrepreneurship and government support led to rapid growth in the manufacturing sector and a corresponding decline in agriculture during the latter part of the nineteenth century.

The Post–World War II Economy

Japan's economic development following World War II was truly remarkable, especially when viewed in light of the condition of the country at the conclusion of hostilities in 1945.

> The war economy, which had been starved, pounded and beaten virtually to its knees by mid-summer of 1945, came to a standstill upon surrender. There was no longer purpose to ninety percent of end-product output. Oriented wholly for war, facing a completely uncertain future, with no incentive or authority for reconversion to peace-time purposes, silent war plants, desolate of workers, remained only so much economic debris, part to be salvaged for reparations, part to be slowly turned to meet reconstruction needs, and part to rot unused and unprotected from the elements.[5]

Not only did the Japanese recognize the importance of rebuilding war-ravaged economic structures, but they emphasized the introduction of innovative processes. "The truth of Japan's dizzying climb out of poverty is that, unencumbered by ideological baggage and having little regard for her own economic history, Japan wrote her own success story. She filled the blank landscape with new institutions and new relationships of her own devising."[6] This approach did not involve the expenditure of large sums of money on research in basic science; Japan concentrated instead on the best prospects for commercial success. They relied on the research and development efforts of other countries and then bought the finished product or process, often at bargain-basement prices, when it had reached a state of significant market potential.

Japan's economic success has been attributed to many factors, ranging from national character to restrictive international trade practices to a skilled labor force. Another plus is that Japan has not been burdened with heavy military expenditures; it spent only 1 percent of GDP on defense during the Cold War years compared to 6 percent in the United States.[7] "Japan's decision-makers have run their country for well over a century now with three objectives: independence, survival, and control—the independence of their country from foreign domination, their own survival as a ruling elite, and their continued control of key economic and political levers."[8]

One of the distinguishing characteristics of the Japanese economic boom was an emphasis on capital expansion at the expense of both public and private consumption. The financial resources generated by economic growth were reinvested to produce further growth. Neither the social infrastructure nor the working public was a prime beneficiary. Investment in education, welfare, and retirement did not match the overall rate of growth. The high personal savings rate together with forced savings through high prices continues today. Richard Katz notes: "Firms took their newfound profits and reinvested them in new factories and equipment. Not the frugality of the Japanese households, but the increased profits of Japanese corporations created Japan's extraordinary national savings."[9] The share of national income received by labor has not kept pace with economic growth.[10] The emphasis on capital formation has come at the expense of personal consumption. "The average Japanese was working hard to subsidize exports."[11]

Japan's national development was based on an industrial development policy that "involves the government's use of its authority and resources to administer policies that address the needs of specific sectors and industries (and, if necessary, those of specific companies) with the aim of raising the productivity of factor inputs."[12] The goals of this policy included increasing economic efficiency, reducing excess competition, and protecting basic materials production for the domestic economy.[13]

The government has famously acted to protect Japanese agriculture and industry, especially fledgling industry, from foreign competition.[14] On occasion, the government has encouraged a reduction in production capacity.[15] Following the 1973 OPEC decision to increase the price of petroleum, the Japanese aluminum industry could not compete with countries possessing their own cheaper sources of energy. As a result of the pullback, aluminum refining capacity in Japan was reduced 97 percent by 1987.[16] At the same time, the decision to reduce dependence on petroleum led Japan to develop alternative energy sources, including nuclear, and spurred the manufacture of fuel-efficient cars.

In seeking to explain the rise of Japan to the position of a major economic power, much has been made of the unity among labor, business, and government.[17] "The emergence of government-guided capitalism was one of the two major elements of the new economic order that transformed Japan after the war. The other was a novel style in relations between workers and management. Its essence was an uncommon harmony between them within the structure of the company."[18] The importance of top-to-bottom socioeconomic solidarity may be overstated. Of perhaps greater importance to Japan's success was the relative absence of divisive and adversarial relationships. Intra-industrial price competition is minimized thanks to government policy that views this American-favored practice as disorderly.[19] Class consciousness and conflict over class-related issues are less significant than in the West. If the tiny fractions of the population who are either very rich or very poor are excluded, the distance between the top and the bottom of the earnings pyramid is not great.[20]

Another reason for the stability of the system has been the extent of vertical integration among businesses. The big companies that make automobiles or electronic equipment are topped by investment banks and rely on hundreds of suppliers, which are tightly integrated into a production system. The reason this system has worked so well is because there are so few opportunities for stoppages to occur within it. During the time Japan was experiencing rapid economic growth, Western economies faced frequent labor problems. American producers had to stockpile parts from suppliers, even those it owned, because of potential strikes. This can lead to storage costs, inventory control problems, and other bottlenecks.

Finally, the emphasis on trade. The high priority given to exports is a function of economic reality. Most industrial raw materials must be purchased abroad, and to pay for them Japan relies on the sale of its own manufactured goods to other countries. It is not the case, however, that the Japanese economy is totally dependent on trade for its survival. Despite the attention given to exports, the backbone of the economy is the domestic market.[21] This is increasingly the case.[22]

Several of the strengths of the Japanese economy attracted particular attention in the business world. These include, first, an emphasis on quality control, ironically based on methods developed in the United States. Second, the Japanese took advantage of an inventory control system called "just-in-time production" to reduce costs, a process developed by the Toyota Motor Company in the 1930s. In this process, a manufacturer maintains only enough parts on the production line to keep it running for a short time, as little as one hour. Third, there is "close cooperation in the movement of new technologies and products from concept to production."[23] Fourth, there is the cooperative relationship between subcontractors and the larger enterprise. Fifth is an emphasis on continuous change in product design and the processes of manufacturing. Improvements are continuous rather the result of one major breakthrough.[24] Sixth is a corporate philosophy which places less emphasis on short-term profits in favor of long-term market share. Finally, there is the substantial worker commitment to the welfare of the company. There are fewer ranks from top to bottom and there is greater cooperation across functional departments.[25]

Japan led in the development and use of industrial robots, resulting in the use of more cost-cutting tools than in the rest of the world combined. Japan also took the lead over its foreign competitors in areas of computer-controlled manufacturing processes. Automation not only reduces labor costs by cutting the number of workers needed, but it increases product quality and reliability. Such technical achievements are possible because of the availability of engineers and technicians, especially electrical engineers, making possible Japan's achievements in the field of consumer electronics.[26]

Modern economic progress requires substantial investment in the search for new materials, processes, and technologies. The United States has historically spent more on research and development than has Japan, but much of that has gone into military-related activities. Half of the American research and development budget comes from the federal government and half to two-thirds of that goes to military-related research.[27] There is considerable activity in space-related research, a source of important innovations. American space technology became increasingly military in its applications during the Reagan administration, which also favored missile defense in the form of the Strategic Defense Initiative (SDI).[28] After the September 11, 2001, attacks, massive amounts of money were committed to "homeland security" in addition to an expanded military budget. Japan participates in research on missile defense. At first, the Japanese were interested not in the military applications of SDI but in possible spin-offs of marketable products. This is consistent with a strategy calling for development of technologies that show promise for aiding in the future needs of the nation, such as energy.[29] Tokyo's attitude changed when North Korea developed a nuclear capability and an effective delivery system.

Employment and Compensation Systems

Rapid economic development after the war was helped by the existence of a reservoir of industrial manpower in the form of underemployed agricultural workers. Here again, the Japanese experience is different from that found elsewhere in the world. Many third world countries also have surplus agricultural labor, but this manpower pool is largely illiterate and lacks the skills necessary for industrial employment. Moreover, Japanese workers have a high incentive to learn new skills and are able to do so thanks to the existence of educational opportunities provided by business and industry.

Among the important factors determining social status in Japan, in addition to education, are age and gender. Of the three, only education is something over which the individual has some measure of control. Nevertheless all of them are significant manpower variables. The rigidities of age differentials that characterize Japanese society would startle Americans used to laws against age discrimination and a powerful political lobby representing senior citizens. Compulsory retirement at fifty or fifty-five is common, and the retirement benefits are comparatively modest.[30] This does not mean that workers are just callously thrown onto the human "scrap heap." Retirement does not necessarily mean unemployment, and many workers, especially in the white-collar categories, find other work, although probably at lower pay. Most workers who have retired from larger firms find work in small and medium-sized firms, where three-fourths of the workers forty-five years of age and older are employed.[31] There are fewer retirees in Japan than in other industrialized countries, but this will change with the aging of the population.[32] It is also true that pressure from the aging workforce has led to liberalization of retirement policies, and many employees are now retained beyond age sixty.[33]

The Japanese save a higher percentage of their incomes compared to the populations of other industrialized countries. Workers save for retirement because benefits are insufficient. Japanese savers put only 10 percent in stocks and mutual funds. Most goes into bank deposits that earn less than 1 percent. This is not only due to conservative practices and risk-aversion but to the fact that under Japan's system most stocks must be bought in lots of 1,000, which would require a substantial outlay.[34]

With a low birthrate and an aging population, Japan faces a shortage of unskilled and semi-skilled labor. The shortage is being met by immigrants, a situation that itself has generated political controversy, as immigration is not encouraged. The Japanese do not warm to the idea of expanding immigration on the grounds that it would be socially and culturally disruptive.[35] Many enter the country anyway, attracted by the possibility of employment. The Justice Ministry estimated that there were 70,000 illegal immigrants working in the country in 1989 and more than twice that many by the turn of the century. These people take jobs considered "dirty, dangerous, or demeaning" by the Japanese.

The salary system covering both workers and managers does not entail the wide disparities in levels of compensation that prevails in the United States.[36] Top executives in Japan rarely receive more than $200,000 a year including benefits compared to the multimillion-dollar packages received by the elite of American business.[37]

Japanese management defines corporate interest in much broader terms than is generally true in the West, where profit is the main issue. There is a greater concern for ensuring long-term viability and market share, not just short-term profits.[38] The health of the firm is seen in the general context of the national welfare rather than the other way around. The government is not there to be exploited or perceived as a threat, depending on circumstances, but as a partner. Overall management philosophy stresses public good over private gain. Individual self-aggrandizement is certainly not part of this philosophy as reflected in the fact that top Japanese executives make considerably less than do their American counterparts. Indeed, the high level of compensation received by American executives is one of the shortcomings of American business as viewed by the Japanese, and by many Americans as well.

The Export Economy

Postwar Japan maintained high import barriers, using tariffs, quotas, and control of foreign exchange to offset chronic trade deficits. But as its balance of payments strengthened, Japan began to feel increasing international pressure to lower import barriers and liberalize trade.

Japan's national prosperity has been linked to the maintenance of an export economy with a perpetual balance-of-payments surplus. This has been a highly satisfactory arrangement for the United States, which regularly buys more than it sells abroad, and since the Japanese accept payment in dollars, they recycle them back to the United States to fund additional imports. "The importance of the current account surplus is so imbedded in the thinking of Japan's decision-makers that to secure it they have been willing to sacrifice much of the prosperity that could otherwise have been theirs. They have seen to it that the surplus was not consumed domestically; instead, they have invested it overseas, where it finances the deficits of trading partners."[39]

The Japanese economy in general and the employment system in particular are not immune to the changes that are affecting other countries. When economies slump, demand for Japanese exports does too. The tremendous pressures exerted on Japan by its trading partners produce adjustments in the domestic economy. For certain sectors of the economy, these adjustments have been traumatic. Major dislocations at the international level, especially since the Asian currency crisis in the late 1990s, have made economic transformation all the more painful. Japan has endured a prolonged economic slump.

What is it that has kept Japan from being an "open" trade partner? Formal tariff barriers are out of fashion, so the main obstacles to imports into Japan are procedural in nature.[40] Lengthy and cumbersome customs procedures increase costs and delays to importers. The Japanese often insist on their own standards, testing, and certification procedures, duplicating in many cases those employed in other countries. In the interest of promoting a national development policy, the Japanese government purchases from domestic producers even though the costs may be higher than those of foreign sources. Under the law, depressed industries are given preferential and protective treatment. At the other extreme, promising but often risky high-tech industries are cultivated and protected by the government. Foreign applications for patents are sometimes delayed for as long as ten years, allowing Japanese producers time to develop the process or idea to the point of commercial viability. Finally, the distribution system in Japan is notoriously complicated, making it difficult for importers to gain access. The government restricts competition and protects small stores through a labyrinth of licensing requirements. To open a supermarket, for example, requires forty-five different licenses and 200 pages of applications under nineteen different laws. "This includes separate applications to different agencies for licenses to sell meat, fish, milk, bread, tofu, pickles, ice cream, cakes, tea, frozen foods, box lunches and so forth."[41]

An area of dispute between Japan and its trading partners concerns agricultural products. There are two major constraints limiting the ability of the government of Japan to be a more accommodating trade partner in this area. The first is the considerable political influence wielded by the agricultural community. With economic recovery after the war, the rural population declined in both numbers and economic influence. Today only a small percentage of the population is engaged in farming, and many are part-timers who receive only a portion of their income from farming. The agricultural portion of GNP is only 3 percent. Yet Japanese agriculture is highly productive.

Another barrier to liberalized agricultural trade is the public's acceptance of the high cost of food. Restrictive agricultural trade policies endure because of the general political consensus regarding the need for a stable and guaranteed food supply, even if this means paying higher prices than those on the world market.

Boom and Bust

The heady years of seemingly limitless economic success came to an abrupt end when the Bank of Japan (BOJ) reversed policy in order to cool down an overheating Japanese economy. During the 1980s boom, the loosening of regulations and monetary easing by the BOJ had led to a rapid rise in the stock market and in property prices. These conditions fueled considerable overconstruction, in particular in office buildings. When the bubble inevitably burst, rents for these buildings dropped sharply, making it difficult to pay back the bank loans that had been made for their construction.[42] Construction costs in Japan are very high due to collusion among bidders. In order to spread the wealth, they agree in advance on which company will get the contract, freezing out, of course, foreign bidders whose bid may be as much as 45 percent less that those of Japanese companies. According to Katz, "construction lies at the heart of Japan's daisy-chain of inefficiency."[43]

The banking crisis that ensued proved particularly intractable due in part to its magnitude but also to the lack of political will to fix it. Insurance companies were hard hit because they invested heavily in banks. Banks had also made bad loans for foreign purchases. In 1993, a group of Japanese banks led by Mitsubishi Bank sold the Hyatt Regency Wakoloa resort hotel in Hawaii to a Hilton Hotels subsidiary for 25 percent of the construction costs.[44]

Then in the late 1990s, the Asian financial crisis compounded the problem. From 1998 through 2002, the government spent 10.433 trillion yen on failed financial institutions, leaving 8.7 trillion yen remaining in bad loans.[45] The Japanese economy was entering a second decade of stagnation.

The Ministry of Finance took a conservative approach to the bad-debt problem. Rather than a shake-out that would eliminate weaker financial institutions, the MOF kept them afloat so as avoid the ripple effects of bankruptcies and unemployment. The result not only weakened the reputation of the MOF but also that of Japanese banks whose international ratings declined.[46]

Since the 1990s, Japan has seemed unable to climb out of the economic doldrums. Despite international pressure and changes of government in Japan, efforts to bring the structures, policies, and mental habits of Japan's economy into harmony with the realities of the twenty-first century proceeded at a glacial pace.[47] The economic system that had allowed Japan to catch up with and even surpass much of the West was itself now being surpassed by a rising China.

Several recent shocks may be the catalyst that Japan has needed to finally make some of the changes it has postponed for so long. One of these is the global financial crisis that began in the United States in 2007 and subsequently engulfed more and more economies, including Japan. The downturn in demand for Japanese exports, triggering yet another recession, reopened the recurrent debate in Japan on trade liberalization and restructuring as ways to revitalize the economy. China, Japan, and the United States have been championing free trade initiatives for the Asia–Pacific region, and the tide of opinion in Japan may finally be shifting.

Just as Japan seemed to be making a good recovery from the 2008–2009 recession, the country suffered another series of shocks—this time, literally. In March 2011, a 9.0-magnitude earthquake followed by tsunami devastated northeast Japan and flooded the Fukushima nuclear power complex, disabling both the cooling system and the backup systems that kept the nuclear fuel from melting down. It will be up to Japan's political leadership either to make this disaster the starting point for major reconstruction efforts and the development of new power supply systems that will lessen or even end Japan's reliance on nuclear power, or to instead continue on a course of indecision and half-measures.

17

Government and Politics

Japan is a democracy and has been at least since the end of World War II, when commitment to the adoption of a democratic form of government had been made a condition of surrender. Democracy requires a formula for controlling political power, usually articulated in the form of a written constitution that places the source of governing authority outside government itself. Among the institutions considered most important in maintaining democracy is, first, a system of popular elections to make the government in some way accountable to the people. The second institution is a judiciary that is capable of making independent judgments, free from coercion from other branches of government. The third is a legislative process that draws its authority from and is ultimately responsible to the citizenry.

The constitution that took effect in May 1947 states clearly that sovereignty resides in the Japanese people, not the emperor, who is now essentially a symbolic figure. The political system more closely resembles the British form of parliamentary government then the American system.

The Legislative System

Legislatures are typically slow, cumbersome, and contentious. Never have the virtues of democracy been preserved, for long at any rate, when the government has been the exclusive province of executive authority. The existence of a legislature, the members of which owe their position to the voters rather than to the executive, is an effective, although by no means infallible, protector of democratic interests.

Although patterned after the British "Westminister" model, the Japanese legislature—the Diet—does not possess the supreme power of the state as does the British Parliament.[1] Nor does it have the kind of independence that characterizes many legislatures and especially the United States Congress. The system of "checks and balances," so dear to Americans, is typically not a fixture of parliamentary systems, including Japan's. Power is shared among the legislature, the "government," that is, the cabinet, and the bureaucracy. The legislative process is an important mechanism serving as a focal point of public discussion and opinion-formation and in maintaining popular support for the overall governing process.[2] The Japanese are not unfamiliar with

General Douglas MacArthur and Emperor Hirohito

legislatures. Experience with legislative bodies goes back at least as far as the 1889 constitution, and the present arrangement is basically a refinement of practices developed in the 1920s.

Members of the Diet tend to have a lot in common. Most members come from the world of business. Others are bureaucrats; organized labor is the third most common background. Family background is also a common feature of Diet members. Nearly 40 percent of the Liberal Democratic Party (LDP) candidates in the 1990 lower house election were children of Diet members.[3] This phenomenon reflects the influence of support groups (*koenkai*) in selecting candidates that are inclined to choose relatives of the previous occupant of the seat.[4]

The upper house of the Diet, called the House of Councillors, is the successor to the prewar House of Peers, a body that was made up mainly of the hereditary nobility. Today the upper house has 242 members who serve six-year terms. Of these, 146 are chosen from the forty-seven prefectures and two are selected from Okinawa. In addition, 96 seats are contested nationally and awarded under a system of proportional representation. Half the seats in the House of Councillors are contested in elections held at fixed three-year intervals.

Since the 1983 election, councillors from the national constituency have been selected by a process in which voters cast their ballots for a party rather than for an individual candidate. It was initially thought the new system would diminish the "popularity contest" aspect of upper house elections. This has not proven to be the case, however, as parties try to recruit well-known figures to run under their banner. Small parties have been less successful in attracting famous people to run and are disadvantaged by the proportional representation system; seats are allocated on the basis of the size of the total party vote.

The electoral procedure for the lower house, called the House of Representatives, was replaced following the 1993 election. Today, 300 members are chosen from single-member districts and 180 by a system of proportional representation. Members serve a four-year term, although the lower house may be dissolved at any time by decision of the prime minister, in which case a general election is held early. Each member of the Diet can expect at least one committee assignment. Junior members may be given choice committee assignments, such as Agriculture, in order to put them in a position to build good relationships with their constituents. Senior members, who already have strong organizations, take the less politically rewarding committees such as Foreign Affairs.[5] According to the rules, committee chairmen are elected in each house from members of the committee but, in practice, they are appointed by the Speaker in consultation with the parties. Chairmen have extensive formal powers governing the procedural operation of the committees.[6]

All legislatures have their own distinctive formal and informal styles of operation. In Japan, the dominance of the LDP throughout most of the postwar period has worked to define the legislative process. The governing party is not always able to get its way. The opposition can prevent enactment of legislation if it is unified and has public support. Compromise is usually reached through intensive and prolonged bargaining. On occasion, the government has locked out the opposition, for example in 1960 when rancorous debate prevented a vote on the renewal of the Mutual Security Treaty with the United States. If it has been excluded from the process where the government's legislation is drafted and its own proposals stand no chance of success, the opposition may try to force concessions by methods that can include obstructionism.[7] They may filibuster or engage in an "ox walk," a procedure whereby members take an inordinate amount of time to walk a short distance to cast their ballots.

Long service within the Diet makes it possible for some members to develop influence based on policy expertise. Some of these Diet members have knowledge of their own preferred area of policy that rivals that of the most senior bureaucrats from the relevant ministry. This expertise can lead to committee assignments in the Diet and to important positions in the LDP's

Policy Affairs Research Council (PARC). These "policy-specialized cliques" are called *zoku* and are another important element in the linkage among the public, the legislature, and the ministries.[8]

The Prime Minister and the Cabinet

In a parliamentary system, the chief executive, or prime minister, is also leader of the legislative branch, more specifically the lower house. Ministers, a majority of whom must be chosen from among members of the Diet, are appointed and removed by the prime minister. Japanese ministers normally do not remain in office long. From the 1970s until the end of the century, there was a turnover in the office of prime minister about every two years. The pattern was broken, temporarily, following the election victory of a multiparty coalition in 1993, when there were three prime ministers in one twelve-month period. It was broken again, by an LDP prime minister, Junichiro Koizumi, who served more than five years from 2001 to 2006. Since Koizumi's retirement, prime ministerial tenure has been approximately one year.

Changes in the various ministerial assignments are even more frequent. From 1964 to 1987, the average term of office for a cabinet minister was less than a year.[9] The frequent change in cabinet ministers means they lack sufficient time to gain full control over their ministries. A minister is not likely to have much personal influence, deferring rather to his subordinate officials because "he might be on hand barely long enough to find his way around the building."[10]

Unlike China or the Koreas, Japanese politics has not involved a "cult of personality." Japanese politicians, Koizumi being one exception, have not been colorful or charismatic. Top government leaders tend to possess the same kinds of personal qualities and attainments as business leaders.[11] They are men of ability in the management and organizational sense, but as public figures, they are rather bland.[12] Achieving the prime ministership or a major cabinet position may be the capstone of one's political career, but "the Japanese prime minister has less real power than any head of government in the Western world, or in most countries of Asia."[13]

The Bureaucracy

A distinguishing feature of the Japanese parliamentary system is the influence typically exercised by the bureaucracy in shaping public policy compared to other institutions such as parties or the legislature. "For what it is worth, Japanese bureaucrats are frequently more influential than bureaucrats in dictatorships."[14] The exact extent of this power derives from a variety of sources.

Japanese Prime Ministerial Tenures Since the 1994 Electoral Reform

Prime Minister	Party	Term
Morihiro Hosokawa	Japan New	August 1993–April 1994
Tsutomu Hata	Renewal	April 1994–June 1994
Tomiichi Murayama	Socialist	June 1994–January 1996
Ryutaro Hashimoto	LDP	January 1996–November 1996
Ryutaro Hashimoto	LDP	November 1996–July 1998
Keizo Obuchi	LDP	July 1998–April 2000
Yoshiro Mori	LDP	April 2000–July 2000
Yoshiro Mori	LDP	July 2000–April 2001
Junichiro Koizumi	LDP	April 2001–November 2003
Junichiro Koizumi	LDP	November 2003–September 2005
Junichiro Koizumi	LDP	September 2005–September 2006
Shinzo Abe	LDP	September 2006–September 2007
Yasuo Fukuda	LDP	September 2007–September 2008
Taro Aso	LDP	September 2008–September 2009
Yukio Hatoyama	DPJ	September 2009–June 2010
Naoto Kan	DPJ	June 2010–September 2011
Yoshihiko Noda	DPJ	September 2011–

LDP: Liberal Democratic Party: DPJ: Democratic Party of Japan

Public agencies actively cultivate clientele groups that in turn support the agencies' existence and activities.[15] The rapid turnover at the ministerial level allows bureaucrats to build organizational strength. An important source of bureaucratic power comes from the issuance of ordinances and ministerial communications. While these are technically clarifications and interpretations of the law, they can be so significant as to revise the original intent of the law.[16] As Chalmers Johnson observed: "The politicians reign and the bureaucrats rule."[17]

The power of the bureaucracy is the product of longstanding political style and traditions. The bureaucracy was an important element of the political modernization process during the last half of the nineteenth century. Moreover, the bureaucracy as an institution was basically unaffected by World War II and the subsequent Occupation. "The historical record shows that little direct effort at bureaucratic reform was ever considered by the United States."[18] But despite its significance in the political system, the bureaucracy is smaller and costs much less than the administrative structures in many other countries.

Important interpersonal connections are maintained by the practice of officials rotating among bureaucracy, business, and politics. A similar practice, called the "revolving door," draws frequent criticism in the United States, where retired public officials or military officers obtain jobs with private industry, often those with whom they had dealt in their former capacities. Far from being condemned, this is a normal aspect of administrative life in Japan, which is generally viewed with favor, as the term for it—"descent from heaven" (*amakudari*)—would imply.[19] Retirees from the public service, often at an early age, join private industry or in some cases "special legal entities" such as public corporations.[20] Some go into party politics, and for them the most promising avenue to elected office is the national constituency of the House of Councillors, where a broad organizational base is an advantage.[21] The practice of leaving public service to pursue a second career in business or politics is not only condoned but expected. For one reason, this practice contributes to the effective operation of the policy-making process. Personal contacts, the more extensive the better, are the medium through which negotiation and consensus decision making are achieved.

The efficiency of the bureaucracy is one of the reasons Japan enjoyed its long run of political stability and economic success. Until the economic difficulties of the 1990s, the bureaucracy was able to deliver the services demanded of it by the public. Then the bureaucracy, and especially the Ministry of Finance, lost much of its luster. The decline of the bureaucracy, among other things, enhanced the role of the governing party in the policy process.[22] The bureaucracy became a target for political criticism and the budgetary ax. Job opportunities in the public service are few and advancement is slow. Meanwhile, fewer than 5 percent of those taking the higher civil service exam pass it in any given year and once there, civil servants must wait at least twenty years before attaining the level of bureau chief.[23] Competition among candidates for employment is fierce and is getting more so since efforts to keep public expenditures down means limited expansion of personnel opportunities.[24] If and when the public begins expecting more and better services, the demands on the bureaucracy will intensify.

The Legal System

The Japanese legal system as it exists today is patterned after that of continental Europe. The French court system was introduced in 1875 and German influence was pronounced after the adoption of the Meiji constitution in 1889. The influence of the Anglo-American legal tradition was added after World War II.[25] The substance of the law is also similar to that in Europe except as pertains to family matters, in which the tradition of Confucian ethics prevails. Neither the adversarial system nor jury trials are used, although currently a sort of hybrid jury system is being developed that adds six randomly selected citizens to the panel of three judges hearing serious criminal cases. Legal precedent is not binding in subsequent cases as it is in the United States, where the doctrine of *stare decisis* is used. Japanese courts, while not totally indifferent to precedent, are likely to decide on the basis of "the prevalent sociopolitical climate of a given moment."[26] In the inquisitorial system employed in Japan, judges are not passive referees but may take an active part in seeking out the facts. Judges also render verdicts. Prosecutors are career civil servants. The role of lawyers is generally limited to that of advisor to their clients rather than being their champions.

The constitution invests the Supreme Court with all judicial power but also authorizes the establishment of lesser courts. The result is a judicial system arranged hierarchically. The Supreme Court is composed of fifteen judges, fourteen of whom are appointed by the cabinet from a list provided by the Court itself. The chief justice is normally influential in the process of selecting the other justices.[27] The chief justice is appointed by the emperor, upon recommendation by the cabinet, a procedure that is presumed to give the job more prestige. The Court sits as the Grand Bench, involving all fifteen justices to hear cases of special importance, especially constitutional issues. More often the work of the Court is conducted by the Petty Benches, composed of five justices who consider routine cases submitted for review.

The Supreme Court typically does not hold public hearings in which opposing attorneys argue their cases and answer questions from the justices. Hearings are held in criminal cases when the Court is likely to reverse a lower court judgment, in capital punishment cases, and in reviewing public security incidents.[28]

Until American influence was felt, the Supreme Court published only the majority opinion, as in the European tradition. But not all cases have the decision published, only those considered significant.[29] Now concurring and dissenting opinions are published. Lower courts publish only majority opinions.[30]

The Supreme Court's role is to oversee the judicial system by determining the rules of procedure and practice and to hear cases on appeal from the lower courts. There are eight High Courts corresponding to geographical regions. Next are District Courts (roughly one per prefecture with the exception of Hokkaido, which has four) with more than 200 branches. At the lowest level are Summary Courts, with three judges each, which handle minor criminal and civil cases. Summary Courts are distinct from the courts at higher levels in that the justices of Summary Courts are not career judges but rather are similar to American justices of the peace. Decisions of Summary Courts can be appealed only as far as the High Court.[31]

Another system is that of the Family Courts, which structurally parallel the District Courts. Family Courts adjudicate domestic complaints, such as inheritance, divorce, and juvenile matters.

Japan is not known as a litigious society. Informal approaches to conflict resolution are preferred because of the embarrassment associated with a public airing of controversy. "There is abundant evidence that in the conduct of their daily lives, the Japanese are at pains to avoid contention and confrontation."[32] To retain the services of a lawyer is an admission that the usual and proper way of dealing with a problem has failed. Hence the legal profession is not nearly as large or as prestigious as in the United States. The size of the legal profession has not been limited only by demand for legal services. The government, as a matter of policy, put restrictions on the numbers of lawyers.[33]

In 2003, the Ministry of Education approved the establishment of U.S.-style law schools with the intention of increasing the number of legal practitioners in Japan. Until these reforms, there were no postgraduate law schools in Japanese universities; almost all licensed lawyers received their training from the Supreme Court's Legal Training and Research Institute. Admission to the two-year program was extremely competitive for a relatively small number of slots. Top graduates might go on to become judges.[34] Others became prosecutors or went into private practice. Many legal functions, such as drawing up contracts, have been handled in Japan by nonlicensed lawyers who have received an undergraduate level of education from a faculty of law in one of the universities. The newly expanded legal training system is intended to make legal services more broadly available and better meet the needs of Japanese and other multinational corporations.[35]

While the complexity of modern society encourages the use of formal legal procedures,[36] in Japan there is a reluctance to employ the adversarial procedures that such methods imply. The Japanese tend to see conflicts in shades of gray rather than in black-and-white, right-and-wrong terms, and many petty offenses are never prosecuted. Legal confrontation disrupts community solidarity and causes personal embarrassment by making conflicts open and public. The Japanese still prefer to settle conflicts through backroom deals, the use of elaborate rituals, or other modes of alternative dispute resolution. Overall, the system is weighted in favor of the government. "When sued, the Japanese government always wins."[37]

The Political Party System

Political parties appeared in Japan after the Meiji Restoration in 1868. The first real party was founded in 1874, followed by a second in 1882. Factors shaping Japanese political parties include social values and myths, customs and traditions, and the ways in which people identify themselves in the social order. Another factor is formal political structure.[38] In the parliamentary model, the legislative and executive branches are combined in that the prime minister and the cabinet provide leadership for the legislature and the bureaucracy. A third factor is the type of system used to elect people to the legislature. There are many such systems, ranging from single-member districts in which election requires a plurality to proportional representation systems whereby seats are apportioned on the basis of the percentage of votes received by each political party.

Two important aspects of political parties are organization and ideology.[39] The organization of the LDP is loosely based on individual politicians, and there is considerable division and factionalism within the party. The importance of ideology for the LDP and its backers is minimal. The same might be said about the more recently formed Democratic Party of Japan (DPJ), many of whose members once belonged to the LDP. All Japanese political parties have national organizations, with the first subdivision occurring at the prefectural level. Generally, these prefectural units "implement national party directives, coordinate activities of lower party units, formulate party policies on problems specific to a prefecture, supervise the work of party-endorsed assemblymen and recommend the endorsement of Diet candidates to the national parties."[40]

The long success of the Liberal Democratic Party was attributable to its favorable record in promoting economic prosperity.[41] Good economic times play well in all democracies; bad times spell trouble for the party in power. The LDP's good fortune was also due to the absence of viable competition. The formation of voting blocs based on social or ethnic divisions is largely missing. The absence of these factors also means that an important source of political competition is lacking. Class identity is not a powerful influence on voting behavior either.[42] While younger voters tended to favor progressive parties, they were also less likely to vote. Women tended to be more conservative than men.[43]

On January 24, 1994, during a brief period when a coalition of opposition parties held the majority, parliament approved legislation changing Japan's electoral system. A combination of single-member voting and proportional representation replaced the multiple-member district arrangement. These changes were expected to make independent or "floating" voters more important in election outcomes.[44] Indeed, the years since the reform saw the revitalization of the opposition in the form of the Democratic Party of Japan, which would sweep the LDP from power in 2009.

The Liberal Democratic Party

Officially organized in 1955, the LDP can trace its lineage as far back as the 1870s. The mainstream of major Japanese political parties, in which the LDP squarely fits, has been in the moderate to conservative part of the political spectrum. The philosophy of the LDP favors a centralized and efficient government exercising an important role in the economy. This is to be achieved by a management approach to public policy that closely approximates that employed in business. The ideology of the LDP substitutes an economic definition of national security for a military one. The party achieved its greatest success in promoting the reestablishment of Japan's importance in the world arena almost entirely by economic means. The LDP has always maintained close ties to business, especially larger corporations, as well as agrarian interests and the bureaucracy. This relationship supported the development of an effective national economic policy but also encouraged corruption. Japan's substantial economic growth under the tutelage of the LDP also served to insulate the party from accountability by the voters.[45]

The LDP divided into factions immediately upon its formation in 1955. Factions consist of members of the Diet who commit themselves to the leadership of a senior party figure. To attain such a leadership position requires influential connections with the business community and the bureaucracy, and the ability to raise money. Membership in a faction is necessary not only for support in getting elected but as a channel for political advancement. Factions are also decisive in the process of selecting the party leadership, especially the party president. Top party posts are usually shared among all major factions in proportion to their strength. Factions fill the strong psychological requirement for participation in a group.[46] Membership in factions tends to be stable. Moreover, changing factions means loss of seniority, which is determined by the number of times an individual has been elected to the Diet as a member of a given faction.[47] Those who change factions find themselves in the company of others with junior standing and little influence. The opportunity to add members to a faction is found among those running for office for the first time. Factions within the LDP are not rigid, and membership in them does not preclude interaction with members of other factions. For decades, the fluidity of relations between members of different LDP factions was an important— and often the only—source of opposition and competition within the political elite.[48] The importance of the oppositional role of factions looms even larger in the context of the general weakness of interparty competition. The public, however, views factions as serving the personal ambitions of politicians rather than the public interest. The power wielded by faction leaders has less to do with their political leadership skills or expertise in areas of public policy than with their ability to raise money.[49]

On October 20, 1996, new elections to the lower house were held using for the first time the Public Office Election Law passed in 1994. In 1993, the LDP had been removed from power, and a plethora of new parties emerged. The LDP government was replaced by a seven-party coalition, a government that lasted only from April until June 1994, when a new coalition composed of the LDP, the Japan Socialist Party (JSP), and the New Party Sakigake established a government with the prime ministership going to the head of the JSP, but his party had a comparatively weak showing in the July 1995 upper house elections. The realigned government was once again headed by a member of the LDP.

For the Socialists to enter a coalition with the LDP may seem odd, given the strong left-wing ideological position long held by the JSP. But by this time, the party was trying to redefine itself. The LDP's alliance with the Socialists is probably easier to explain. For one thing, the LDP has "few, if any, inviolable principles." Since compromising on policy matters is not a problem, the LDP could do whatever was necessary to get back into power.

By the new millennium most of the new parties had either merged or simply gone out of existence. Two new parties came into being. The Democratic Party of Japan (Minshuto) was formed in 1998 through a merger of four small liberal or social-democratic parties. A new Liberal Party (Jiyuto) formed a coalition with the LDP in 1999. In the 2000 election, the LDP was once more back on top. In 2003, Jiyuto merged with the DPJ, adding momentum to the latter's rise.

The Japan Socialist Party

In the years immediately after the war, the political environment favored parties that were philosophically left of center. One factor working in favor of the left was the New Deal liberalism of the American Occupation. Progressive political groups also benefited from a purge undertaken in January 1946 that focused on the conservatives because of their association with the activities of imperial Japan. The Japan Socialist Party (JSP), established in October 1945, was the first postwar political party to form. In 1947, it led a minority government. It also augmented its power by placing its people in important positions in the bureaucracy. But the Socialists soon dissipated their strength quarreling among themselves. They had serious philosophical and organizational problems, the party had only been in existence a short time, and they had little understanding of the operation of parliament.[50] In addition, they took over a government faced with an almost insurmountable crisis: wages and prices were rising rapidly, labor was becoming increasingly militant, and there was a food shortage. The Socialists were unable to enact their agenda; the only measure they were able to get through the Diet was a watered-down program calling for state control of coal mining that passed in November 1947. Actually it only meant modernization of machinery at the taxpayers' expense, while the mines themselves were soon returned to private hands.

Throughout the 1950s the Socialists found themselves and their ideas under conservative assault. In 1952 an important legislative battle was fought against the Subversive Activities Prevention bill. This measure was nominally directed against Communists but the Socialists feared it was a potential threat to anyone with left-wing political views. The conservatives mounted an attack against one of the most important bases of Socialist strength—the teachers' union. The confrontation between conservatives and the union began in 1952 over school board elections. Later the government moved to make school board members subject to appointment by heads of local bodies rather than by election. As if they did not have enough trouble with conservative plots to undermine their strength, the Socialists suffered from other handicaps. One of these was labor union radicalism that weakened their popular appeal and even alienated some moderate elements within the party. The JSP's neutral posture vis-à-vis the excesses of the Cultural Revolution in China in the late 1960s, a matter of considerable interest to the Japanese public, cost the party additional support. Its attack on the evils of capitalism, an essential ingredient of socialist doctrine, was politically untimely, given the significant rate of economic growth that was widely beneficial to Japanese society. As a result of these and other factors, the chances of the Socialists by themselves or in league with other parties replacing the LDP declined.

By 1960, the JSP was confronted again with a split in its ranks. Many members of the party, especially younger ones, did not have ties and loyalties dating back to the prewar era. Nor did they have the unshakable faith in doctrinaire socialist principles that characterized their older colleagues. They also opposed the extremes of union pressure. These factors combined to provoke a rebellion, leading moderate elements to leave the JSP and form the Democratic Socialist Party (DSP). The DSP modeled itself on the kind of socialism found in Western Europe. It held out little attraction to the radical left; but neither did its mild socialism capture the imagination of the public. As a result, it had only limited success.

The process of redesigning the party began in earnest in January 1986 when the JSP adopted a program that explicitly renounced Soviet- and East

European–style socialism in favor of a "social democratic philosophy." Instead of references to Marxism-Leninism, the term scientific socialism was employed. Dictatorship of the proletariat was dropped in favor of workers' power.[51] At its fifty-fifth regular party convention in 1990, the party dropped from its rules language advocating "socialist revolution" in favor of "social democracy."[52] In a major retreat, the party backed away from its long-held position favoring unarmed neutrality as the basis of Japan's foreign policy.[53] They were also divided over the United States–Japan security agreement. The Self-Defense Force was a major bone of contention within the JSP, with the left wing opposing it and the rest of the party taking a more moderate view. The JSP faced a dilemma: to move closer to the center of the political spectrum and thus become a more effective electoral force seemed to compromise its principles and alienate or even drive out the left wing of the party.

In the end, that is almost what happened. After its brief fling with power in the coalition governments of the mid-1990s, the JSP changed its name to the Social Democratic Party of Japan. The left kept control of the party. It was the moderate members who broke ranks—to join the newly formed DPJ.

The Clean Government Party

The Clean Government Party, or Komeito, is the only party in postwar Japan with links to a religious organization. Its sponsor, Soka Gakkai, the laymen's affiliate of the Nicheren sect of Buddhism, was founded on November 18, 1930. Leaders of Soka Gakkai are committed to the goal of fusing Buddhism with politics. The Komeito worked toward the realization of this goal by seeking "the structural changes in society that will produce a social, economic and political environment in which *Nicheren Shoshu* can be fully accepted."[54]

Soka Gakkai first entered politics in 1955 when its cultural department put up fifty-three candidates in local elections and all but one were victorious. The Komeito was formed in 1964 but it did not enter lower house elections until 1967. The Komeito claimed to represent all people. In fact, however, the Komeito was never broadly representative of the population but reflected its parent organization's emphasis on the socially marginalized. The party appealed especially to women, younger people, unskilled workers, and those with comparatively less education.[55]

The Japan Communist Party

The Japan Communist Party (JCP) was founded on July 15, 1922, with the encouragement and financial support of the Soviet Union. The party always closely followed Moscow's lead, although the success of the Chinese Communist Revolution in 1949 also influenced the JCP's development.[56] Then in the 1980s and 1990s the party moved closer to the model of Euro-communism. This meant a political line largely independent of both Moscow and Beijing and an effort to identify itself with nationalist ideals.

The JCP has been divided between those who favor peaceful coexistence and advocates of violent revolution. A majority of the party has tended toward the former view, and present-day Communists are almost exclusively concerned with peace issues. The party has had little ideological appeal among the general public. Instead it focuses on controversial issues such as the alliance with the United States and has had some attraction for members of the peace movement.

As a party committed to an ideological position, the JCP has suffered even more than other opposition parties from the ideological neutrality of the Japanese voter. The JCP's link with the Soviet Union made it, in the view of many Japanese, a tool of a foreign power and a highly objectionable one at that. The excesses of the Cultural Revolution and the 1989 Tiananmen incident discredited Chinese communism.

In June 2003 a proposal was submitted to the Central Committee Plenum of the JCP calling for extensive revisions in the party's manifesto. The changes were significant, including the substitution of "democratic reform" for the party's goal of "socialist revolution." The phrase "U.S. imperialism," which appears in the old document thirty-two times, now appears only once. "Japanese monopoly capital," used twenty times in the old manifesto, was dropped altogether.[57]

The Democratic Party of Japan

The Democratic Party of Japan (DPJ) was formed during the politically turbulent years that followed the bursting of the Japanese financial bubble in the 1990s. For a brief period from August 1993 to June 1994, a coalition of opposition parties led by former LDP member Morihiro Hosokawa was able to form a governing majority in the lower house. In January 1994, the coalition succeeded in passing a major reform that changed the system of representation for elections to the lower house. Hosokawa and his successor, Tsotumo Hata, were, however, unable to form a stable government, and the LDP soon began its comeback. The Japan Socialist Party left the coalition of small opposition parties and entered into a coalition with the LDP and the Sakigake. When Socialist prime minister Tomiichi Murayama resigned in January 1996, worn down by a difficult year dealing with the Kobe earthquake and a deadly sarin gas attack on the Tokyo subway carried out by a bizarre

Seats Won by the LDP and the DPJ in Elections Since the 1994 Electoral Reform

Election	House	LDP	DPJ
7-23-1995	HC	110	—
6-12-1998	HC	44	27
7-29-2001*	HC	64	26
7-11-2004	HC	49	50
7-29-2007	HC	37	60
7-11-2010	HC	51	44
10-20-1996	HR	239	52
6-25-2000*	HR	223	127
11-9-2003	HR	237	177
9-11-2005	HR	296	113
8-30-2009	HR	119	308

LDP: Liberal Democratic Party: DPJ: Democratic Party of Japan; HC: House of Councillors; HR: House of Representatives.

*Effective for the 2000–2001 elections, the number of seats in the House of Councillors was 242 and the House of Representatives has 480 seats. Members of both houses are elected by a mix of local individual candidacies and a smaller share of seats awarded under proportional representation.

cult called Aum Shinrikyo ("Supreme Truth"), LDP leader Ryutaro Hashimoto took the prime ministership.

By 1998, several of the small opposition parties and their leaders had combined their forces to create an enlarged Democratic Party of Japan, intended to offer a more formidable and competitive reformist alternative to the LDP. The DPJ was clearly to the left of the LDP, but it was not a strongly ideological party—which is not surprising, given its creation out of so many small parties. It called its guiding principle "democratic centrism."

During the Koizumi years (2001–2006), the LDP (and Japan) had an energetic, effective, and—unusually for Japan—charismatic leader. But each of Koizumi's three successors held the prime ministership for only a year, and support for the LDP fell so steeply that the party postponed the next general election for as long as it could.

In 2007 the DPJ gained control of the upper house of the Diet, but the party's real breakthrough came in the 2009 general election, with a sweeping victory that gave the DPJ control of the lower house, and the prime ministership. During its brief time in power, the DPJ has not yet been able to gain a firm footing as a governing party. Prime Minister Yukio Hatoyama served for less than a year, and his successor, Naoto Kan, held on for only a bit longer, enduring criticism over what was perceived to be a passive and ineffectual response to the March 2011 disaster and the nuclear crisis at Fukushima. In September 2011, the winner of the DPJ leadership election, Yoshihiko Noda, became prime minister, pledging to "work hard" on Japan's recovery from the disaster as well as the impact of the global financial crisis.

Toward a Two-Party System?

Ever since the brief rupture of the LDP's virtual monopoly on political power in Japan, and the electoral reform enacted in January 1994, political scientists have been watching to see whether the new rules of the game would facilitate the emergence of a two-party system in Japan.[58] That may be what is happening now, but it is too soon to say that the DPJ will endure as the second major party. Not long after the DPJ took power, Reuters reported (April 5, 2010) poll results showing that half of the Japanese voting public does not consider itself affiliated with either party. The DPJ's 2009 victory was a repudiation of the LDP and a response to the DPJ's promise of reform, but it is not yet clear that the DPJ will prove itself capable of being an effective governing party.[59]

18

Contemporary Issues

The first task facing the postwar government of Japan was to lift the country out of the wreckage left in the aftermath of the war. By any measure, these efforts were a resounding success, especially in economic terms. But twenty-first-century Japan is no longer the economic dynamo that in the late 1970s seemed to be on a trajectory to surpass the United States. Today's Japan faces not only economic but demographic, social, environmental, and security challenges.

Population

Among the distinguishing characteristics of Japan is a high degree of homogeneity. Racial, linguistic, religious, and other forms of social distinction that influence politics and public policy in many countries are almost entirely lacking in Japan, although there are some small minority groups and a growing population of immigrants, mainly from other Asian countries. Class has little political significance, as about 90 percent of the population consider themselves middle class.

Another important feature of Japanese society is the age profile. The median age is increasing, as it is in most of the advanced industrial societies. The birthrate is low, and as the population ages, there are proportionally fewer workers and taxpayers to support more retirees. While this may mean there is less demand for public services such as law enforcement and education, there is more need for health care and income supports. The Japanese are also exceptionally long-lived. Japanese women have the longest life expectancy of any country in the world, around 86 years. Men, too, live longer than those in most other countries, to around 79 years.

Since awakening to the problem, Japanese governments have sought ways to encourage families to have more children, for example by spurring employers to adopt more family-friendly policies. One election pledge that the Democratic Party of Japan (DPJ) made, and kept, was to implement a per-child allowance for families with young children. The new policy had a secondary purpose, insofar as it supported consumption; but the same economic stagnation that made this aspect of the child allowance policy potentially beneficial also makes it difficult to sustain an adequate level of payments to have much impact on the birth rate. Urban Japan's high female labor-market participation rate, high cost of living, and typically small living quarters are not conducive to large families. In many other highly industrialized societies, single motherhood has become increasingly common; but this is not as true in Japan, where some eighty percent of single mothers are divorced. Female-headed households are at the bottom of the income scale. Only a third receive child support, and litigation over the issue is rare.[1]

Article 25 of the Japanese constitution states: "All people shall have the right to maintain the minimum standards of wholesome and cultured living. In all spheres of life, the State shall use its endeavors for the promotion and extension of social welfare and security, and of public health." All Japanese citizens are obliged to enroll in employment-related or publicly sponsored pension and health care systems. Contributions to public systems are on a sliding scale, and patients also pay a portion of the cost of medical services and prescriptions while the government pays the balance, a little over 70 percent. Prices are tightly regulated, with the result that coverage is nearly universal while health costs take up only about 8 percent of GDP—roughly half the level of health expenditures in the United States.

The problem with the system, in Japan as in other developed countries, is that the workforce is a declining percentage of the population, and the imbalance between contributors to and recipients of health services and pensions is growing rapidly as baby boomers retire. Meanwhile, pension funds have been negatively affected by investment losses, and no one expects future gains to be robust enough to make up for the actuarial gap. Taxes in Japan are high, and highly progressive, yet government debt is already twice the GDP. Debt is likely to rise further as the government deals with the aftermath of the Fukushima disaster.

Education

One area of public policy that has long attracted international attention is Japan's approach to education. In the nineteenth and early twentieth centuries, educational philosophy was an integral part of Japan's tightly knit sociopolitical system centered on the emperor. A high premium was placed on loyalty in this system, and education provided rigorous socialization. The government promoted orthodox beliefs and a proper public orientation toward the state. During World War II, there were even more vigorous attempts to promote ideological orthodoxy and military values. Emphasis on intellectual conformity fell heavily on education.

After the war, the American Occupation authorities sought an overhaul of the process and substance of Japanese education. Its philosophy contained three basic principles: equal opportunity, broad knowledge aimed at personal enlightenment, and respect for academic freedom and autonomy. Central-ized control of education was ended and authority transferred to elected school boards at the prefectural and major city levels.[2] American educa-tional ideas and philosophies were introduced, the curriculum was revised, and textbooks were rewritten and published by private publishing houses. Japanese conservative and nationalist circles have always pushed back on these policies. History textbooks have been an ongoing battleground. In late 2006, Prime Minister Shinzo Abe succeeded in gaining passage of revisions to the Fundamental Law of Education to, among other things, make it more reflective of traditional Japanese values and a "correct understanding" of Japanese history.

There was considerable public support for education reform, as an earlier movement to make schooling less stressful and the curriculum more flex-ible seemed to have led to a decline of Japanese students' traditionally high international rankings. For the Japanese, education is an important factor in defining social status. An important predictor of educational attainment is family, and today it is rare for a child in a family with low educational at-tainment to change his or her social position by gaining the "right kind" of education. By the same token, it is likely that a person from a family with a high-status educational background will acquire the same kind of education as have other members of the family.

The achievement of near universal literacy and high levels of educational performance, at least as measured by standardized exams, are not attributable to lavish financial support. Japan spends 3.5 percent of GDP on primary and secondary education, compared to an average figure closer to 5 percent in other industrialized countries. The most important influence in shaping overall edu-cational attainment is the general social value and expectation that everyone will be able to read. Another factor is intellectual discipline and commitment on the part of students. On the whole, Japanese students take their schooling more seriously than do their American counterparts. Even if a Japanese stu-dent has neither great intellectual curiosity nor a commitment to learning for its own sake, he or she will try hard in order to avoid the embarrassment of a poor showing.[3]

Up to high school, students are treated more or less equally. It is common for students of all ability levels to be in the same class following the same pace of instruction. Teachers and parents do not accept the notion that there are fundamental differences in ability among students. Differences in performance are not seen as the result of aptitude but of a lack of effort.

From high school on, the stress is on merit in a process designed to identify the most gifted and highly motivated.[4] The egalitarian approach to educa-tion gives way to a rigorous sorting process, in which students are grouped together on the basis of ability, motivation, and job orientation. After ninth grade, students take examinations that funnel them into senior high schools and vocational schools of varying quality. Students may have to travel some distance from home in order to attend the school of their choice. Grades and teacher recommendations count, but the most important factor is the entrance examination. Not all students, of course, are "driven" by the desire to achieve high educational status; only about 10 percent have such aspirations.[5] Students receive a heavy dose of math and science, and in these subjects they compare favorably with their counterparts anywhere in the world. Japanese students are committed to the mastery of a vast amount of material. There is a popular adage that a student who spends more than four hours sleeping will definitely not get into one of the top universities.

In both process and content the educational system is geared to the passing of examinations. "No single event, with the possible exception of marriage, determines the course of a young man's life as much as entrance examinations, and nothing, including marriage, requires as many years of planning and hard work,"[6] Ezra Vogel observed in the 1960s, and that remains largely true today. Examinations are decisive in gaining admission to the better high schools and, especially, universities. Students must begin preparing for these examinations as early as the primary grades or even before, if they ever hope to pass the entrance examination to a top university. Each university has its own examination, so failing one means that a student may try for another. The examination may also be retaken, which many do several times, hoping to gain admission to the institution of their choice. The exams themselves are of two kinds. The first is a standardized test—The Unified Screening Test—introduced in 1979 in an attempt to simplify the entrance process to national universities. It lasts one day and all students take it irrespective of which university or college they are seeking to enter. This exam was supposed to replace the exams given by individual universities. In practice, it has simply been added on as another exam, with the universities regarding it as a way of weeding out the unqualified. The second exam or series of exams is prepared by the individual universities and may take two or three days to complete.

Compared to the time and effort spent qualifying for advanced study, once having entered an institution of higher learning students discover that the demands made of them are diminished substantially. The course work is not demanding and, once admitted, a student is virtually guaranteed a diploma. The years of higher education for students are more like a welcome pause before entering the pressured environment of employment and married life. By contrast, in the United States, getting into college may be relatively easy but getting through is another matter. Fewer than 50 percent of those who enter American colleges and universities ever receive a bachelor's degree.

The issue of educational quality at the university level is a matter of serious concern, given the fact that the knowledge race is not only accelerating but has more participants. Japan achieved its advanced industrial status by buying many technologies from abroad and making successful commercial applications out of them; the focus was on engineering. Since the 1990s, more attention has been devoted to the promotion of technological innovation, research and development, and theoretical or basic science.

Environmental Issues

Nowadays people think first of China when it comes to environmental degradation, air and water pollution, toxic waste dumping, and the selling of food or other products containing deadly chemicals. During its industrial high-growth years in the 1950s and 1960s, water supplies and air poisoned by toxic chemical wastes took a heavy human toll in Japan. In 1971 an Environmental Agency was established; in 2001 it was raised to the cabinet level as the Ministry of Environment. Over these decades, real progress has been made in pollution control.

The greatest environmental disaster to hit Japan occurred in March 2011, when a massive earthquake and tsunami destroyed the nuclear power complex at Fukushima in northeast Japan, causing nuclear meltdown and radiation contamination of the surrounding area. Postwar Japan, having experienced the devastating effects of atomic power after the bombings of Hiroshima and Nagasaki in 1945, renounced any future effort to develop atomic weapons. But the country embraced nuclear power as a way to compensate for its lack of oil and gas resources. Before the accident at Fukushima, Japan relied on nuclear energy for 30 percent of its electric power. That created powerful incentives for companies and the government to resist pressures to increase and strictly enforce safety requirements for the siting, building, and operation of nuclear power plants, in consideration of the country's seismic risks. Today Japan faces the enormous costs of cleaning up the devastation in the northeast and resettling those who will never be able to return to their homes. The larger question is the future of nuclear power in Japan and the potentials for development of alternative energy sources.[7]

Foreign Relations

The legacy of the war endures as a theme not only in Japan's domestic politics but in its relations with its neighbors, particularly those that were subject to colonial domination or wartime occupation by Japanese forces. As Japan set about reestablishing international diplomatic ties and trade relations, it became necessary to issue apologies and expressions of regret for damage done. Even Prime Minister Junichiro Koizumi, a nationalist, made such statements on several occasions, but he also reignited old angers by making annual visits to the Yasukuni Shrine, in Tokyo, a Shinto memorial to those who died in service of the empire, including some of the top war criminals executed by the Allied Forces after the war. Another recurring irritant is the treatment of the war in some Japanese history textbooks that downplay, ignore, or deny wartime atrocities and Japan's role as aggressor. While the U.S.-Japan alliance has endured, trade frictions have caused considerable tensions at times.

Relations with Neighbors

Physical isolation and the absence of desirable commodities, resources, and market potential helped spare Japan from foreign invasion and exploitation. To accomplish its own economic modernization, however, Japan needed to rely on external sources of supply for raw materials.[8] The effort to accomplish this goal through military conquest culminated in Japan's defeat in 1945.

Once the Occupation ended in 1952, Japan initiated a cautious campaign to rebuild its overseas connections. From the very outset, these overtures had a decidedly trade-oriented character. The Japanese signed a treaty with Taiwan in 1952 and made sizable investments that partially offset the demand for reparations. Reparations were paid to some countries, such as Burma in 1954, while agreements were reached with other countries under which they would receive quantities of capital goods: the Philippines, 1956; Indonesia, 1958; Laos and Cambodia, 1959; Thailand, 1962; and South Korea, 1965. These agreements helped smooth the way to the opening and development of markets in Southeast Asia. Restoring normal relations, however, proved difficult, because the acts of brutality committed by the Japanese army against the people of conquered Asian countries had left a legacy that was difficult to overcome.[9] Even though decades have passed since the end of the war, distrust of the Japanese endures in many Asian countries.

It was particularly desirable for Japan to establish good relations with the People's Republic China, given its size, its population, and its drive for economic development. From the end of the war to the 1970s, however, relations between the two countries were minimal. This was not because of Japan's history of aggression so much as the fact that Japan was obliged to align with U.S. foreign policy. Washington officially regarded the Communist takeover of China as illegitimate and maintained that the "legal" government of China was the Nationalist regime on Taiwan. Meanwhile, China, having broken with the Soviet Union in 1960, had few friends and seemed little interested in acquiring any. Two things changed all this. One was the restructuring of

America's cold war foreign policy, in order to outflank the Soviet Union as the United States was secretly negotiating an end to the Vietnam War. President Richard Nixon traveled to China in February 1972, and the two countries proclaimed the goal of normalizing relations. The second impetus to change was the death of Mao Zedong in 1976, and the decision of his successors to prioritize national development.

Under these altered circumstances, Japan opened diplomatic relations with China. Two agreements were signed in 1978: the Sino-Japanese Treaty of Peace and Friendship and the Sino-Japanese Long Term Trade Agreement. These agreements facilitated the development of commercial links between the two countries and significant direct investment by Japanese. Despite some fits and starts, China today is Japan's largest export market. China recently surpassed Japan to become the world's second largest economy (when it comes to per capita GDP, however, Japan at $34,000 is more than four and a half times greater than China at a little over $7,500).

On the political level, relations have been rockier, as each country is highly suspicious of the other's regional ambitions. The Japanese are concerned about China's military modernization efforts and its rapid buildup of naval power. Meanwhile Japan's alliance with the United States and steady expansion of its own defense capabilities—which today are quiet robust—fuel distrust in Beijing.

China's growing military strength has not been the only catalyst for Japan's efforts to enhance its security. Another has been the unpredictable and frequently provocative behavior of North Korea, now presumed to be building nuclear weapons capacity that threatens both South Korea and Japan.[10] This has spurred Japan to joint development of anti-missile defense systems with the United States.

After North Korea withdrew from the Nuclear Non-Proliferation Treaty in 2003, China, Japan, South Korea, the Russian Federation, and the United States launched a series of "six-party talks" to attempt to negotiate an agreement with North Korea to shut down its nuclear facilities. To date, the talks have been unavailing. In 2009 North Korea resumed its military provocations as well as its nuclear program, expelled nuclear inspectors, and announced that it had pulled out of the talks. As the post–Kim Jong Il transition unfolds, it is impossible to predict how the opaque North Korean regime will conduct foreign relations.

Although relations between Japan and South Korea continue to be clouded by lingering resentment of Japan's harsh colonial regime as well as its greater economic clout, the two U.S. allies face many of the same external threats and may find their way to closer cooperation in the future.

Japan's relations with Russia are vexed by an ongoing territorial dispute.

Japan had signed a neutrality pact with the Soviet Union in April 1941, but on August 8, 1945, the Soviets entered the war on the side of the United States and its allies, and pushed into Manchuria, Inner Mongolia, northern Korea, southern Sakhalin, and the Kuril Islands. Japan views the Soviet entry into the war as opportunistic. The Soviets further added to Japanese ire by prolonging their advance into September, after the emperor's surrender statement of August 15. Soviet brutality against Japanese nationals in captured territory and the detention of nearly 600,000 prisoners of war, in some cases for years, contributed to Japanese bitterness toward the Russians. The Soviet Union refused to sign the Treaty of Peace with Japan in 1951, citing numerous objections, but in 1954, the Soviet Union announced it was prepared to normalize relations with Japan. After extensive and difficult negotiations, all outstanding issues between the two countries were settled with the exception of the territorial question. In a joint declaration issued on October 19, 1956, the state of war was ended and normal diplomatic relations were established.[11]

Relations between the two countries have remained chilly into the post-Soviet period, despite Japan's interest in participating in the development of the Russian Far East. The region is rich in natural resources, but Russia's financial and technical capability to develop them fully is lacking. The Japanese frequently express interest in the possibilities of investment in the region, but little has actually been accomplished for several reasons, including the unresolved Northern Territories issue.

Japan lost many territories as a result of World War II. Taiwan, which it had controlled for five decades, reverted to China. The Koreans achieved their independence from Japanese colonial rule in 1945. The United States occupied Okinawa, which it returned in 1972, and a host of lesser islands in the Pacific. Japan dropped its claim to southern Sakhalin in the 1952 peace treaty, without recognizing Soviet annexation of the territory. The Soviets also took those islands in the Kuril chain under Japanese control and repatriated the 16,000 Japanese citizens living there. The Japanese consider four of the islands—Etorofu, Kunashiri, Shikotan, and Habomai—legitimately theirs, and they continue to seek their return. Japanese interest in the islands is sharpened by the fact that they are located in one of the world's richest fishing areas, but their main significance is their strategic location and their relevance to Japanese national pride.

Until 1988, the Soviets refused to accept the idea that the Kuril issue was something dividing the two countries. A Soviet "peace offensive" in Asia, the pressing need for Japanese financial and technical help for Soviet economic reforms, and a proposed visit by President Mikhail Gorbachev to Japan in spring 1991 briefly created an atmosphere in which it seemed that some movement on the Northern Territories issue was possible, but that hope died with the end of the Soviet Union. Russia shows no interest in reopening the issue today.

Relations with the United States

The first concern of the Occupation authorities in postwar Japan was to end permanently the country's capacity for military aggression. Article 9 of Chapter II of the constitution that took effect in 1947 reads:

> Aspiring sincerely to an international peace based on justice and order, the Japanese people forever renounce war as a sovereign right of the nation and the threat or use of force as means of settling international disputes.
>
> In order to accomplish the aim of the preceding paragraph, land, sea, and air forces, as well as other war potential, will never be maintained. The right of belligerency of the state will not be recognized.

After the Communist victory over Chiang Kaishek in China and the breakout of war in Korea, however, the United States rethought the problem of Japan's vulnerability, to the extent of urging Japan to establish self-defense forces. The United States guaranteed Japan's security in a 1951 Mutual Security Treaty, a Mutual Defense Assistance Agreement signed in 1954, and a Treaty of Mutual Cooperation and Security signed in 1960, providing for an ongoing U.S. military presence in Japan. Today that presence numbers approximately 40,000 military personnel concentrated in bases on Okinawa (returned to Japanese control in 1972). Local dissatisfaction with the heavy presence of U.S. troops, who are immune from criminal prosecution, has been a heated political issue. Japan shares the cost of maintaining these U.S. forces.

Although Japanese majority opinion has long embraced pacificism, the strictures of Article 9 have been reevaluated and retested as circumstances have changed. In a controversial move that seemed to test the constitutional limits, Prime Minister Koizumi, a strong supporter of U.S. President George Bush's Global War on Terror, committed Japan's Self-Defense Forces to support missions in both Iraq and Afghanistan. Less controversial has been the recognition that Japan needs to fortify itself against the rising power of China and the rogue behavior of North Korea. In January 2007, Japan's Defense Agency was elevated to cabinet status as the Ministry of Defense, with support from both the Liberal Democratic Party and the Democratic Party of Japan.

The renewal of the Japan-U.S. military alliance in 1960 was strongly opposed both by the nationalist right and the neutralist left. That opposition softened over time, especially after U.S. President Richard Nixon laid out what became known as the "Nixon Doctrine" in a televised speech delivered on November 3, 1969. In the president's own words:

> First, the United States will keep all of its treaty commitments.
> Second, we shall provide a shield if a nuclear power threatens the freedom of a nation allied with us or of a nation whose survival we consider vital to our security.
> Third, in cases involving other types of aggression, we shall furnish military and economic assistance when requested in accordance with our treaty commitments. But we shall look to the nation directly threatened to assume the primary responsibility of providing the manpower for its defense.

At that time, Japan's export economy was prospering, while the United States was preoccupied with seeking ways to withdraw from the war in Southeast Asia and open up relations with China. These developments promised to loosen the U.S. reins and make it easier for the Japanese to pursue their own interests—which they proceeded to do. This would soon lead to a new kind of tension with the United States.

Under Japan's export-led economic growth model, domestic consumption was kept low and high rates of savings were channeled into high rates of investment in strategically targeted industries. While the exchange rate was used to keep the yen undervalued and the prices of exported products artificially low, protectionist measures kept the domestic market shielded from price-competitive imports. This strategy was so effective that, by the late 1970s and early 1980s, Japan's exports dwarfed imports, and Japanese companies had "virtually taken over the U.S. textile, radio, recorder, television, shoe, and machine tool industries and were making big inroads in the auto, heavy machinery, tire, semiconductor, computer, telecommunications, steel, and other advanced industries."[12]

To some extent, American trade problems are self-inflicted. In the 1950s and 1960s, the United States, in the interest of containing the Soviet Union, pursued a policy of promoting solidarity among its allies. One aspect of this solidarity was to restrict trade with the Soviet Bloc. As an inducement to cooperate with this policy, the United States allowed its trade partners access to the American market while permitting these partners to retain barriers to American goods.[13] At the time, America's trade partners were so weak and the United States so strong that this was not seen as a serious problem. But as America's allies prospered, trade imbalances grew, and the United States shifted from a creditor to a debtor nation. Needless to say, this was extremely distressing to the United States and led to continuous efforts to renegotiate the rules of the game, particularly "fair trade" and exchange rate issues—the same issues that today cause friction between the United States and China. In January 1995, both the United States and Japan became members of the newly founded World Trade Organization, which was founded to promote liberalization and transparency of trade policies and serve as a forum for dispute resolution. The People's Republic of China won admission five years later, in 2000.

Americans have long believed that Japan suppresses imports by means of non-tariff barriers, while the Japanese have seen U.S. difficulties as resulting from too much spending, too little saving, and poor quality standards attributable in part to poor public education. For their part, Japanese governments see it as their responsibility to gain competitive advantages for Japanese producers rather than making it easier for foreign companies to make inroads in the Japanese market.

Today, Japan, like China, effectively subsidizes U.S. deficits by accepting dollars as payment and reinvesting those dollars back in the United States.[14] Meanwhile, Americans tend to lose sight of the fact that Japan, quite unlike the United States, is highly dependent on imports for its most critical needs: raw materials, energy, and even food.

Appendices

The appendices reproduce the preambles and initial chapters of the current constitutions of the People's Republic of China, the Republic of Korea (South Korea), the Democratic People's Republic of Korea (North Korea), and Japan. Constitutional amendments and revisions are provided or described.

These excerpts were selected as official statements of general principles and, as such, revealing of the nature of the regimes. Comparing them is a worthwhile exercise. The full texts of the constitutional documents, including the provisions describing institutional and other arrangements, may be easily accessed online.

APPENDIX 1

The Constitution of the People's Republic of China

The Chinese Constitution excerpted here is that of December 4, 1982, as translated in People's Daily. *It is interesting to note that the 1982 Constitution largely restores the governing structures laid out in the first, 1954 Constitution. The intervening 1975 Constitution reflected the institutional ruptures of the Cultural Revolution period; the 1978 Constitution was a transitional document drafted after Mao's death in 1976. The 1982 Constitution, including the Preamble and Chapter I: General Principles, as reproduced here, has been amended four times. Amendments to the relevant sections of the 1982 text can be found below the excerpts. The amendments are well worth reading as documentation of China's rapid changes.*

PREAMBLE

China is one of the countries with the longest histories in the world. The people of all nationalities in China have jointly created a splendid culture and have a glorious revolutionary tradition.

Feudal China was gradually reduced after 1840 to a semi-colonial and semi-feudal country. The Chinese people waged wave upon wave of heroic struggles for national independence and liberation and for democracy and freedom.

Great and earth-shaking historical changes have taken place in China in the 20th century.

The Revolution of 1911, led by Dr Sun Yat-sen, abolished the feudal monarchy and gave birth to the Republic of China. But the Chinese people had yet to fulfill their historical task of overthrowing imperialism and feudalism.

After waging hard, protracted and tortuous struggles, armed and otherwise, the Chinese people of all nationalities led by the Communist Party of China with Chairman Mao Zedong as its leader ultimately, in 1949, overthrew the rule of imperialism, feudalism and bureaucrat capitalism, won the great victory of the new-democratic revolution and founded the People's Republic of China. Thereupon the Chinese people took state power into their own hands and became masters of the country.

After the founding of the People's Republic, the transition of Chinese society from a new-democratic to a socialist society was effected step by step. The socialist transformation of the private ownership of the means of production was completed, the system of exploitation of man by man eliminated and the socialist system established. The people's democratic dictatorship led by the working class and based on the alliance of workers and peasants, which is in essence the dictatorship of the proletariat, has been consolidated and developed. The Chinese people and the Chinese People's Liberation Army have thwarted aggression, sabotage and armed provocations by imperialists and hegemonists, safeguarded China's national independence and security and strengthened its national defense. Major successes have been achieved in economic development. An independent and fairly comprehensive socialist system of industry has in the main been established. There has been a marked increase in agricultural production. Significant progress has been made in educational, scientific, cultural and other undertakings, and socialist ideological education has yielded noteworthy results. The living standards of the people have improved considerably.

Both the victory of China's new-democratic revolution and the successes of its socialist cause have been achieved by the Chinese people of all nationalities under the leadership of the Communist Party of China and the guidance of Marxism-Leninism and Mao Zedong Thought, and by upholding truth, correcting errors and overcoming numerous difficulties and hardships. The basic task of the nation in the years to come is to concentrate its effort on socialist modernization. Under the leadership of the Communist Party of China and the guidance of Marxism- Leninism and Mao Zedong Thought, the Chinese people of all nationalities will continue to adhere to the people's democratic dictatorship and follow the socialist road, steadily improve socialist institutions, develop socialist democracy, improve the socialist legal system and work hard and self-reliantly to modernize industry, agriculture, national defense and science and technology step by step to turn China into a socialist country with a high level of culture and democracy.

The exploiting classes as such have been eliminated in our country. However, class struggle will continue to exist within certain limits for a long time to come. The Chinese people must fight against those forces and elements, both at home and abroad, that are hostile to China's socialist system and try to undermine it.

Taiwan is part of the sacred territory of the People's Republic of China. It is the lofty duty of the entire Chinese people, including our compatriots in Taiwan, to accomplish the great task of reunifying the motherland.

In building socialism it is imperative to rely on the workers, peasants and intellectuals and unite with all the forces that can be united. In the long years of revolution and construction, there has been formed under the leadership of the Communist Party of China a broad patriotic united front that is composed of democratic parties and people's organizations and embraces all socialist working people, all patriots who support socialism and all patriots who stand for reunification of the motherland. This united front will continue to be consolidated and developed. The Chinese People's Political Consultative Conference is a broadly representative organization of the united front, which has played a significant historical role and will continue to do so in the political and social life of the country, in promoting friendship with the people of other countries and in the struggle for socialist modernization and for the reunification and unity of the country.

The People's Republic of China is a unitary multi-national state built up jointly by the people of all its nationalities. Socialist relations of equality, unity and mutual assistance have been established among them and will continue to be strengthened. In the struggle to safeguard the unity of the nationalities, it is necessary to combat big-nation chauvinism, mainly Han chauvinism, and also necessary to combat local-national chauvinism. The state does its utmost to promote the common prosperity of all nationalities in the country.

China's achievements in revolution and construction are inseparable from support by the people of the world. The future of China is closely linked with that of the whole world. China adheres to an independent foreign policy as well as to the five principles of mutual respect for sovereignty and territorial integrity, mutual non-aggression, non-interference in each other's internal affairs, equality and mutual benefit, and peaceful coexistence in developing diplomatic relations and economic and cultural exchanges with other countries; China consistently opposes imperialism, hegemonism and colonialism, works to strengthen unity with the people of other countries, supports the oppressed nations and the developing countries in their just struggle to win and preserve national independence and develop their national economies, and strives to safeguard world peace and promote the cause of human progress.

This Constitution affirms the achievements of the struggles of the Chinese people of all nationalities and defines the basic system and basic tasks of the state in legal form; it is the fundamental law of the state and has supreme legal authority. The people of all nationalities, all state organs, the armed forces, all political parties and public organizations and all enterprises and undertakings in the country must take the Constitution as the basic norm of conduct, and they have the duty to uphold the dignity of the Constitution and ensure its implementation.

CHAPTER I. GENERAL PRINCIPLES

Article 1. The People's Republic of China is a socialist state under the people's democratic dictatorship led by the working class and based on the alliance of workers and peasants. The socialist system is the basic system of the People's Republic of China. Sabotage of the socialist system by any organization or individual is prohibited.

Article 2. All power in the People's Republic of China belongs to the people. The organs through which the people exercise state power are the National People's Congress and the local people's congresses at different levels. The people administer state affairs and manage economic, cultural and social affairs through various channels and in various ways in accordance with the law.

Article 3. The state organs of the People's Republic of China apply the principle of democratic centralism. The National People's Congress and the local people's congresses at different levels are instituted through democratic election. They are responsible to the people and subject to their supervision. All administrative, judicial and procuratorial organs of the state are created by the people's congresses to which they are responsible and under whose supervision they operate. The division of functions and powers between the central and local state organs is guided by the principle of giving full play to the initiative and enthusiasm of the local authorities under the unified leadership of the central authorities.

Article 4. All nationalities in the People's Republic of China are equal. The state protects the lawful rights and interests of the minority nationalities and upholds and develops the relationship of equality, unity and mutual assistance among all of China's nationalities. Discrimination against and oppression of any nationality are prohibited; any acts that undermine the unity of the nationalities or instigate their secession are prohibited. The state helps the areas inhabited by minority nationalities speed up their economic and cultural development in accordance with the peculiarities and needs of the different minority nationalities. Regional autonomy is practiced in areas where people of minority nationalities live in compact communities; in these areas organs of self- government are established for the exercise of the right of autonomy. All the national autonomous areas are inalienable parts of the People's Republic of China. The people of all nationalities have the freedom to use and develop their own spoken and written languages, and to preserve or reform their own ways and customs.

Article 5. The state upholds the uniformity and dignity of the socialist legal system. No law or administrative or local rules and regulations shall contravene the constitution. All state organs, the armed forces, all political parties and public organizations and all enterprises and undertakings must abide by the Constitution and the law. All acts in violation of the Constitution and the law must be investigated. No organization or individual may enjoy the privilege of being above the Constitution and the law.

Article 6. The basis of the socialist economic system of the People's Republic of China is socialist public ownership of the means of production, namely, ownership by the whole people and collective ownership by the working people. The system of socialist public ownership supersedes the system of exploitation of man by man; it applies the principle of 'from each according to his ability, to each according to his work.

Article 7. The state economy is the sector of socialist economy under ownership by the whole people; it is the leading force in the national economy. The state ensures the consolidation and growth of the state economy.

Article 8. Rural people's communes, agricultural producers' co-operatives, and other forms of co- operative economy such as producers' supply and marketing, credit and consumers co-operatives, belong to the sector of socialist economy under collective ownership by the working people. Working people who are members of rural economic collectives have the right, within the limits prescribed by law, to farm private plots of cropland and hilly land, engage in household sideline production and raise privately owned livestock. The various forms of co-operative economy in the cities and towns, such as those in the handicraft, industrial, building, transport, commercial and service trades, all belong to the sector of socialist economy under collective ownership by the working people. The state protects the lawful rights and interests of the urban and rural economic collectives and encourages, guides and helps the growth of the collective economy.

Article 9. Mineral resources, waters, forests, mountains, grassland, unreclaimed land, beaches and other natural resources are owned by the state, that is, by the whole people, with the exception of the forests, mountains, grassland, unreclaimed land and beaches that are owned by collectives in accordance with the law. The state ensures the rational use of natural resources and protects rare animals and plants. The appropriation or damage of natural resources by any organization or individual by whatever means is prohibited.

Article 10. Land in the cities is owned by the state. Land in the rural and suburban areas is owned by collectives except for those portions which belong to the state in accordance with the law; house sites and private plots of cropland and hilly land are also owned by collectives. The state may in the public interest take over land for its use in accordance with the law. No organization or individual may appropriate, buy, sell or lease land, or unlawfully transfer land in other ways. All organizations and individuals who use land must make rational use of the land.

Article 11. The individual economy of urban and rural working people, operated within the limits prescribed by law, is a complement to the socialist public economy. The state protects the lawful rights and interests of the individual economy. The state guides, helps and supervises the individual economy by exercising administrative control.

Article 12. Socialist public property is sacred and inviolable. The state protects socialist public property. Appropriation or damage of state or collective property by any organization or individual by whatever means is prohibited.

Article 13. The state protects the right of citizens to own lawfully earned income, savings, houses and other lawful property. The state protects by law the right of citizens to inherit private property.

Article 14. The state continuously raises labor productivity, improves economic results and develops the productive forces by enhancing the enthusiasm of the working people, raising the level of their technical skill, disseminating advanced science and technology, improving the systems of economic administration and enterprise operation and management, instituting the socialist system of responsibility in various forms and improving organization of work. The state practices strict economy and combats waste. The state properly apportions accumulation and consumption, pays attention to the interests of the collective and the individual as well as of the state and, on the basis of expanded production, gradually improves the material and cultural life of the people.

Article 15. The state practices economic planning on the basis of socialist public ownership. It ensures the proportionate and co-ordinated growth of the national economy through overall balancing by economic planning and the supplementary role of regulation by the market. Disturbance of the orderly functioning of the social economy or disruption of the state economic plan by any organization or individual is prohibited.

Article 16. State enterprises have decision-making power in operation and management within the limits prescribed by law, on condition that they submit to unified leadership by the state and fulfill all their obligations under the state plan. State enterprises practice democratic management through congresses of workers and staff and in other ways in accordance with the law.

Article 17. Collective economic organizations have decision-making power in conducting independent economic activities, on condition that they accept the guidance of the state plan and abide by the relevant laws. Collective economic organizations practice democratic management in accordance with the law, with the entire body of their workers electing or removing their managerial personnel and deciding on major issues concerning operation and management.

Article 18. The People's Republic of China permits foreign enterprises, other foreign economic organizations and individual foreigners to invest in China and to enter into various forms of economic co-operation with Chinese enterprises and other economic organizations in accordance with the law of the People's Republic of China. All foreign enterprises and other foreign economic organizations in China, as well as joint ventures with Chinese and foreign investment located in China, shall abide by the law of the People's Republic of China. Their lawful rights and interests are protected by the law of the People's Republic of China.

Article 19. The state develops socialist educational undertakings and works to raise the scientific and cultural level of the whole nation. The state runs schools of various types, makes primary education compulsory and universal, develops secondary, vocational and higher education and promotes pre-school education. The state develops educational facilities of various types in order to wipe out illiteracy and provide political, cultural, scientific, technical and professional education for workers, peasants, state functionaries and other working people. It encourages people to become educated through self- study. The state encourages the collective economic organizations, state enterprises and undertakings and other social forces to set up educational institutions of various types in accordance with the law.

The state promotes the nationwide use of Putonghua (common speech based on Beijing pronunciation).

Article 20. The state promotes the development of the natural and social sciences, disseminates scientific and technical knowledge, and commends and rewards achievements in scientific research as well as technological discoveries and inventions.

Article 21. The state develops medical and health services, promotes modern medicine and traditional Chinese medicine, encourages and supports the setting up of various medical and health facilities by the rural economic collectives, state enterprises and undertakings and neighborhood organizations, and promotes sanitation activities of a mass character, all to protect the people's health. The state develops physical culture and promotes mass sports activities to build up the people's physique.

Article 22. The state promotes the development of literature and art, the press, broadcasting and television undertakings, publishing and distribution services, libraries, museums, cultural centres and other cultural undertakings, that serve the people and socialism, and sponsors mass cultural activities. The state protects places of scenic and historical interest, valuable cultural monuments and relics and other important items of China's historical and cultural heritage.

Article 23. The state trains specialized personnel in all fields who serve socialism, increases the number of intellectuals and creates conditions to give full scope to their role in socialist modernization.

Article 24. The state strengthens the building of socialist spiritual civilization through spreading education in high ideals and morality, general education and education in discipline and the legal system, and through promoting the formulation and observance of rules of conduct and common pledges by different sections of the people in urban and rural areas. The state advocates the civic virtues of love for the motherland, for the people, for labor, for science and for socialism; it educates the people in patriotism, collectivism, internationalism and communism and in dialectical and historical materialism; it combats the decadent ideas of capitalism and feudalism and other decadent ideas.

Article 25. The state promotes family planning so that population growth may fit the plans for economic and social development.

Article 26. The state protects and improves the living environment and the ecological environment, and prevents and controls pollution and other public hazards. The state organizes and encourages afforestation and the protection of forests.

Article 27. All state organs carry out the principle of simple and efficient administration, the system of responsibility for work and the system of training functionaries and appraising their work in order constantly to improve quality of work and efficiency and combat bureaucratism. All state organs and functionaries must rely on the support of the people, keep in close touch with them, heed their opinions and suggestions, accept their supervision and work hard to serve them.

Article 28. The state maintains public order and suppresses treasonable and other counter- revolutionary activities; it penalizes actions that endanger public security and disrupt the socialist economy and other criminal activities, and punishes and reforms criminals.

Article 29. The armed forces of the People's Republic of China belong to the people. Their tasks are to strengthen national defense, resist aggression, defend the motherland, safeguard the people's peaceful labor, participate in national reconstruction, and work hard to serve the people. The state strengthens the revolutionization, modernization and regularization of the armed forces in order to increase the national defense capability.

Article 30. The administrative division of the People's Republic of China is as follows: (1) The country is divided into provinces, autonomous regions and municipalities directly under the Central Government; (2) Provinces and autonomous regions are divided into autonomous prefectures, counties, autonomous counties and cities; (3) Counties and autonomous counties are divided into townships, nationality townships and towns. Municipalities directly under the Central Government and other large cities are divided into districts and counties. Autonomous prefectures are divided into counties, autonomous counties, and cities. All autonomous regions, autonomous prefectures and autonomous counties are national autonomous areas.

Article 31. The state may establish special administrative regions when necessary. The systems to be instituted in special administrative regions shall be prescribed by law enacted by the National People's Congress in the light of the specific conditions.

Article 32. The People's Republic of China protects the lawful rights and interests of foreigners within Chinese territory, and while on Chinese territory foreigners must abide by the law of the People's Republic of China. The People's Republic of China may grant asylum to foreigners who request it for political reasons.

Amendments to the 1982 Constitution

AMENDMENT ONE

(Approved on April 12, 1988, by the 7th National
People's Congress at its 1st Session)

1. Article 11 of the Constitution shall include a new paragraph which reads: "The State permits the private sector of the economy to exist and develop within the limits prescribed by law. The private sector of the economy is a complement to the socialist public economy. The State protects the lawful rights and interests of the private sector of the economy, and exercises guidance, supervision and control over the private sector of the economy."

2. The fourth paragraph of Article 10 of the Constitution, which provides that "no organization or individual may appropriate, buy, sell or lease land or otherwise engage in the transfer of land by unlawful means," shall be amended as: "no organization or individual may appropriate, buy, sell or otherwise engage in the transfer of land by unlawful means. The right to the use of land may be transferred according to law."

AMENDMENT TWO

(Approved on March 29, 1993, by the 8th National
People's Congress at its 1st Session)

3. The last two sentences of the seventh paragraph of the Preamble which reads "The basic task of the nation in the years to come is to concentrate its effort on socialist modernization. Under the leadership of the Communist Party of China and the guidance of Marxism-Leninism and Mao Zedong Thought, the Chinese people of all nationalities will continue to adhere to the people's democratic dictatorship and follow the socialist road, steadily improve socialist institutions, develop socialist democracy, improve the socialist legal system and work hard and self-reliantly to modernize industry, agriculture, national defense and science and technology step by step to turn China into a socialist

country with a high level of culture and democracy," shall be amended as: "China is at the primary stage of socialism. The basic task of the nation is, according to the theory of building socialism with Chinese characteristics, to concentrate its effort on socialist modernization. Under the leadership of the Communist Party of China and the guidance of Marxism-Leninism and Mao Zedong Thought, the Chinese people of all nationalities will continue to adhere to the people's democratic dictatorship and follow the socialist road, persevere in reform and opening to the outside, steadily improve socialist institutions, develop socialist democracy, improve the socialist legal system and work hard and self-reliantly to modernize industry, agriculture, national defense and science and technology step by step to turn China into a socialist country with prosperity and power, democracy and culture."

4. At the end of the tenth paragraph of the Preamble, add "The system of multi-party cooperation and political consultation led by the Communist Party of China will exist and develop in China for a long time to come."

5. Article 7 which reads "The State economy is the sector of socialist economy under ownership by the whole people; it is the leading force in the national economy. The State ensures the consolidation and growth of the State economy," shall be changed to: "The State-owned economy, that is, the socialist economy under ownership by the whole people, is the leading force in the national economy. The State ensures the consolidation and growth of the State-owned economy."

6. The first item of Article 8 which reads "Rural people's communes, agricultural producers' cooperatives, and other forms of cooperative economy such as producers', supply and marketing, credit and consumers' cooperatives, belong to the sector of socialist economy under collective ownership by the working people. Working people who are members of rural economic collectives have the right, within the limits prescribed by law, to farm plots of cropland and hilly land allotted for private use, engage in household sideline production and raise privately-owned livestock," shall be amended as: "Rural household-based contract responsibility system with remuneration linked to output, and other forms of cooperative economy such as producers', supply and marketing, credit and consumers' cooperatives, belong to the sector of socialist economy under collective ownership by the working people. Working people who are members of rural economic collectives have the right, within the limits prescribed by law, to farm plots of cropland and hilly land allotted for private use, engage in household sideline production and raise privately-owned livestock."

7. Article 15 which reads "The State practices economic planning on the basis of socialist public ownership. It ensures the proportionate and coordinated growth of the national economy through overall balancing by economic planning and the supplementary role of regulation by the market. Disturbance of the orderly functioning of the social economy or disruption of the State economic plan by any organization or individual is prohibited," shall be changed to: "The state has put into practice a socialist market economy. The State strengthens formulating economic laws, improves macro adjustment and control and forbids according to law any units or individuals from interfering with the social economic order."

8. Article 16 which reads "State enterprises have decision-making power in operation and management within the limits prescribed by law, on condition that they submit to unified leadership by the State and fulfill and their obligations under the State plan. State enterprises practice democratic management through congresses of workers and staff and in other ways in accordance with the law," shall be revised as: "Stated-owned enterprises have decision-making power in operation and management within the limits prescribed by law. State-owned enterprises practice democratic management through congresses of workers and staff and in other ways in accordance with the law."

9. Article 17 which reads "Collective economic organizations have decision-making power in conducting independent economic activities, on condition that they accept the guidance of the State plan and abide by the relevant laws. Collective economic organizations practice democratic management in accordance with the law, with the entire body of their workers electing or removing their managerial personnel and deciding on major issues concerning operation and management," shall be amended as: "Collective economic organizations have decision-making power in conducting independent economic activities, on condition that they abide by the relevant laws. Collective economic organizations practice democratic management, elect or remove their managerial personnel and decide on major issue concerning operation and management according to law."

AMENDMENT THREE

(Approved on March 15, 1999, by the 9th National
People's Congress at its 2nd Session)

The original text of paragraph seven in the Preamble of the Constitution is: "Both the victory of China's new-democratic revolution and the successes of its socialist cause have been achieved by the Chinese people of all nationalities under the leadership of the Communist Party of China and the guidance of

Marxism-Leninism and Mao Zedong Thought, and by upholding truth, correcting errors and overcoming numerous difficulties and hardships. China is currently in the primary stage of socialism. The basic task of the nation is to concentrate its effort on socialist modernization in accordance with the theory of building socialism with Chinese characteristics. Under the leadership of the Communist Party of China and the guidance of Marxism-Leninism and Mao Zedong Thought, the Chinese people of all nationalities will continue to adhere to the people's democratic dictatorship, follow the socialist road, persist in reform and opening-up, steadily improve socialist institutions, develop socialist democracy, improve the socialist legal system and work hard and self-reliantly to modernize industry, agriculture, national defense and science and technology step by step to turn China into a powerful and prosperous socialist country with a high level of culture and democracy."

It is revised into: "Both the victory of China's new-democratic revolution and the successes of its socialist cause have been achieved by the Chinese people of all nationalities under the leadership of the Communist Party of China and the guidance of Marxism-Leninism and Mao Zedong Thought, and by upholding truth, correcting errors and overcoming numerous difficulties and hardships. China will stay in the primary stage of socialism for a long period of time. The basic task of the nation is to concentrate its efforts on socialist modernization by following the road of building socialism with Chinese characteristics. Under the leadership of the Communist Party of China and the guidance of Marxism-Leninism, Mao Zedong Thought and Deng Xiaoping Theory, the Chinese people of all nationalities will continue to adhere to the people's democratic dictatorship, follow the socialist road, persist in reform and opening-up, steadily improve socialist institutions, develop a socialist market economy, advance socialist democracy, improve the socialist legal system and work hard and self-reliantly to modernize industry, agriculture, national defense and science and technology step by step to turn China into a powerful and prosperous socialist country with a high level of culture and democracy."

One section is added to Article Five of the Constitution as the first section: "The People's Republic of China practices ruling the country in accordance with the law and building a socialist country of law."

The original text of Article Six of the Constitution is: "The basis of the socialist economic system of the People's Republic of China is socialist public ownership of the means of production, namely, ownership by the whole people and collective ownership by the working people." "The system of socialist public ownership supersedes the system of exploitation of man by man; it applies the principle of 'from each according to his ability, to each according to his work'."

It is revised into: "The basis of the socialist economic system of the People's Republic of China is socialist public ownership of the means of production, namely, ownership by the whole people and collective ownership by the working people. The system of socialist public ownership supersedes the system of exploitation of man by man; it applies the principle of 'from each according to his ability, to each according to his work'." "During the primary stage of socialism, the State adheres to the basic economic system with the public ownership remaining dominant and diverse sectors of the economy developing side by side, and to the distribution system with the distribution according to work remaining dominant and the coexistence of a variety of modes of distribution."

The original text of the first section in Article Eight of the Constitution is: "The rural household-based output-related contracted responsibility system and other forms of the cooperative economy such as producers', supply and marketing, credit and consumers' cooperatives belong to the sector of the socialist economy under collective ownership by the working people. Working people who are members of rural economic collectives have the right, within the limits prescribed by law, to farm plots of cropland and hilly land allotted for private use, engage in household sideline production and raise privately owned livestock."

It is revised into: "Rural collective economic organizations practice the double-tier management system that combines unified and separate operations on the basis of the household-based output-related contracted responsibility system. Various forms of the cooperative economy in rural areas such as producers', supply and marketing, credit and consumers' cooperatives belong to the sector of the socialist economy under collective ownership by the working people.

Working people who are members of rural economic collectives have the right, within the limits prescribed by law, to farm plots of cropland and hilly land allotted for private use, engage in household sideline production and raise privately owned livestock."

The original text of Article 11 of the Constitution is: "The individual economy of urban and rural working people, operating within the limits prescribed by law, is a complement to the socialist public economy. The State protects the lawful rights and interests of the individual economy." "The State guides, helps and supervises the individual economy by exercising administrative control." "The State permits the private economy to exist and develop within the limits prescribed by law. The private economy is a complement to the socialist public economy. The State protects the lawful rights and interests of the private economy, and guides, supervises and administers the private economy."

It is revised into: "Individual, private and other non-public economies that exist within the limits prescribed by law are major components of the socialist market economy." "The State protects the lawful rights and interests of individual and private economies, and guides, supervises and administers individual and private economies."

The original text of Article 28 of the Constitution is: "The State maintains public order and suppresses treasonable and other counter-revolutionary activities; it penalizes actions that endanger public security and disrupt the socialist economy and other criminal activities, and punishes and reforms criminals."

It is revised into: "The State maintains public order and suppresses treasonable and other criminal activities that endanger State security; it penalizes actions that endanger public security and disrupt the socialist economy and other criminal activities, and punishes and reforms criminals.

AMENDMENT FOUR

(Approved on March 14, 2004, by the 10th National
People's Congress at its 2nd Session)

1. "... along the road of building socialism with Chinese characteristics..." and "...under the guidance of Marxism-Leninism, Mao Zedong Thought and Deng Xiaoping Theory..."

Revised to: "... along the road of Chinese-style socialism..." and "...under the guidance of Marxism-Leninism, Mao Zedong Thought, Deng Xiaoping Theory and the important thought of 'Three Represents'..."

2. Seventh paragraph of the Preamble: After "... to modernize the industry, agriculture, national defence and science and technology step by step..."

Is added: "... promote the co-ordinated development of the material, political and spiritual civilizations..."

3. The second sentence of the 10th paragraph of the Preamble: "In the long years of revolution and construction, there has been formed under the leadership of the Communist Party of China a broad patriotic united front that is composed of the democratic parties and people's organizations and embraces all socialist working people, all patriots who support socialism, and all patriots who stand for the reunification of the motherland. This united front will continue to be consolidated and developed."

After "... a broad patriotic united front that is composed of the democratic parties and people's organizations and embraces all socialist working people..." is added "... all builders of socialism, ..."

4. Third paragraph of Article 10: "The State may, in the public interest, requisition land for its use in accordance with the law."

Revised to: "The State may, in the public interest and in accordance with the provisions of law, expropriate or requisition land for its use and shall make compensation for the land expropriated or requisitioned."

5. Second paragraph of Article 11:"The State protects the lawful rights and interests of the individual and private sectors of the economy, and exercises guidance, supervision and control over individual and the private sectors of the economy."

Revised to: "The State protects the lawful rights and interests of the non-public sectors of the economy such as the individual and private sectors of the economy. The State encourages, supports and guides the development of the non-public sectors of the economy and, in accordance with law, exercises supervision and control over the non-public sectors of the economy."

6. Article 13: "The State protects the right of citizens to own lawfully earned income, savings, houses and other lawful property." and "The State protects according to law the right of citizens to inherit private property."

Revised to: "Citizens' lawful private property is inviolable" and "The State, in accordance with law, protects the rights of citizens to private property and to its inheritance" and "The State may, in the public interest and in accordance with law, expropriate or requisition private property for its use and shall make compensation for the private property expropriated or requisitioned."

7. Article 14 has a fourth paragraph added: "The State establishes a sound social security system compatible with the level of economic development."

8. Article 33 [All persons holding the nationality of the People's Republic of China are citizens of the People's Republic of China. All citizens of the People's Republic of China are equal before the law. Every citizen enjoys the rights and at the same time must perform the duties prescribed by the Constitution and the law.] has a third paragraph added: "The State respects and preserves human rights."

The Constitution of the Republic of Korea

The Preamble and Chapter I: General Principles of the Constitution of the Republic of Korea, reproduced below, are from the eighth revision of South Korea's Constitution, as ratified in October 1987. Appearing in the 1987 version, for the first time, is a commitment to seek Korean reunification by peaceful means (Article 4). The Preamble of the first, 1948 Constitution declared the goal "To establish a democratic system of government eliminating evil social customs of all kinds, to afford equal protection to every person and to provide for the fullest development of the capacity of each individual in all the fields of political, economic, social and cultural life." The General Principles in Chapter I declared that the Republic of Korea shall be a democratic republic and that "the sovereignty of the Republic of Korea shall reside in the people, from whom all state authority emanates." By and large, the revisions and amendments to the Constitution of 1948 can be understood as maneuvers by incumbent political leaders to amass power or to forestall a transfer of power according to the constitutionally prescribed procedure.

PREAMBLE

We, the people of Korea, proud of a resplendent history and traditions dating from time immemorial, upholding the cause of the Provisional Government of the Republic of Korea born of the March First Independence Movement of 1919 and the democratic ideals of the April Revolution of 1960, having assumed the mission of democratic reform and peaceful unification of our homeland and having determined to consolidate national unity with justice, humanitarianism and brotherly love, and to destroy all social vices and injustice, and to afford equal opportunities to every person and provide for the fullest development of individual capabilities in all fields, including political, economic, social and cultural life by further strengthening the free and democratic basic order conducive to private initiative and public harmony, and to help each person discharge those duties and responsibilities concomitant to freedoms and rights, and to elevate the quality of life for all citizens and contribute to lasting world peace and the common prosperity of mankind and thereby to ensure security, liberty and happiness for ourselves and our posterity forever, do hereby amend, through national referendum following a resolution by the National Assembly, the Constitution, ordained and established on July 12, 1948, and amended eight times subsequently.

October 29, 1987

CHAPTER I. GENERAL PROVISIONS

Article 1

1. The Republic of Korea shall be a democratic republic.

2. The sovereignty of the Republic of Korea shall reside in the people, and all state authority shall emanate from the people.

Article 2

1. Nationality in the Republic of Korea shall be prescribed by Act.

2. The State shall protect its citizens abroad as provided by Act.

Article 3

The territory of the Republic of Korea shall consist of the Korean peninsula and its adjacent islands.

Article 4

The Republic of Korea shall seek national unification, and shall formulate and carry out peaceful unification policy based on the free and democratic basic order.

Article 5

1. The Republic of Korea shall endeavor to maintain international peace and shall renounce any war of aggression.

2. The national Armed Forces shall be charged with the sacred mission of national security and the defense of the land and their political neutrality shall be observed.

Article 6

1. Treaties duly concluded and promulgated under the Constitution and generally recognized rules of international law shall have the same force and effect of law as domestic laws of the Republic of Korea.

2. Status of aliens shall be guaranteed in accordance with international laws and treaties.

Article 7

1. Public officials shall be servants of the people and shall be responsible to the people.

2. Status and political neutrality of public officials shall be guaranteed as prescribed by Act.

Article 8

1. Establishment of political parties shall be free and the plural party system shall be guaranteed.

2. Political parties shall be democratic in their objectives, organization and activities, and shall have necessary organizational arrangements to participate in the formation of political will of the people.

3. Political parties shall be protected by the State as provided by statute and may receive subsidy for operation from the State as prescribed by Act.

4. If the purposes or activities of a political party are contrary to the democratic basic order, the Government may bring an action for its dissolution in the Constitutional Court, and the political party may be dissolved by decision of the Constitutional Court.

Article 9

The State shall strive to sustain and develop cultural heritages and to enhance national culture.

The Socialist Constitution of the Democratic People's Republic of Korea

The Preamble and Chapter I below are excerpted from the Socialist Constitution of the Democratic People's Republic of Korea as adopted in December 1972 and amended in 1992, 1998, and 2009. The Preamble to the 1998 version, amended after Kim Il Sung's death in 1994, enshrined the "Great Leader" as the "Eternal President of the Republic." The most recent changes, adopted after Kim Jong Il suffered a stroke in 2008, re-inforced the legitimacy of his rule by officially identifying the chairman of the National Defense Commission (a title held by Kim) as "supreme leader" of North Korea (Article 100). In Article 3, Kim Jong Il's "songun," or military-first policy, is elevated for the first time in the Constitution to appear alongside Kim Il Sung's principle of "juche," or self-reliance. The 2009 version of the Constitution notably excludes any reference to communism or Marxism-Leninism, but introduces no changes of an economic nature. The 2009 revisions were adopted in April but not publicly announced until September 2009.

PREAMBLE

The Democratic People's Republic of Korea is a juche-based socialist fatherland that embodies the idea and leadership of the great leader Comrade Kim Il Sung.

The great leader Comrade Kim Il Sung is the founder of the DPRK and the father of socialist Korea.

Comrade Kim Il Sung founded the immortal juche idea, and by organizing and leading the anti-Japanese revolutionary struggle under its banner, established glorious revolutionary traditions and achieved the historic cause of the fatherland's liberation. He founded the DPRK on the basis of laying a solid foundation for building an independent and sovereign state in the fields of politics, economy, culture, and military.

Comrade Kim Il Sung reinforced and developed the Republic into a popular masses-centered socialist country and a socialist state of independence, self-support, and self-defense by putting forward a juche-oriented revolutionary line and wisely leading various stages of the social revolution and construction work.

Comrade Kim Il Sung clarified the fundamental principles of state building and state activities; established the most superior state and social system, political method, and system and method of social management; and provided a firm foundation for achieving the wealth, power, and prosperity of the socialist fatherland and for succeeding to and completing the juche revolutionary cause.

Comrade Kim Il Sung, regarding the idea of "Serving the people as heaven" as his motto, was always with the people, devoted his whole life to them, took care of and led the people with his noble politics of benevolence, and thus turned the whole society into one big, single-heartedly united family.

The great leader Comrade Kim Il Sung is the sun of the nation and the lodestar of the fatherland's reunification. Comrade Kim Il Sung set forth the country's reunification as the supreme task of the nation and devoted all his efforts and energies to its realization. While consolidating the Republic into a powerful and mighty fortress for the fatherland's reunification, Comrade Kim Il Sung presented fundamental principles and methods of the fatherland's reunification and developed the movement for the fatherland's reunification into a pan-national movement, and thus paved the road for accomplishing the cause of the fatherland's reunification with the united strength of the entire nation.

The great leader Comrade Kim Il Sung clarified the basic idea of the DPRK's foreign policy, expanded and developed the country's external relations with this as a basis, and enabled the Republic to highly display its international authority. Comrade Kim Il Sung, as a veteran statesman of the world, pioneered a new era of independence, engaged in energetic activities for the reinforcement and development of the socialist movement and the nonaligned movement, as well as for global peace and friendship among the peoples, and made an immortal contribution to mankind's cause of independence.

Comrade Kim Il Sung was a genius in ideology and theory and in the art of leadership, an ever-victorious, iron-willed brilliant commander, a great revolutionary and politician, and a great human being.

Comrade Kim Il Sung's great idea and achievements in leadership are the eternal treasures of the DPRK revolution and serve as a basic guarantee for the affluence and prosperity of the DPRK.

Under the leadership of the Workers Party of Korea [WPK], the DPRK and the Korean people will hold the great leader Comrade Kim Il Sung in high esteem as the eternal president of the Republic and complete the juche revolutionary cause to the end by defending, carrying forward, and developing Comrade Kim Il Sung's idea and achievements.

The DPRK Socialist Constitution is the Kim Il Sung constitution, in which the great leader Comrade Kim Il Sung's juche-oriented idea of state building and his achievements in state building have been made into law.

CHAPTER I. POLITICS

Article 1. The DPRK is an independent socialist state representing the interests of all the Korean people.

Article 2. The DPRK is a revolutionary state, which has inherited the brilliant traditions established in the glorious revolutionary struggle against the imperialist aggressors to achieve the fatherland's liberation and the freedom and happiness of the people.

Article 3. The DPRK considers the juche idea and the military-first idea, which are person-centered worldviews and revolutionary ideas for achieving the independence of the popular masses, as the guiding principles of its activities.

Article 4. The sovereignty of the DPRK shall be vested in the working people, which include workers, farmers, soldiers, and working intellectuals. The working people shall exercise their sovereignty through their representative organs—the Supreme People's Assembly [SPA] and the local people's assemblies at all levels.

Article 5. All state organs of the DPRK shall be organized and managed on the principle of democratic centralism.

Article 6. The organs of sovereignty at all levels, from the county people's assembly to the SPA, shall be elected on the principle of universal, equal, and direct suffrage by secret ballot.

Article 7. Deputies to the organs of sovereignty at all levels shall have close ties with their constituents and shall be accountable to them for their work. Constituents may recall a deputy they have elected at any given time in the event the latter loses confidence.

Article 8. The social system of the DPRK is a man-centered social system whereby the working popular masses are the masters of everything, and everything in society serves the working popular masses. The state shall safeguard the interests of, and respect and protect the human rights of the working people, including workers, farmers, soldiers, and working intellectuals, who have been freed from exploitation and oppression and have become the masters of the state and society.

Article 9. The DPRK shall struggle to achieve the complete victory of socialism by strengthening the people's regime in the northern half of Korea and by vigorously waging the three revolutions—ideological, technological, and cultural—to achieve the fatherland's reunification on the principle of independence, peaceful reunification, and grand national unity.

Article 10. The DPRK shall base itself on the political and ideological unity of all the people, based on the worker-farmer alliance led by the working class. The state shall revolutionize all members of the society and turn them into the working class by intensifying the ideological revolution, and shall turn the whole of society into a single collective united in comradeship.

Article 11. The DPRK shall carry out all its activities under the leadership of the WPK.

Article 12. The state shall adhere to the class line and strengthen the dictatorship of the people's democracy, and thus firmly protect the people's sovereignty and socialist system from the maneuvers for destruction by hostile elements at home and abroad.

Article 13. The state shall embody the mass line and implement in all work the Ch'o'ngsan-ri spirit and method, whereby the upper echelons assist the lower echelons, solutions to problems are sought among the masses, and the voluntary enthusiasm of the masses is aroused by giving priority to the political work, the work with people.

Article 14. The state shall vigorously carry out mass movements, including the Movement To Win the Three-Revolution Red Flag, and accelerate the socialist construction to the maximum.

Article 15. The DPRK shall protect the democratic national rights of Korean compatriots overseas and their legitimate rights and interests as recognized by international law.

Article 16. The DPRK shall guarantee the legitimate rights and interests of foreigners in its territory.

Article 17. Independence, peace, and friendship are the basic ideas of the DPRK's foreign policy and the principles of its external activities. The state shall establish diplomatic and political, economic, and cultural relations with all the countries that treat our country in a friendly manner, on the principles of complete equality and independence, mutual respect and noninterference in each other's internal affairs, and reciprocity. The state shall unite with the peoples of the world who espouse independence and shall actively support and encourage the struggle of the peoples of all countries to oppose all forms of aggression and interference in others' internal affairs and to achieve the sovereignty of their countries and national and class liberation.

Article 18. The laws of the DPRK are a reflection of the intents and interests of the working people and serve as a basic weapon in state administration. Respect for the law and its strict observation and execution is the duty of all organs, enterprises, organizations, and citizens. The state shall perfect the socialist legal system and strengthen the socialist law-abiding life.

The Constitution of Japan

Japan's postwar or "Peace" Constitution, drafted by two U.S. Army officers tasked by General Douglas MacArthur, and then revised by Japanese officials, was passed by the Diet in October 1946 as an amendment to the Meiji Constitution of 1889. Of signal importance was establishment of the principle of popular sovereignty. The Constitution was accepted by the Emperor on November 3, 1946, and came into effect on May 3, 1947. It has never been amended.

PREFACE

We, the Japanese people, acting through our duly elected representatives in the National Diet, determined that we shall secure for ourselves and our posterity the fruits of peaceful cooperation with all nations and the blessings of liberty throughout this land, and resolved that never again shall we be visited with the horrors of war through the action of government, do proclaim that sovereign power resides with the people and do firmly establish this Constitution. Government is a sacred trust of the people, the authority for which is derived from the people, the powers of which are exercised by the representatives of the people, and the benefits of which are enjoyed by the people. This is a universal principle of mankind upon which this Constitution is founded. We reject and revoke all constitutions, laws, ordinances, and rescripts in conflict herewith.

We, the Japanese people, desire peace for all time and are deeply conscious of the high ideals controlling human relationship, and we have determined to preserve our security and existence, trusting in the justice and faith of the peace-loving peoples of the world. We desire to occupy an honored place in an international society striving for the preservation of peace, and the banishment of tyranny and slavery, oppression and intolerance for all time from the earth. We recognize that all peoples of the world have the right to live in peace, free from fear and want.

We believe that no nation is responsible to itself alone, but that laws of political morality are universal; and that obedience to such laws is incumbent upon all nations who would sustain their own sovereignty and justify their sovereign relationship with other nations. We, the Japanese people, pledge our national honor to accomplish these high ideals and purposes with all our resources.

CHAPTER I: THE EMPEROR

Article 1:
The Emperor shall be the symbol of the State and the unity of the people, deriving his position from the will of the people with whom resides sovereign power.

Article 2:
The Imperial Throne shall be dynastic and succeeded to in accordance with the Imperial House Law passed by the Diet.

Article 3:
The advice and approval of the Emperor in matters of state, and the Cabinet shall be responsible therefor.

Article 4:
The Emperor shall perform only such acts in matters of state as are provided for in this Constitution and he shall not have powers related to government. The Emperor may delegate the performance of his acts in matters of state as may be provided for by law.

Article 5:
When, in accordance with the Imperial House Law, a Regency is established, the Regent shall perform his acts in matters of state in the Emperor's name. In this case, paragraph one of the preceding Article will be applicable.

Article 6:
The Emperor shall appoint the Prime Minister as designated by the Diet. The Emperor shall appoint the Chief Judge of the Supreme Court as designated by the Cabinet.

Article 7:
The Emperor shall, with the advice and approval of the Cabinet, perform the following acts in matters of state on behalf of the people: (1) Promulgation of amendments of the constitution, laws, cabinet orders and treaties. (2) Convocation of the Diet. (3) Dissolution of the House of Representatives. (4) Proclamation of general election of members of the Diet. (5) Attestation of the appointment and dismissal of Ministers of State and other officials as provided for by law, and of full powers and credentials of Ambassadors and Ministers. (6) Attestation of general and special amnesty, commutation of

punishment, reprieve, and restoration of rights. (7) Awarding of honors. (8) Attestation of instruments of ratification and other diplomatic documents as provided for by law. (9) Receiving foreign ambassadors and ministers. (10) Performance of ceremonial functions.

Article 8:
No property can be given to, or received by, the Imperial House, nor can any gifts be made therefrom, without the authorization of the Diet.

CHAPTER II: RENUNCIATION OF WAR

Article 9:
Aspiring sincerely to an international peace based on justice and order, the Japanese people forever renounce war as a sovereign right of the nation and the threat or use of force as means of settling international disputes. In order to accomplish the aim of the preceding paragraph, land, sea, and air forces, as well as other war potential, will never be maintained. The right of belligerency of the state will not be recognized.

Notes

Chapter 1. The Confucian Tradition

1. H.G. Creel, *Confucius and the Chinese Way* (New York: Harper & Row, 1949), 189.

2. John King Fairbank and Merle Goldman, *China: A New History*, 2d enlarged edition (Cambridge, MA: Harvard University Press, 2006), 51–52.

3. Ibid., 52.

4. Ibid., 52–53.

5. Immanuel C.Y. Hsu, *The Rise of Modern China*, 5th edition (New York: Oxford University Press, 1995), 74.

6. Fairbank and Goldman, *China: A New History*, 53.

7. Ibid.

8. Ibid.

9. Ibid., 108.

10. Ibid., 115.

11. R.H. Tawney, *Land and Labor in China* (Boston: Beacon Press, 1966), 66.

12. Hsu, *The Rise of Modern China*, 6.

13. Joseph Needham, *The Grand Titration: Science and Society in East and West* (Toronto: University of Toronto Press, 1969), 87.

14. Ibid., 91.

15. Ibid., 211.

16. Charles O. Hucker, "Political Institutions," in John Meskill, *An Introduction to Chinese Civilization* (Lexington, MA: D.C. Heath, 1973), 552.

17. Fairbank and Goldman, *China: A New History*, 47.

18. Ibid., 112–13.

19. Ibid., 138.

Chapter 2. China and the West

1. Immanuel C.Y. Hsu, *The Rise of Modern China*, 5th edition (New York: Oxford University Press, 1995), 96.

2. Ibid., 142.

3. Ibid., 169.

4. Jonathan D. Spence, *God's Chinese Son: The Taiping Heavenly Kingdom of Hong Xiuquan* (New York: W.W. Norton, 1996), xxi.

5. Ibid.

6. Hsu, *The Rise of Modern China*, 221.

7. Ibid., 344.

8. Ibid., 306.

9. Ibid., 412.

10. John King Fairbank and Merle Goldman, *China: A New History*, 2d enlarged edition (Cambridge, MA: Harvard University Press, 2006), 229–30.

11. Hsu, *The Rise of Modern China*, 436.
12. Ibid., 402.
13. Ibid., 403.
14. Ibid., 494.

Chapter 3. Revolution

1. John King Fairbank, *The Great Chinese Revolution: 1800–1985* (New York: Harper & Row, 1987).
2. John King Fairbank and Merle Goldman, *China: A New History*, 2d enlarged edition (Cambridge, MA: Harvard University Press, 2006), 298.
3. Ibid., 353.
4. Sterling Seagrave. *The Soong Dynasty* (New York: Harper & Row, 1985), 8.
5. Ibid., 9.
6. Immanuel C.Y. Hsu, *The Rise of Modern China*, 5th edition (New York: Oxford University Press, 1995), 526.
7. O. Edmund Clubb, *20th Century China* (New York: Columbia University Press, 1964), 186–187.
8. Lucien Bianco, *Origins of the Chinese Revolution, 1915–1949* (Stanford: Stanford University Press, 1971), 124.
9. Fairbank and Goldman, *China: A New History*, 331.
10. William R. Nester, *Power Across the Pacific: A Diplomatic History of American Relations with Japan* (Basingstoke: Macmillan, 1996), 105.
11. A. Morgan Young, *Imperial Japan* (Westport, CT: Greenwood Press, 1938), 203–205.
12. Hisahiko Okazaki, *A Grand Strategy for Japanese Defense* (Lanham, MD: University Press of America, 1986), 63–64.
13. Hugh Borton, *Japan's Modern Century: From Perry to 1970* (New York: Ronald Press, 1970), 371.
14. Sadako Ogata, *Defiance in Manchuria: The Making of Japanese Foreign Policy, 1931–1932* (Berkeley: University of California Press, 1964), 59.
15. Borton, *Japan's Modern Century*, 373.
16. James B. Crowley, *Japan's Quest for Autonomy: National Security and Foreign Policy* (Princeton: Princeton University Press, 1966), 181.
17. Ogata, *Defiance in Manchuria*, 170.
18. Ibid., 171.
19. Louise Young, *Japan's Total Empire: Manchuria and the Culture of Wartime Imperialism* (Berkeley: University of California Press, 1998), 101.
20. Crowley, *Japan's Quest for Autonomy*, 181–82.
21. Ibid., 185–86.
22. Ogata, *Defiance in Manchuria*, 176.
23. Lincoln Li, *The Japanese Army in North China, 1937–1941* (Tokyo: Oxford University Press, 1975), 11.
24. James William Morley, *The China Quagmire: Japan's Expansion on the Asian Continent, 1933–41* (New York: Columbia University Press, 1983), 290.
25. Parks M. Coble, *Facing Japan: Chinese Politics and Japanese Imperialism, 1931–1937* (Cambridge, MA: Harvard University Press, 1991), 379.
26. John Hunter Boyle, *China and Japan at War, 1937–1945: The Politics of Collaboration* (Stanford: Stanford University Press, 1972), 106–7.

27. Coble, *Facing Japan*, 379.
28. Morley, *The China Quagmire*, 435.
29. Bianco, *Origins of the Chinese Revolution*, 130.
30. Ibid., 139.
31. Fairbank and Goldman, *China: A New History*, 339.

Chapter 4. Maoism

1. John King Fairbank and Merle Goldman, *China: A New History*, 2d enlarged edition (Cambridge, MA: Harvard University Press, 2006), 374.
2. Ibid., 302.
3. Ibid., 380.
4. Ibid., 387.
5. Ibid., 403.
6. Ibid., 437.
7. Ibid., 395.

Chapter 5. China After Mao

1. Immanuel C.Y. Hsu, *The Rise of Modern China*, 5th edition (New York: Oxford University Press, 1995), 950.
2. Benjamin Yang, *Deng: A Political Biography* (Armonk, NY: M.E. Sharpe, 1998), 110.
3. Hsu, *The Rise of Modern China*, 841.
4. Ibid., 872.
5. Tzu-yang Chao quoted in ibid.
6. Ibid., 951.
7. Ibid., 977.
8. Ibid., 909.
9. Merle Goldman, "Politically Engaged Intellectuals in the 1990s," in Richard Louis Edmonds, ed., *The People's Republic of China After 50 Years* (New York: Oxford University Press), 142.
10. For the three rules, see Chapter 5.
11. Hsu, *The Rise of Modern China*, vii.
12. James C.F. Wang, *Contemporary Chinese Politics: An Introduction*, 7th edition (Upper Saddle River, NJ: Pearson Education, 2002), 87.
13. Ibid., 96.
14. Ibid., 99.
15. Ibid., 133.
16. Kenneth Lieberthal, *Governing China: From Revolution Through Reform* (New York: W.W. Norton, 1995), 169.
17. Ibid., 89.
18. Ibid., 90.
19. Wang, *Contemporary Chinese Politics*, 92.
20. Ibid., 94.
21. Ibid., 161.
22. Ibid., 161–62.
23. Ibid., 173.
24. Ibid., 173–74.

25. Lieberthal, *Governing China*, 299.
26. Wang, *Contemporary Chinese Politics*, 140.
27. Ibid., 152.
28. Harold M. Tanner, *Strike Hard! Anti-Crime Campaigns and Chinese Criminal Justice 1979–1985* (Ithaca, NY: Cornell University Press, 1999), 58.
29. Yingyi Situ and Weizheng Liu, "An Overview of the Chinese Criminal Justice System," in Obi N.I. Ebbe, ed., *Comparative and International Criminal Justice Systems: Policing, Judiciary, and Corrections* (Boston: Butterworth-Heinemann, 1996), 134.
30. Wang, *Contemporary Chinese Politics*, 147.
31. Ibid., 148.
32. Tanner, *Strike Hard!*, 142.
33. Ibid., 134.
34. Ibid., 157.
35. Ibid., 149.
36. Ibid., 26.

Chapter 6. Contemporary Issues

1. John King Fairbank and Merle Goldman, *China: A New History*, 2d enlarged edition (Cambridge, MA: Harvard University Press, 2006), 360.
2. Ibid., 363.
3. Ibid.
4. Ibid., 368.
5. June Teufel Dreyer, *China's Political System: Modernization and Tradition*, 4th ed. (New York: Pearson, 2004), 287–89.
6. Ibid., 312.

Chapter 7. In the Shadow of China

1. Totemism is the identification with a particular object in the natural world and is thought to strengthen solidarity within a group and define that group as distinct from others.
2. Carter J. Eckert et al., *Korea, Old and New: A History* (Cambridge, MA: Harvard University Press, 1990), 11.
3. Ibid., 18–19.
4. Ibid., 14.
5. Edward A. Olsen, *Korea, The Divided Nation* (Westport, CT: Praeger Security International, 2005), 14.
6. Eckert et al., *Korea Old and New*, 21.
7. Young Whan Kihl, *Transforming Korean Politics: Democracy, Reform, and Culture* (Armonk, NY: M.E. Sharpe, 2005), 41.
8. Robert T. Oliver. *A History of the Korean People in Modern Times: 1800 to the Present* (Newark, DE: University of Delaware Press, 1993), 22–23.
9. Geir Helgesen, "The Case for Moral Education," in Daniel A. Bell and Chaebong Ham, eds., *Confucianism for the Modern World* (Cambridge: Cambridge University Press, 2003), 162.
10. Lew et al., "Affective Networks and Modernity: The Case of Korea," in Bell and Ham, *Confucianism in the Modern World*, 202.

11. Ibid., 203.

12. Ibid., 205.

13. Immanuel C.Y. Hsu, *The Rise of Modern China*, 5th edition (New York: Oxford University Press, 1995), 132–33.

14. Ibid., 332.

15. Oliver, *A History of the Korean People*, 50.

16. Ibid., 54.

17. Shin, Gi-Wook, "Asianism in Korea's Politics of Identity," *Inter-Asia Cultural Studies* 6 (November 4, 2006): 618.

18. Ibid., 620.

19. Ibid., 625.

20. Oliver, *A History of the Korean Peoples*, 31–32.

Chapter 8. Korea and Imperialism

1. Robert T. Oliver, *A History of the Korean People in Modern Times: 1800 to the Present* (Newark, DE: University of Delaware Press, 1993), 36.

2. Ibid., 56–57.

3. Ibid., 88.

4. Ibid., 94.

5. Bruce Cumings, *The Origins of the Korean War: Liberation and the Emergence of Separate Regimes, 1945–1947* (Princeton: Princeton University Press, 1987), 9.

6. Ibid., 11.

7. Oliver, *A History of the Korean People*, 147.

8. Ibid., 120.

9. Cumings, *The Origins of the Korean War*, 48.

10. Ibid., 55–56.

11. Ibid., 29.

12. Ibid., 82.

Chapter 9. Partition and War

1. Bruce Cumings, *The Origins of the Korean War: Liberation and the Emergence of Separate Regimes, 1945–1947* (Princeton: Princeton University Press, 1987), 38.

2. John L. Snell et al., *The Meaning of Yalta: Big Three Diplomacy and the New Balance of Power* (Baton Rouge: Louisiana State University Press, 1956), 193–95.

3. Ibid., 196–97.

4. Kim Baum and James I. Matray, *Korea and the Cold War: Division, Destruction, and Disarmament* (Claremont, CA: Regina Books, 1993), 37.

5. Cordell Hull, *The Memoirs of Cordell Hull,* as quoted in ibid., 40.

6. William Stueck, *The Korean War: An International History* (Princeton: Princeton University Press, 1995), 16–18.

7. Snell et al., *The Meaning of Yalta,* 191.

8. Baum and Matray, *Korea and the Cold War,* 44.

9. Samuel S. Kim, *The Two Koreas and the Great Powers* (Cambridge: Cambridge University Press, 2006), 237.

10. Cumings, *The Origins of the Korean War*, 125.

11. Ibid., 67.

12. Harry G. Summers, Jr., *Korean War Almanac* (New York: Facts On File, 1990), 158.

13. Cumings, *The Origins of the Korean War*, 125.

14. Ibid., 403.

15. Baum and Matray, *Korea and the Cold War*, 51.

16. Robert T. Oliver, *A History of the Korean People in Modern Times: 1800 to the Present* (Newark, DE: University of Delaware Press, 1993), 191.

17. Donald Stone MacDonald, *The Koreans: Contemporary Politics and Society* (Boulder, CO: Westview Press, 1966), 44.

18. Oliver, *A History of the Korean People*, 186.

19. Baum and Matray, *Korea and the Cold War*, 59.

20. Cumings, 390.

21. Oliver, *A History of the Korean People*, 170.

22. Ibid., 171.

23. Ibid.

24. Ibid., 173.

25. Ibid., 174.

26. Kim, *The Two Koreas and the Great Powers*, 114–15.

27. Henry A. Kissinger, *Diplomacy* (New York: Simon & Schuster, 1994), 475.

28. Steven W. Hook and John Spanier, *American Foreign Policy Since World War II*, 17th edition (Washington, DC: Congressional Quarterly Press, 2007), 15–19.

29. Ibid., 479.

30. T.R. Fehrenback, *This Kind of War* (Dulles, VA: Brassey's, 1994), 7.

31. Ibid.

32. Ibid., 49.

33. Ibid., 65.

34. Kissinger, *Diplomacy*, 484.

35. Henry Kissinger has a high regard for MacArthur, whom he describes as "America's most talented general of this century." Ibid., 480.

36. Kissinger suggests Chinese intervention could have been prevented had there been established "some kind of buffer zone along the Chinese border. That was never attempted." Ibid., 482. On the other hand, MacArthur suggested that the UN forces might cross the Yalu into China. His public questioning of U.S. policy led to his dismissal by President Truman.

37. Kissinger, *Diplomacy*, 488–89.

38. Kim, *The Two Koreas and the Great Powers*, 240–41.

39. Park Jae-kyu, "North Korea Since 2000 and Prospects for Inter-Korean Relations," *Korea Policy Review* 2(2) (2006): 13–19. Also found in Andrei Lankov, "The Natural Death of North Korean Stalinism," *Asia Policy* 1 (January 2006): 95–121.

40. Lankov, "The Natural Death of North Korean Stalinism," 105–7.

41. Ibid., 107.

42. Park, "North Korea Since 2000," 14.

43. Ibid., 19; Lankov "The Natural Death of North Korean Stalinism," 120.

44. Bruce Cumings, *Korea's Place in the Sun: A Modern History* (New York: W.W. Norton, 1997), 25.

Chapter 10. Korea and the Cold War

1. Bruce Cumings, *The Origins of the Korean War: Liberation and the Emergence of Separate Regimes, 1945–1947* (Princeton: Princeton University Press, 1981), 25.

2. Robert T. Oliver, *A History of the Korean People in Modern Times: 1800 to the Present* (Newark, DE: University of Delaware Press, 1993), 84; Harry G. Summers, Jr., *Korean War Almanac* (New York: Facts On File, 1990), 230–32.

3. Carter J. Eckert et al., *Korea, Old and New: A History* (Cambridge, MA: Harvard University Press, 1990), 232–33.

4. Ibid., 233.

5. Ibid.

6. Ibid., 235–36.

7. Ibid., 236.

8. Ibid.

9. Summers, *Korean War Almanac*, 230. Summers states Rhee was jailed prior to Chae-Pil's second exile.

10. Eckert et al., *Korea Old and New*, 274.

11. Summers, *Korean War Almanac*, 230.

12. Ibid., 230.

13. Hahm Pyong Choon, *Korean Jurisprudence: Politics and Culture* (Seoul: Yonsei University Press, 1986), 506.

14. Eckert et al., *Korea Old and New*, 272.

15. Ibid., 274–75.

16. Ibid., 276.

17. Ibid., 280.

18. Summers, *Korean War Almanac*, 230.

19. Don Oberdorfer, *The Two Koreas: A Contemporary History* (Boston: Addison-Wesley, 1997), 8.

20. Eckert et al., *Korea Old and New*, 341.

21. Bruce C. Cumings, *The Origins of the Korean War: Liberation and the Emergence of Separate Regimes, 1945–1947* (Princeton: Princeton University Press, 1987), 431.

22. Ibid., 349.

23. William Stueck, *The Korean War: An International History* (Princeton: Princeton University Press, 1995), 213–14.

24. Oberdorfer, *The Two Koreas*, 10.

25. Hahm, *Korean Jurisprudence*, 195.

26. Eckert et al., *Korea Old and New*, 349–51.

27. Ibid., 354–55.

28. Ibid., 348.

29. Bruce Cumings, *Korea's Place in the Sun: A Modern History* (New York: W.W. Norton, 1997), 224.

Chapter 11. The Hermit Kingdom

1. Harry G. Summers, Jr., *Korean War Almanac* (New York: Facts On File, 1990), 157.

2. Don Oberdorfer, *The Two Koreas: A Contemporary History* (Boston: Addison-Wesley, 1997), 16–17.

3. Charles K. Armstrong, *The North Korean Revolution, 1945–1950* (Ithaca, NY: Cornell University Press, 2003), 39.

4. Ibid., 55.

5. Ibid., 43.

6. Bruce C. Cumings, *The Origins of the Korean War: Liberation and the Emergence of Separate Regimes, 1945–1947* (Princeton: Princeton University Press, 1987), 414.

7. Ibid., 399.

8. Summers, *Korean War Almanac*, 158.

9. Oberdorfer, *The Two Koreas*, 17.

10. Ibid., 21.

11. Armstrong, *The North Korean Revolution*, 225.

12. Cumings, *The Origins of the Korean War*, 416.

13. Armstrong, *The North Korean Revolution*, 75.

14. Ibid., 99.

15. Ibid., 146.

16. Ibid., 4.

17. Ibid., 40.

18. Edward A. Olsen, *Korea, The Divided Nation* (Westport, CT: Praeger Security International, 2005), 106.

19. Armstrong, *The North Korean Revolution*, 159.

20. Olsen, *Korea*, 108.

21. Oberdorfer, *The Two Koreas*, 346.

22. Ibid. Armstrong, *The North Korean Revolution*, 159.

23. Ibid., 347.

24. Ibid., 348.

25. Bruce Cumings, *Korea's Place in the Sun: A Modern History* (New York: W.W. Norton, 1997), 416.

26. Oberdorfer, *The Two Koreas*, 349–50.

27. Cumings, *Korea's Place in the Sun*, 415.

28. Oberdorfer, *The Two Koreas*, 350.

29. Marcus Noland, *Avoiding the Apocalypse: The Future of the Two Koreas* (Washington, DC: Institute for International Economics, 2004), 62. *Juche* is defined as national self-reliance.

30. Ibid., 42.

31. Elizabeth Wishnick, "Russian–North Korean Relations: A New Era?" in Samuel S. Kim and Tai Hwan Lee, eds., *North Korea and Northeast Asia* (Lanham, MD: Rowman and Littlefield, 2002), 143.

32. Ibid., 126.

33. Andrei Lankov, "The Natural Death of North Korean Stalinism," *Asia Policy* 1 (January 2006): 101–2.

34. Ibid., 107.

35. Ibid., 117.

36. Noland, *Avoiding the Apocalypse*, 116–21.

37. Alexandre Y. Mansourov, "Emergence of the Second Republic: The Kim Regime Adapts to the Challenge of Modernity," in Young Whan Kihl and Hong Nack Kim, eds. *North Korea: The Politics of Survival* (Armonk, NY: M.E. Sharpe, 2006), 37.

38. Ibid., 71.

39. Larry Niksch, "North Korea's Weapons of Mass Destruction," in Kihl and Kim, *North Korea*, 109.

40. Noland, *Avoiding the Apocalypse*, 10.

41. Energy consumption in North Korea is marked by considerable inefficiency. The deteriorating condition of the power grid leads to substantial losses. "For the most part, it appears that, because of the lack of monitoring devices, the North Koreans have no idea how much electricity makes it to end users." Ibid., 144.

42. Ibid., 160.

43. Eric Yong-Joong Lee, "The Six-Party Talks and the North Korean Nuclear Dispute Resolution under the IAEA Safeguards Regime," *Asian-Pacific Law and Policy Journal* 5(1): 114.

44. Kim, *The Two Koreas and the Great Powers*, 262–63.

45. Samuel S. Kim, "Sino-North Korean Relations in the Post–Cold War World," in Kihl and Kim, *North Korea*.

46. Samuel S. Kim, *The Two Koreas and the Great Powers* (Cambridge: Cambridge University Press, 2006), 174–75.

47. Ibid., 201.

48. In the 1970s and 1980s, several Japanese disappeared under suspicious circumstances. It was suspected some had been kidnapped by North Korea. On September 11, 2002, North Korea acknowledged it had abducted Japanese citizens. The purpose was to provide identity for North Korean agents and to teach these agents to speak and act like Japanese. Kim Jong Il acknowledged and apologized for the abductions. Five abductees eventually returned to Japan. Others, presumably, were no longer alive.

49. Hong Nack Kim, "Japanese–North Korean Relations Under the Koizumi Government," in Kihl and Kim, *North Korea*, 165.

50. Young W. Kihl, *Transforming Korean Politics: Democracy, Reform, and Culture* (Armonk, NY: M.E. Sharpe, 2004), 240.

51. Myonwoo Lee, "Japanese–North Korean Relations: Going in Circles," in Kim and Lee, *North Korea and Northeast Asia*, 89.

52. Samuel S. Kim and Tai Hwan Lee, "Chinese–North Korean Relations: Managing Asymmetrical Interdependence," in Kim and Lee, *North Korea and Northeast Asia*, 113.

53. Samuel S. Kim, "North Korea and Northeast Asia in World Politics," in Kim and Lee, *North Korea and Northeast Asia*, 39.

54. Noland, *Avoiding the Apocalypse*, 251.

Chapter 12. Asian Tiger

1. Robert T. Oliver, *A History of the Korean People in Modern Times: 1800 to the Present* (Newark, DE: University of Delaware Press, 1993), 287.

2. Hyug Baeg Im, "The US Role in Korean Democracy and Security Since the Cold War Era," *International Relations of the Asia-Pacific* 6 (2006): 166.

3. Oliver, *A History of the Korean People*, 323.

4. Ibid., 310–11.

5. Young W. Kihl, *Transforming Korean Politics: Democracy, Reform, and Culture* (Armonk, NY: M.E. Sharpe, 2004), 134.

6. Ibid., 144.

7. Ibid., 251.

8. Samuel S. Kim, *Korea's Democratization* (New York and Cambridge: Cambridge University Press, 2003), xv.

9. Samuel S. Kim, "Korea's Democratization in the Global-Local Nexus," in ibid., 4.

10. Chan Wook Park, "Legislative-Executive Relations and Legislative Reforms," in Larry Jay Diamond and Doh C. Shin, eds., *Institutional Reforms and Democratic Consolidation in Korea* (Stanford, CA: Hoover Institution Press, 2000), 83.

11. Kim, "Korea's Democratization in the Global-Local Nexus," 24.

12. Sunhyuk Kim, "Civil Society in Democratizing Korea," in Kim, *Korea's Democratization*, 104.

13. Hoon Jaung, "Electoral Politics and Political Parties," in Diamond and Shin, *Institutional Reforms and Democratic Consolidation in Korea*, 51.

14. Eun Mee Kim, "Reforming the *Chaebols*," in ibid., 171.

15. Mark Andrew Abdollahian, Jacek Kugler, and Hilton R. Root, "Economic Crisis and the Future of Oligarchy," in ibid., 202.

Chapter 13. Japan in Isolation

1. Herschel Webb, *The Japanese Imperial Institution in the Tokugawa Period* (New York: Columbia University Press, 1968), 9.

2. Bob Tadashi Wakabayashi, *Anti-Foreignism and Western Learning in Early Modern Japan: The New Theses of 1825* (Cambridge, MA: Harvard University Press, 1986), 22.

3. Webb, *The Japanese Imperial Institution*, 162.

4. Marius B. Jansen, "The Ruling Class," in Marius B. Jansen and Gilbert Rozman, eds., *Japan in Transition: From Tokugawa to Meiji* (Princeton: Princeton University Press, 1986), 71. For a discussion of the legitimation of the shogun see Ronald A. Toby, *State and Diplomacy in Early Modern Japan* (Princeton: Princeton University Press, 1984), 53–109.

5. Webb, *The Japanese Imperial Institution*, 129.

6. Neil S. Fujita, *Japan's Encounter with Christianity: The Catholic Mission in Pre-Modern Japan* (New York: Paulist Press, 1991), 9.

7. Mary Elizabeth Berry, *Hideyoshi* (Cambridge, MA: Harvard University Press, 1982), 111–31.

8. Webb, *The Japanese Imperial Institution*, 73.

9. Berry, *Hideyoshi*, 104.

10. Ibid.

11. Michio Umegaki, *After the Restoration: The Beginning of Japan's Modern State* (New York: New York University Press, 1988), 22.

12. Fujita, *Japan's Encounter with Christianity*, 9.

13. Donald Calman, *The Nature and Origins of Japanese Imperialism: A Reinterpretation of the Great Crisis of 1873* (London: Routledge, 1992), 313–14.

14. Toby, *State and Diplomacy in Early Modern Japan*, 5–11.

15. Johann Arnason, "Paths to Modernity: The Pecularities of Japanese Feudalism," in Gavan McCormack and Yoshio Sugimoto, eds., *The Japanese Trajectory: Modernization and Beyond* (Cambridge: Cambridge University Press, 1988), 235–63.

16. Bob Tadashi Wakabayashi, "A Bakumatsu 'Greater East Asia War'?" in

Joshua A. Fogel, *Late Qing China and Meiji Japan* (Norwalk, CT: EastBridge, 2004), 2–3.

17. Fogel, *Late Qing China*, vii.

Chapter 14. Japan and the World

1. Hugh Borton, *Japan's Modern Century: From Perry to 1970*, 2nd edition (New York: The Ronald Press Co., 1970), 40–41.

2. Michael A. Barnhart. *Japan and the World Since 1868* (London: Edward Arnold, 1995), 6–7.

3. Ibid., 7.

4. Bob Tadashi Wakabayashi, *Anti-Foreignism and Western Learning in Early Modern Japan: The New Theses of 1825* (Cambridge, MA: Harvard University Press, 1986), 90.

5. Neil S. Fujita, *Japan's Encounter with Christianity: The Catholic Mission in Pre-Modern Japan* (New York: Paulist Press, 1991), 257–65.

6. Conrad Totman, *The Collapse of the Tokugawa Bakufu, 1862–1868* (Honolulu: University of Hawaii Press, 1980), 430–43.

7. Tessa Morris-Suzuki, *The Technological Transformation of Japan: From the Seventeenth to the Twenty-first Centuries* (Cambridge: Cambridge University Press, 1994), 34.

8. James W. White, Michip Umegaki, and Thomas Havens, *The Ambivalence of Nationalism* (Lanham, MD: University Press of America, 1990), 187.

9. J.W. Dower, *Empire and Aftermath* (Cambridge, MA: Harvard University, Council on East Asian Studies, 1979), 34.

10. White, Umegaki, and Havens, *The Ambivalence of Nationalism*, 63.

11. Michael Montgomery, *Imperialist Japan* (London: Christopher Helm, 1987), vii.

12. James B. Crowley, *Japan's Quest for Autonomy* (Princeton: Princeton University Press, 1966), 4.

13. Ibid.

14. Richard J. Mitchell, *Thought Control in Prewar Japan* (Ithaca: Cornell University Press, 1976), 21.

15. Carol Gluck, *Japan's Modern Myths: Ideology in the Late Meiji Period* (Princeton: Princeton University Press, 1985), 3.

16. Elise K. Tipton, *The Japanese Police State: The Tokko in Interwar Japan* (Honolulu: University of Hawaii Press, 1990), 17.

17. Ibid., 59.

18. Gluck, *Japan's Modern Myths*, 17.

19. Misako Hane, *Modern Japan: A Historical Survey* (Boulder, CO: Westview Press, 1986), 227–43.

20. Tipton, *The Japanese Police State*, 18.

21. Mitchell, *Thought Control in Prewar Japan*, 23–25. This special political role for the police originated in France at the time of Napolean. Ibid., 45.

22. Ibid., 22.

23. Ibid., 62.

24. Theodore Mcnelly, "The Japanese Constitution: Child of the Cold War," *Political Science Quarterly* 74 (June 1959): 195.

25. Edwin O. Reischauer and Albert M. Craig, *Japan: Tradition and Transformation* (Boston: Houghton Mifflin, 1978), 245.

26. Interestingly, this authoritarian rule was achieved without the mass application of terror that usually attends such processes. Widespread arrests, executions, and forced labor in concentration camps were not visited on the Japanese citizenry. Mitchell, *Thought Control in Prewar Japan*, 191.

27. Morris-Suzuki, *The Technological Transformation of Japan*, 41.

28. Michael A. Barnhart, *Japan Prepares for War: The Search for Economic Security, 1919–1941* (Ithaca, NY: Cornell University Press, 1987), 115–35.

29. The most notorious example of this racial bias occurred during World War II when Japanese-Americans were interned because they were considered a security threat. Americans of German or Italian extraction did not suffer a similar fate.

30. The term Manchuria was a shorthand term used by Westerners and Japanese to refer to the northeastern provinces of China and illustrates their political and imperialistic perspective. It suggests that China and Manchuria were separate entities, which is not really the case. Gavan McCormack, *Chang Tso-lin in Northeast Asia, 1911–1928: China, Japan and the Manchurian Idea* (Stanford, CA: Stanford University Press, 1974), 4.

31. Barnhart, *Japan Prepares for War*, 83.

32. Ben-ami Shillony, *Revolt in Japan: The Young Officers and the February 6, 1936 Incident* (Princeton: Princeton University Press, 1973), 13.

33. Crowley, *Japan's Quest for Autonomy*, 176.

34. John Toland, *The Rising Sun: The Decline and Fall of the Japanese Empire* (New York: Bantam Books, 1971), 1–22.

35. Tadashi Fukutake, *The Japanese Social Structure: Its Evolution in the Modern Century* (Tokyo: Tokyo University Press, 1982), 73.

36. Barnhart, *Japan Prepares for War*, 56.

37. Kenneth B. Pyle, *The Making of Modern Japan* (Lexington, MA: D.C. Heath, 1978), 147.

Chapter 15. Japan at War

1. Lincoln Li, *Japanese Army in North China: July 1937–December, 1941: Problems of Political and Economic Control* (Tokyo: Oxford University Press, 1975), 122.

2. Michael Barnhart, *Japan Prepares for War: The Search for Economic Security, 1919–1941* (Ithaca, NY: Cornell University Press, 1987), 146.

3. John Hunter Boyle, *Japan and China at War, 1937–1945: The Politics of Collaboration* (Stanford, CA: Stanford University Press, 1972), 119.

4. Michael Barnhart, *Japan and the World Since 1868* (London: Edward Arnold, 1995), 103.

5. Barnhart, *Japan Prepares for War*, 86.

6. William R. Nester, *Across the Pacific: A Diplomatic History of American Relations with Japan* (New York: New York University Press, 1996), 84–85.

7. Barnhart, *Japan and the World Since 1868*, 133.

8. Nester, *Across the Pacfic*, 134.

9. Louise Young, *Japan's Total Empire: Manchuria and the Culture of Wartime Imperialism* (Berkeley: University of California Press, 1998), 103.

10. Barnhart, *Japan and the World Since 1868*, 73.

11. Nobuya Bamba, *Japanese Diplomacy in a Dilemma: New Light on Japan's China Policy* (Vancouver: University of British Columbia Press, 1972), 376.

12. Ibid., 377.

13. Candee Yale Maxon, *Control of Japanese Foreign Policy* (Berkeley: University of California Press, 1957), 214. "[T]he rhetoric of the China conflict had launched the empire [Japan] on a perilous mission, one inspired by an imperial ideology which was not circumscribed by careful even credible strategic calculations." James B. Crowley, *Japan's Quest for Autonomy: National Security and Foreign Policy, 1930–1938* (Princeton: Princeton University Press, 1966), 378.

14. Young, *Japan's Total Empire*, 69.

15. Barnhart, *Japan and the World Since 1868*, 107.

16. Young, *Japan's Total Empire*, 24; Gavan McCormack, *Chang Tso-lin in Northeast China, 1911–1928: China, Japan, and the Manchurian Idea* (Stanford: Stanford University Press, 1974), 144.

17. James William Morley, *The China Quagmire: Japan's Expansion on the Asian Continent, 1933–1941* (New York: Columbia University Press, 1983), 30.

18. Barnhart, *Japan and the World Since 1868*, 117.

19. Mark R. Peattie, *Ishiwara Kanji and Japan's Confrontation with the West* (Princeton: Princeton University Press, 1975), 152.

20. Young, *Japan's Total Empire*, 307–8.

21. Ibid., 4.

22. W.G. Beasley, *Japanese Imperialism: 1894–1945* (Oxford: Clarendon Press, 1987), 155.

23. Richard Storry, *The Double Patriots: A Study of Japanese Nationalism* (Boston: Houghton Mifflin, 1956), 112.

24. Young, *Japan's Total Empire*, 40.

25. Sadako Ogata, *Defiance in Manchuria: The Making of Japanese Foreign Policy, 1931–1932* (Berkeley: University of California Press, 1964), 100.

26. The undermining of civilian authority would eventually compromise the military itself. "The mistrust and defiance of authority at the root of the radical reform movement made the military ascendancy that followed vulnerable to the same phenomena." Ogata, *Defiance in Manchuria,* xvi. See also Storry, *The Double Patriots*, 192.

27. Young, *Japan's Total Empire*, 138.

28. Li, *The Japanese Army in North China*, 29.

29. J. W. Dower, *Empire and Aftermath* (Cambridge, MA: Harvard University Press, Council on East Asian Studies, 1979), 281.

30. Young, *Japan's Total Empire*, 128.

31. Morley, *The China Quagmire*, 328.

32. Young, *Japan's Total Empire*, 31.

33. Ibid., 31. Ramon H. Myers, "Japanese Imperialism in Manchuria: The South Manchuria Railway Company, 1906–1933," in Duus et al., *The Japanese Informal Empire in China*, 109.

34. Crowley, *Japan's Quest for Autonomy*, 195.

35. Boyle, *China and Japan at War*, 107.

36. Ibid., 130.

37. Nakagane Katsuji, "Manchukuo and Economic Development," in Duus et al., *The Japanese Informal Empire*, 157.

38. William H. Elsbree, *Japan's Role in Southeast Asian Nationalist Movements: 1940–1945* (New York: Russell and Russell, 1953), 15.

39. The French were not the only ones failing to appreciate the full implications of modern warfare. With regard to the British, Niall Furgeson notes: "Too much emphasis was placed on morale, courage, and discipline, not enough on fire-power and tactics." *The Pity of War* (Boulder, CO: Basic Books, 1999), 306.

40. Hisako Okazaki, *A Grand Strategy for Japanese Defense* (Lanham, MD: University Press of America, 1986), 131.

41. Tessa Morris-Suzuki, *The Technological Transformation of Japan: From the Seventeenth Century to the Twenty-first Centuries* (New York: Cambridge University Press, 1994), 157.

42. Elsbree, *Japan's Role in Southeast Asian Nationalist Movements*, 34.

43. Young, *Japan's Total Empire*, 433.

44. Beasley, *Japanese Imperialism*, 195.

45. Elsbree, *Japan's Role in Southeast Asian Nationalist Movements*, 10.

46. Ibid., 42.

47. Ibid., 164.

48. The Japanese sought to implement the theories of the American strategist Alfred Thayer Mahan.

Chapter 16. The Japanese Miracle

1. "Japanese companies seem to have enjoyed extraordinary latitude in their technical relationship with western companies, largely, no doubt, because Europeans and Americans were still quite unable to conceive of Japan as a serious competitor in technologically advanced industries." Tessa Morris-Suzuki, *The Technological Transformation of Japan: From the Seventeenth to the Twenty-first Centuries* (New York: Cambridge University Press, 1994), 112.

2. Jean Courdy, *The Japanese* (New York: Harper & Row, 1984), 226.

3. H.W. Brands, Jr., "The United States and the Reemergence of Independent Japan," *Pacific Affairs* 59 (Fall 1986): 400; Morris-Suzuki, *The Technological Transformation of Japan*, 23.

4. Harry D. Harootunian, "The Progress of Japan and the Samurai Class," *Pacific Historical Review* 28 (August 1959): 266.

5. Jerome B. Cohen, *Japan's Economy in War and Reconstruction* (Minneapolis: University of Minnesota Press, 1949), 417.

6. William Chapman, *Inventing Japan: The Making of a Postwar Civilization* (Englewood Cliffs, NJ: Prentice-Hall, 1991), 96.

7. Chalmers Johnson, *MITI and the Japanese Miracle: The Growth of Industrial Policy, 1925–1975* (Stanford: Stanford University, 1985), 239.

8. Akiko Mikuni and R. Taggart Murphy, *Japan's Policy Trap: Dollars, Deflation and the Crises of Japanese Finance* (Washington, DC: Brookings Institution, 2002), 3.

9. Richard Katz, *Japan—The System That Soured: The Rise and Fall of the Japanese Economic Miracle* (Armonk, NY: M.E. Sharpe, 1998), 202.

10. Ardath W. Burks, *Japan: A Postindustrial Power*, 2nd edition (Boulder, CO: Westview Press, 1984), 157.

11. Ibid., 190.

12. Daniel K. Okimoto, *Between MITI and the Market: Japanese Industrial Policy for High Technology* (Stanford, CA: Stanford University Press, 1989), 8.

13. "But to the Japanese elite, competition carries with it the deadly whiff of disorder and loss of control. Asking Japan's governing elite to embrace competition

is like asking the Pentagon to embrace radical pacificism." Mikuni and Murphy, *Japan's Policy Trap*, 245.

14. James C. Abegglen and George Stark, Jr., *Kaisha: The Japanese Corporation* (New York: Basic Books, 1985), 23–30.

15. See Richard J. Samuels, "The Industrial Destructuring of the Japanese Aluminum Industry," *Pacific Affairs* (Fall 1983): 495–509.

16. Mark C. Tilton, *Restrained Trade: Cartels in Japan's Basic Materials Industries* (Ithaca, NY: Cornell University Press, 1966), 50.

17. See, for example, Ezra F. Vogel, *Japan as Number One: Lessons for America* (Cambridge, MA: Harvard University Press, 1979), especially Chapter 5.

18. Chapman, *Inventing Japan*, 107.

19. Johnson, *MITI and the Japanese Miracle*, 81.

20. Ibid., 239.

21. Ibid., 16.

22. Bela Belassa and Marcus Noland, *Japan in the World Economy* (Washington, DC: Institute of International Economics, 1988), 16. In point of fact, trade is a larger component of the German economy than it is in Japan.

23. Edward J. Lincoln, *Japan: Facing Economic Maturity* (Washington, DC: Brookings Institution, 1988), 48.

24. Ibid.

25. Ibid.

26. Ezra F. Vogel, "Pax Nipponica?" *Foreign Affairs* (Spring 1986): 753.

27. Ellen L. Frost, *For Richer, For Poorer: The New U.S.-Japan Relationship* (New York: Council on Foreign Relations, 1986), 46.

28. Vogel, "Pax Nipponica?" 754.

29. Frost, *For Richer, For Poorer*, 60.

30. Tomoko Hamada, "Corporation, Culture, and Environment: The Japanese Model," *Asian Survey* 25 (December 1985): 12–85.

31. Norma Chalmers, *Industrial Relations in Japan: The Peripheral Workforce* (London: Routledge, 1989), 54.

32. Randall S. Jones, "The Economic Implications of Japan's Aging Population," *Asian Survey* (September 1988): 962.

33. Lincoln, *Japan*, 11.

34. Katz, *Japan—The System That Soured*, 334.

35. The Japanese seek to avoid what they consider the mistakes of others on the matter of immigration. "Let's learn from the German lesson" refers to the cultural conflicts that developed when Turkish and other nationalities entered Germany as "guest workers" to overcome a labor shortage. *Japan Times Weekly Overseas Edition.* July 1, 1988, p. 4.

36. Among industrialized countries, Japan ranks at the top in terms of the equitability of income distribution. Okimoto, *Between MITI and the Market*, 180.

37. Frost, *For Richer, For Poorer*, 41.

38. Okimoto, *Between MITI and the Market*, 42–43.

39. Mikuni and Murphy, *Japan's Policy Trap*, 5.

40. Ronald E. Dolan and Robert L. Worden, eds., *Japan: A Country Study* (Washington, DC: Government Printing Office for the Library of Congress, 1994), pp. 265–66.

41. Mark C. Tilton, "Regulatory Reform and Market Opening in Japan," in Lonny E. Carlile and Mark C. Tilton, eds., *Is Japan Really Changing Its Ways? Regulatory Reform and the Japanese Economy* (Washington, DC: Brookings Institution, 1998), 167.

42. Christopher Wood, *The End of Japan Inc. and How the New Japan Will Look* (New York: Simon & Schuster, 1994), 134.

43. Katz, *Japan—The System That Soured*, 35.

44. Wood, *The End of Japan Inc.*, 137.

45. *Japan Times Online*, May 30, 2003.

46. David L. Asher, "What Became of the Japanese 'Miracle'?" *Orbis* (Spring 1996): 225.

47. Katz, *Japan—The System That Soured*, 4.

Chapter 17. Government and Politics

1. Kan Ori, "The Diet and the Japanese Political System," in Francis R. Valeo and Charles E. Morrison, eds., *The Japanese Diet and the U.S. Congress* (Boulder, CO: Westview Press, 1983), 22.

2. Hans H. Baerwald, *Japan's Parliament: An Introduction* (London: Cambridge University Press, 1974), 124.

3. *Time* (February 19, 1990): 46.

4. Michihiro Ishibashi and Steven R. Reed, "Second Generation Diet Members and Democracy in Japan," *Asian Survey* 32 (April 1992): 366–79.

5. T.J. Pempel, "Uneasy Toward Autonomy: Parliament and Parliamentarians in Japan," in *Parliaments and Parliamentarians in Democratic Politics,* Ezra N. Suleiman, ed. (New York: Holmes and Meier, 1986), 138–39; Edwin Reischauer, *The Japanese* (Cambridge, MA: Harvard University Press, 1984), 254.

6. Pempel, "Uneasy Toward Autonomy," 120.

7. T.J. Pempel, "The Dilemma of Parliamentary Opposition in Japan," *Polity* 8 (Fall 1975): 69–70.

8. Leonard J. Schoppa, *Education Reform in Japan: A Case of Immobilist Politics* (London: Routledge, 1991), 11.

9. J.A.A. Stockwin, "Parties, Politicians and the Political System," in J.A.A. Stockwin et al., eds., *Dynamic and Immobilist Politics in Japan* (Honolulu: University of Hawaii Press, 1988), 42.

10. John Crieghton Campbell, *Contemporary Japanese Budget Politics* (Berkeley: University of California Press, 1977), 151. The average term of a minister is 278 days. Koji Kakizawa, "The Diet and the Bureaucracy: The Budget," in Valeo and Morrison, eds., *The Japanese Diet and the U.S. Congress*, 80. In the Ministry of Justice, the prosecutors "dismiss the minister as 'utterly irrelevant.'" David T. Johnson, *The Japanese Way of Justice: Prosecuting Crime in Japan* (Oxford: Oxford University Press, 2002), 120.

11. Nobutaka Ike, *Japanese Politics: Patron-Client Democracy* (New York: Alfred A. Knopf, Inc., 1972), 26.

12. "Japan, in its fairly long history, has produced few, if any, dictatorial or charismatic leaders of the caliber of Napoleon, Hitler or Peter the Great. Japanese groupism does not permit any individual to shine or stand out." Kanji Haitani, "The Paradox of Japan's Groupism: Threat to Future Competitiveness," *Asian Survey* 30 (March 1990): 241.

13. Karel van Wolferen, *The Enigma of Japanese Politics* (New York: Alfred A. Knopf, Inc., 1989), 146.

14. Jon Woronoff, *Politics: The Japanese Way* (New York: St. Martin's Press, 1986), 122. "Japan has a clearly discernable ruling class. Its members—mainly bureaucrats, top businessmen and one section of the LDP—are all administrators; there

is no room among them for the aspiring statesman." van Wolferen, *The Enigma of Japanese Politics*, 109.

15. For a contrast between the bureaucracy as dominant view versus the party as dominant view, see B.C. Koh, *Japan's Administrative Elite* (Berkeley: University of California Press, 1989), 204–18.

16. T.J. Pempel, *Patterns of Japanese Policymaking: Experiences from Higher Education* (Boulder, CO: Westview Press, 1978), 82–87.

17. Chalmers Johnson, *MITI and the Japanese Miracle: The Growth of Industrial Policy, 1925–1975* (Stanford, CA: Stanford University Press, 1985), 154.

18. T.J. Pempel, "The Tar Baby Target: 'Reform' of the Japanese Bureaucracy," in *Democratizing Japan: The Allied Occupation*, Robert E. Ward and Sadamoto Yoshikazu, eds. (Honolulu: The University of Hawaii Press, 1987), 159.

19. There is also the practice, called "side slip," where a retiree takes a job with another government entity. Those who do this more than once are called "migratory birds." Koh, *Japan's Administrative Elite*, 234–44.

20. Tuvia Blumenthal, "The Practice of Amakudari Within the Japanese Employment System," *Asian Survey* 25 (March 1985): 310–21.

21. Sone Yasunori, "Interest Groups and the Process of Political Decision-making in Japan," in *Constructs for Understanding Japan*, Yoshio Sugimoto and Ross E. Mouer, eds. (London: Kegan Paul International, 1989), 271.

22. Ronald J. Hrebenar, *Japan's New Party System: The Post-1993 System* (Boulder, CO: Westview Press, 2000), 139.

23. John S. Kim, *Japan's Civil Service System: Its Structure, Personnel, and Politics* (New York: Greenwood Press, 1988), 29, 47.

24. On numbers of civil servants, see Koh, *Japan's Administrative Elite*, 70–71.

25. Hiroshi Itoh, *The Japanese Supreme Court: Constitutional Policies* (New York: Markus Weiner, 1989), 4, 9.

26. Ibid., 155.

27. Lawrence W. Beer, *Freedom of Expression in Japan: A Study in Comparative Law, Politics, and Society* (Tokyo: Kodansha International, 1984), 135.

28. Itoh, *The Japanese Supreme Court*, 82–83.

29. Ibid., 224.

30. Ibid., 103.

31. Ibid., 31.

32. Robert J. Smith, *Japanese Society: Tradition, Self, and Social Order* (Cambridge: Cambridge University Press), 1983, 44.

33. "Japan: Lawyers Wanted. No, Really," *Business Week*, April 3, 2006.

34. Itoh, *The Japanese Supreme Court*, 28.

35. "Japan: Lawyers Wanted."

36. Ibid.

37. J. Mark Ramseyer and Eric B. Rasmussen, *Measuring Judicial Independence: The Political Economy of Judging in Japan* (Chicago: University of Chicago Press, 2003), 82.

38. An early classic study is Junnosoke Masumi and Robert A. Scalapino, *Parties and Politics in Contemporary Japan* (Berkeley and Los Angeles, University of California Press, 1962).

39. See Maurice Duverger, *Political Parties: Their Organization and Activity in the Modern State* (New York: Wiley, 1963).

40. James J. Foster, "Ghost Hunting: Local Party Organization in Japan," *Asian Survey* 22 (September 1982): 845.

41. "With the LDP paying off faithful support groups through the provision of the usual rewards associated with pork barreling—subsidies, public works, contracts, procurements, allocations from the General Accounts Budget, tax breaks, protection against foreign competition, administrative guidance (for example, concerning the stabilization of prices), and favorable legislation—LDP support groups in the labor intensive sectors—farmers, fishermen, local construction firms, real estate interests, distributors, small retailers, and others—reaped the benefits of continual redistribution of income as Japan's industrial economy expanded." Daniel I. Okimoto, *Between MITI and the Market: Japanese Industrial Policy for High Technology* (Stanford, CA: Stanford University Press, 1989), 187–88.

42. Scott C. Flanagan and Bradley M. Richardson, *Japanese Electoral Behavior: Social Cleavages, Social Networks and Partisanship* (London: Sage Publications, 1977), 38.

43. Ibid., 50–51.

44. Ray Christensen, *Ending the LDP Hegemony: Party Cooperation in Japan* (Honolulu: University of Hawaii Press, 2000), 195.

45. As Bowen quips with good reason, the LDP "is neither liberal, nor democratic, nor a party." Roger W. Bowen, *Japan's Dysfunctional Democracy: The Liberal Democratic Party and Structural Corruption* (Armonk, NY: M.E. Sharpe, 2003), 45.

46. Nathaniel B. Thayer, *How the Conservatives Rule Japan* (Princeton: Princeton University Press), 17; Ronald J. Hrebenar, *Japan's New Party System: The Post-1993 System* (Boulder, CO: Westview Press, 2000), 112–18.

47. Haruhiko Fukui, "Japan's Takeshita Takes the Helm," *Current History* 87 (April 1988): 185.

48. See Michael Leiserson, "Political Opposition and Development in Japan," in *Regimes and Opposition*, Robert A. Dahl, ed. (New Haven: Yale University Press, 1973), 372–94.

49. On the subject of money in politics see Yama Taro, "The Recruit Scandal: Learning from the Causes of Corruption," *Journal of Japanese Studies* 16 (Winter 1990): 107–12.

50. Tani Satomi, "The Japan Socialist Party Before the mid-1960s: An Analysis of Its Stagnation," in *Creating Single Party Democracy: Japan's Postwar Political System*, Tetsuya Kataoka, ed. (Stanford, CA: Hoover Institution Press, 1992), 82.

51. Gerald Curtis, *The Japanese Way of Politics* (New York: Columbia University Press, 1988), 29.

52. *Japan Times Weekly Overseas Edition,* April 16–22, 1990, 1.

53. J.A.A. Stockwin, *The Japanese Socialist Reality and Neutralism: A Study of a Political Party and Its Foreign Policy* (London: Cambridge University Press, 1968), 31.

54. James W. White, *The Sokkagakkai and Mass Society* (Stanford, CA: Stanford University Press, 1970), 126.

55. Ronald J. Hrebenar, *The Japanese Party System: From One-Party Rule to Coalition Government* (Boulder, CO: Westview Press, 1986), 152.

56. Robert A. Scalapino, *The Japanese Communist Movement, 1920–1966* (Berkeley: University of California Press, 1967), 19.

57. *Japan Times,* June 22, 2003.

58. Nicholas D. Kristof, "Japan Seeking Way to Evolve 2-Party System," *New York Times*, October 15, 1996. Political scientist Steven R. Reed, of Chuo University in Tokyo, has framed the question in terms of "Duverger's law" that the electoral system tends to determine the number of competitive political parties.

59. Blaine Harden, "Ruling Party Is Routed in Japan," *Washington Post*, August 31, 2009.

Chapter 18. Contemporary Issues

1. J. Sean Curtin, "Japan, Land of Rising Poverty," *Asia Times*, February 11, 2005.

2. Robert A. Fearey, *The Occupation of Japan: Second Phase 1948–50* (New York: Macmillan, 1950), 36–42.

3. Merry White, *The Japanese Educational Challenge: A Commitment to Children* (New York: The Free Press, 1987), 20.

4. Joy Hendry, *Understanding Japanese Society* (London: Routledge, 1989), 91.

5. White, *The Japanese Educational Challenge*, 142.

6. Ezra F. Vogel, *Japan's New Middle Class: The Salaryman and His Family in a Tokyo Suburb* (Berkeley: University of California Press, 1963), 40.

7. Chris Acheson, "The Future of Nuclear Energy in Japan: An Interview with Daniel P. Aldrich," National Bureau of Asian Research, August 1, 2011.

8. Robert A. Scalapino, "Perspectives on Modern Japanese Foreign Policy," in Robert J. Scalapino, ed., *The Foreign Policy of Modern Japan* (Berkeley: University of California Press, 1977), 391.

9. As World War II recedes further into the past, many Japanese see themselves more as victims of the war than its cause. "[M]any young people are amazed when told that neighboring nations suffered also, possibly more, at the hands of the Japanese." Karel van Wolferen, *The Enigma of Japanese Politics* (New York: Alfred A. Knopf, Inc., 1989), 426.

10. Masako Toki, "Japan's Evolving Security Policies: Along Came North Korea's Threats," *Nuclear Threat Initiative Global Security Newswire*, June 4, 2009.

11. Address to the Nation on the War in Vietnam, November 3, 1969).

12. Clyde Prestowitz, "Japan's Enduring Challenge," *Foreign Policy*, December 9, 2011.

13. Hideo Sato, "Japanese-American Economic Relations in Crisis," *Current History* (December 1985): 407–8.

14. Akiko Mikuni and R. Taggart Murphy, *Japan's Policy Trap: Dollars, Deflation and the Crises of Japanese Finance* (Washington, DC: Brookings Institution, 2002), 241.

Index

About the Author

Louis D. Hayes is emeritus professor of Political Science at the University of Montana. He has taught and conducted research in various Asian countries under Fulbright-Hays and other grants. He has previously published *The Struggle for Legitimacy in Pakistan, Introduction to Japanese Politics* (4th edition), and *Japan and the Security of Asia.*